Self, Society, and Womankind

Recent Titles in **Contributions in Women's Studies**

Women's Studies: An Interdisciplinary Collection
Kathleen O'Connor Blumhagen and Walter D. Johnson, editors

Latin American Women: Historical Perspectives
Asunción Lavrin

Beyond Her Sphere: Women and the Professions in American History
Barbara J. Harris

Literary America, 1903-1934: The Mary Austin Letters
T. M. Pearce, editor

The American Woman in Transition: The Urban Influence,
1870-1920
Margaret Gibbons Wilson

Liberators of the Female Mind: The Shirreff Sisters, Educational Reform,
and the Women's Movement
Edward W. Ellsworth

The Jewish Feminist Movement in Germany: The Campaigns of the
Jüdischer Frauenbund, 1904-1938
Marion A. Kaplan

Silent Hattie Speaks: The Personal Journal of Senator Hattie Caraway
Diane D. Kincaid, editor

Women in Irish Society: The Historical Dimension
Margaret MacCurtain and Donncha Ó'Corráin

Margaret Fuller's *Woman in the Nineteenth Century:* A Literary Study of
Form and Content, of Sources and Influence
Marie Mitchell Olesen Urbanski

To Work and to Wed: Female Employment, Feminism, and the Great
Depression
Lois Scharf

Eve's Orphans: Mothers and Daughters in Medieval Literature
Nikki Stiller

Women, War, and Work: The Impact of World War I on Women Workers
in the United States
Maurine Weiner Greenwald

Self, Society, and Womankind

THE DIALECTIC OF LIBERATION

Kathy E. Ferguson

CONTRIBUTIONS IN WOMEN'S STUDIES, NUMBER 17

GREENWOOD PRESS
WESTPORT, CONNECTICUT • LONDON, ENGLAND

Grateful acknowledgment is made to the following sources:

To The University of Chicago Press. Extracts reprinted from *Mind, Self and Society*, by George Herbert Mead by permission of The University of Chicago Press. Copyright 1934 by The University of Chicago, all rights reserved; and reprinted from *The Philosophy of the Act*, by George Herbert Mead by permission of The University of Chicago Press. Copyright 1938, all rights reserved.

To the Public Affairs Press for permission to quote from *The Social Dynamics of George Herbert Mead,* by Maurice Natanson, copyright 1956, all rights reserved.

To Alfred A. Knopf, Inc., for permission to quote from *The Second Sex,* by Simone de Beauvoir, translated by H. M. Parshley. Copyright 1952 by Alfred A. Knopf, Inc.

To *Catalyst* for permission to quote from "Mead, Marx, and Social Psychology," by Richard Ropers, No. 7 (Winter 1973): 42-61.

Library of Congress Cataloging in Publication Data

Ferguson, Kathy E
    Self, society, and womankind.

    (Contributions in women's studies ; no. 17 ISSN 0147-104X)
    Bibliography: p.
    Includes index.
    1. Feminism—Addresses, essays, lectures.
2. Liberty—Addresses, essays, lectures. 3. Liberal-
ism—Addresses, essays, lectures. 4. Socialism—
Addresses, essays, lectures. I. Title. II. Series.
HQ1154.F49   305.4   79-6831
ISBN 0-313-22245-2 lib. bdg.

Library of Congress Catalog Card Number: 79-6831
ISBN: 0-313-22245-2
ISSN: 0147-104X

First published in 1980

Greenwood Press
A division of Congressional Information Service, Inc.
88 Post Road West, Westport, Connecticut 06881

Printed in the United States of America
10 9 8 7 6 5 4 3 2 1

For my father, my mother,
and my family, with many thanks.

"It riles them to believe
that you perceive
the web they weave,
and keep on thinking free."
—The Moody Blues

Contents

Preface   xi

1. Feminism and Contemporary Political Theory   3

2. The Social, Processual Self: G. H. Mead   23

3. Power and Domination in Self-Other Relations   64

4. The Conditions for Liberation   101

5. Liberation and Womankind   128

Bibliography   183

Index   195

Preface

During the 1970s, social commentators frequently proclaimed that the liberation movements of the 1960s, and the questions they raised, were dead. However, I believe that the interest in a liberated human existence is still very much alive and that the commitments which sparked those Days of Rage are still intact. The aim of this book is to contribute to the continuing inquiry into the possibilities for a liberated human community by creating a new theory of feminism, one that builds upon and surpasses existing theories and incorporates the findings of the expanding empirical research in the field.

The issues surrounding women's oppression in our society are part of a larger set of questions about the nature of power, the mechanisms of domination, and the possibilities of freedom for all persons. Thus, a theory of feminism must be anchored within a broader consideration of the nature of oppression and the possibilities for liberation. My analysis is directed at all individuals and groups who are concerned about the questions of freedom and community in contemporary society.

A project such as this one is never wholly the result of one person's efforts; it is more likely to be the synthesis of a great number and variety of contributions. As George Herbert Mead tells us, we are social beings, whose actions and projects are indicators of the multiple voices within us. I would like to single out a few of these ''significant others'' for special thanks, since much of what is sound and viable in this analysis is a result of their influence. Any errors and omissions, of course, are my own.

I would like to thank the Department of Political Science, University of Minnesota, and Siena College for the financial support that enabled me to pursue this research. I also thank my comrades among the theory students at Minnesota, and my colleagues on the Siena faculty, for their intellectual support and their personal encouragement. The Siena College library staff was helpful in meeting my research needs. Chloe Van Aken patiently assisted in typing and retyping the manuscript. Michael J. McGrath and J. Donald Moon were extremely helpful in their editorial capacity, and I thank them both for the scholarly integrity and critical appreciation they brought to their reading of earlier versions of the manuscript. Michael McGrath and Bernard Johnpoll encouraged me toward publication of this manuscript when such encouragement was sorely needed. Among the many friends who contributed to this work both intellectually and personally, I especially wish to thank Steve Sherlock, Donna Sherlock, and Glenn Williams. Finally, I would like to thank three persons whose contributions have been tremendously valuable to me: Michael Weinstein, Mulford Sibley, and Edwin Fogelman, who read the manuscript at various stages and gave insightful criticisms and generous personal support. They have been both teachers and friends.

Self, Society, and Womankind

Feminism and Contemporary Political Theory   1

Twentieth-century political philosophy has inherited many of the legacies of its nineteenth-century predecessor, not the least of these being its two dominant paradigms of liberation: liberalism and Marxism. Liberalism urges the liberation of the individual from unnecessary restrictions through reforms that protect individual rights, while Marxism envisions the historical liberation of all humankind through the destruction of the old order and the creation of a new one. While certainly some modes of contemporary thought lie outside of these paradigms, such as the relatively recent resurgence of anarchism and the various types of existentialism, on the whole these two views of the relation between the individual and the collective have remained dominant in political theory. A brief look at the major contributions to political philosophy in recent decades confirms this notion. The heritage of liberalism is clearly evident in the much-discussed theory of justice proposed by John Rawls, in most of the work coming out of the social sciences, and in the American pragmatism of the first half of this century. Contemporary variations on the Marxist theme are even more ubiquitous: the Frankfurt school theorists, the Freudian-Marxists, the Christian Marxists, and the various Third World revolutionary writers—Mao Tse-tung, Ho Chi Minh, Frantz Fanon, Che Guevara —proceed from a Marxist perspective.

This basic division between the liberal and the Marxist paradigms is further evident in the internal splits among the various liberation movements. In these contexts the division is usually between "re-

formers'' and "revolutionaries" that is, between those who advocate working for change within the existing political/social/
economic structure, and those who wish to overthrow that structure. The black liberation movement, for example, since its inception has been divided between the civil rights workers and the
more militant Black Power advocates.[1] Similarly, the working-class
movement has had to deal with the perennial split between mili-
tants and moderates.

The resurgence of the feminist movement over the last decade
and a half also bears the marks of this ubiquitous split. Many
commentators on the "new feminism," in their efforts to piece
together the prevailing patterns of thought within the many threads
of current feminist analysis, have noted and documented the division. Few, however, have seen that its roots lie in the same basic
distinction that characterizes nearly all of contemporary political
philosophy: the liberal goal of the liberation of the individual by the
reform of existing social structures versus the Marxist vision of class
liberation by the revolutionary overthrow of these structures.[2]

Focusing primarily on the variables of organizational structure
and political style, several authors have defined the current split
within the feminist movement as one between the women's rights
and women's liberation groups.[3] The women's rights groups are
made up of moderate feminists who are engaged in exerting pressure upon the existing social structure, especially the legal system,
in order to eradicate sex discrimination in public institutions. Best
represented by National Organization for Women (NOW), Women's
Equity Action League (WEAL), and various professional women's
associations, these are usually large, structured organizations, often
with a nationwide organizational base. While most of the women in
these groups see the need for fundamental changes in the basic
attitudes and behavior that characterize interpersonal relations
between men and women, they argue that these changes are best
achieved through the piecemeal reform of existing institutions.

The women's liberation branch has its origins in the student
activism and New Left organization of the 1960s. Because these
groups are usually small, decentralized, and loosely structured,
their existence as organizations is more transient. Some of the more
well-known of these have been the Redstockings, the New York

Radical Feminists, and Women's International Terrorists Conspiracy from Hell (WITCH). These women are usually radical and anticapitalist, and their efforts are simultaneously directed toward self-education and consciousness-raising, and toward revolutionary social change.[4] The rights groups are primarily concerned with bringing women into the mainstream of American life, while the liberation feminists are more interested in changing the nature of that life. As one feminist quipped, the distinction can be said to be one between demands to "let us in" and those to "set us free."[5]

The differences between these two groups indicate a fundamental underlying divergence in the political theories that guide them.[6] The women's rights groups are primarily liberal in orientation; their most representative theoretical work, Betty Friedan's *The Feminine Mystique*, has its roots in the liberal tradition and most specifically in the writings of John Stuart Mill. These feminists echo their predecessors in their advocacy of legal equality and equal opportunity as the method by which to end women's subordination. They by and large accept the structure of capitalism and concentrate on bringing women into full participation in the existing political/economic/social institutions.[7]

The liberation branch of the women's movement is divided, sometimes bitterly, into Marxists and non-Marxist radicals. The Marxists, often called "politicos" in New Left circles, argue that women's oppression can only be understood as part of the dynamic of capitalism and thus that feminism must be encompassed within the Marxist critique of capitalist society. Drawing on Engels' *Origins of the Family, Private Property, and the State* for their theoretical analysis, these feminists somewhat reluctantly endorse the existence of an autonomous women's movement, always cautioning that it must not lose sight of its ultimately subordinate place in the broader working-class revolution.[8] The large and growing group of non-Marxist radicals retain an anticapitalist stance but throw their net wider: they advocate an attack on all instances of male domination and define the enemy as "patriarchy" rather than capitalism per se (although capitalism is perhaps the patriarchal system par excellence).[9] These feminists have no specified theoretical foundation for their critique; non-Marxist radical feminism has so far been a perspective in search of a theory.

The ranks of the non-Marxist radicals are growing simply because neither liberalism nor Marxism provides an adequate theoretical base for contemporary feminism. Liberalism's view of liberation is an atomistic one; it advocates state regulation to achieve individual autonomy. The Marxist theory of liberation is a class theory; it advocates reorganization of the means of production in order to meet material (and subsequently other) needs. While each contains a partial truth, neither provides the basis in political philosophy that a thoroughgoing feminism requires. A brief look at the major thrust of both liberalism and Marxism will demonstrate that a new theory of liberation is needed.

Liberalism, since its inception in the contract theory of John Locke and the utilitarianism of Jeremy Bentham and (to some extent) John Stuart Mill, has been an atomistic theory; it views individuals as preformed, autonomous units interacting via contracts to further their narrow economic interests. The close tie between liberal theory and capitalist economic systems is cemented by the possessive quality of liberal individualism.[10] Liberalism defines the individual as the owner of himself and his productive capacities. Social relations are then reduced to relations of exchange between entrepreneurs, and freedom is defined as the ability to conduct market relations. Liberalism objectifies individuals by defining them in terms of ownership. All interactions become commodity relations, and people are made into objects.

The freedom that liberalism offers is one that consists of noninterference by others; it defines boundaries between people and promises equal penalties to any and all who abridge them. Liberty, in this view, lies in the recognition of an arena of thought and action—the "private" realm—in which people are entitled to act without interference. Liberalism claims to emancipate people by proclaiming that differences in wealth, status, education, and the like will not affect their standing as citizens. It then leaves these differences intact. Thus, the status that accrues to males simply by virtue of their sex is not abolished, although its effects within those realms controlled by law may be regulated. Neither are internalized status distinctions disturbed; the definitions of themselves that men and women receive from the society around them, which proclaim to the male of his superiority and convince the female to acquiesce in her oppression, remain unaltered.

Liberalism, by viewing society as composed of separate individuals interacting autonomously with one another, ignores the complex social process by which we *become* who we are. By defining selfhood as an *a priori* condition of ownership rather than a process of social interaction, liberalism in fact perpetuates women's oppression by ignoring the extent to which social norms delimit "women's place" and male-dominated institutions conspire to keep her in it. Women, like men, are social beings formed by the expectations and sanctions of patriarchical society. The liberal definition of self fails to come to grips with the manifold effects of the socializing process by which women internalize the dominant definitions of themselves, so that, until they shake free of this and arrive at their own self-definition, their "choices," market or otherwise, are not free at all. Women are often their own worst enemies because that is what they have been taught to be. The liberal critique of legal inequality between men and women is an important and necessary aspect of the feminist position, but it is not by itself an adequate base for feminist theory. A theory of women's liberation must come to grips with the structural inadequacies of existing institutions. If it is the existing social order, and the processes by which that social order is perpetuated, that account for the oppression of women, then simply advocating the integration of women into that social order will not bring about their liberation.

In abrupt contrast to liberalism's view of liberation as the ability of autonomous individuals to conduct open contractual relations, Marxism offers a view of liberation that focuses on the relation of a class of people to the economic structure that defines them. The original analysis of Marx and Engels defined the first division of labor in society as that between male and female. The subjection of women began when superior technological ability gave men the opportunity to produce goods for exchange rather than consumption. Private property then became dominant and commodity relations superseded community. Women's access to the means of production was cut off, and their labor was redefined as a private service performed for their husbands. Their activities thus lost the status of socially necessary labor performed for the community and was consequently devalued. The solution, of course, from the Marxist perspective, is to integrate women into the public work force and abolish the system of private ownership; women will then be liberated under communism.

Because Marxism's liberation is a *class* theory, Marxist feminists, in order to apply their theory to women, must define women in terms of their relations to the means of production. The Marxist ultimately returns to the importance of developing proletarian class consciousness and building an organizational base for the working-class struggle. The women's movement is important only insofar as it can enlighten a particularly backward part of the labor force to the evils of capitalism. But the fact remains that women, as an entire group, do not occupy any one particular relation to the means of production, even though they are most commonly found in subordinate economic positions. Marxist efforts to define women solely in terms of their relation to the mode of production are so narrow, so ignorant of the complex multiplicity of factors that must be considered simultaneously in order to understand women's oppression adequately, that they border on the absurd. For example, one Marxist defines women as "that group of people which is responsible for the production of simple use values in those activities associated with the home and family"[11]; another urges that the abolition of sexism be accomplished in order to increase the "available labor power."[12] More sensitive and complex Marxist analyses, such as those by Sheila Rowbotham and Juliet Mitchell, are less willing to reduce women to makers of "simple use values," but they still focus exclusively on women as producers. These analyses look closely at the link between capitalist economic forms and women's role in the nuclear family. Women contribute largely unrecognized (because unpaid) labor power, they raise and socialize the next generation of workers, and they provide a refuge for the alienated male worker who seeks escape from the dehumanizing realm of public commodity production into the privacy of his personal/productive unit. These observations are all true, and they are all important aspects of women's oppression. Women are exploited both as producers and as consumers in capitalist society, and their traditional economic dependence has often left them powerless and silent. But even the most generous Marxist perspective on women insists on reducing the dynamic of their oppression to their capacity to work. The "politicos" insist that the abolition of private property, and the inclusion of women in the public sector, will be synonymous with their liberation.[13]

This exclusive focus on the economic aspects of women's oppression, while important, is far too narrow. It fails to consider the multiple dimensions of power relations as they affect women in contemporary society: the ever-present threat of physical violence, the dehumanizing bias in everyday language, the debilitating psychological effects of internalized sex role definitions, the continuing effect of custom, tradition, and religious myths that define women as inferior, and so on. As the experience of the Soviet Union shows, the abolition of most private property and the inclusion of women in the labor force do not guarantee their liberation.[14] As Hilda Scott notes in her study of women in socialist nations, there is a "lag in consciousness" involved here in that the belief in women's inferiority is a deeply ingrained one and has multiple sources that are not all specifically economic.[15]

In a cross-cultural survey of women's labor and status, anthropologist Peggy R. Sanday concludes that women's status in society is not fully determined by her access to the means of production: "female productive activities may be a *necessary* but not sufficient precondition for the development of female power."[16] Furthermore, since most Marxist and neo-Marxist groups are male-dominated affairs, in which feminist concerns are defined as secondary to the working-class struggle, and women are told to "shut up and fight," there is little assurance that women's fate after this hypothetical proletarian victory will be noticeably preferable to that which preceded it. The early radical feminist newsletters of the 1960s and 1970s were replete with enraged accounts of the exclusion of women from meaningful participation in New Left organizations. Jo Freeman reports that when she and Shulamith Firestone tried to include a women's rights plank in the agenda of the 1967 National Conference on New Politics, they were first ignored and were then told by the chair, "cool down, little girl, we have more important things to talk about than women's problems."[17] In Seattle a year later, a male Students for a Democratic Society

(SDS) speaker, in recommending tactics for raising the conscious-ness of poor whites, "noted that sometimes after analyzing societal ills, the men shared leisure time by 'balling a chick together.' He pointed out that such activities did much to enhance the political consciousness of poor white youth. A women in the University of Washington audience asked 'and what did it do for the political consciousness of the chick?' "[18] These are only two examples from a host of angered women, whose reaction to neo-Marxist male chauvinism was often to break away and start independent feminist groups. Many of the Marxist insights are valid and useful in under-standing the economic aspects of women's oppression, but, like liberalism, Marxism alone does not provide an adequate base for a theory of women's liberation.

Before going on to investigate the possibilities that an alternative philosophy of liberation would hold for women, we should attempt to determine the reasons for this continuing dualism in political philosophy. The liberal/Marxist, reform/revolutionary split is basic to all liberation politics, feminism included, because it reflects a fundamental dilemma that is both political and ontological. It is political because, as political actors pursuing some version of liberation as our goal, we must both live in the world and change it. That is, we are torn between the pressure to revise existing struc-tures in order to make them livable, and the need to dismantle those structures that pose barriers to the goal of liberation. While these two activities are not unrelated,[19] there is an unfortunate tension between them, of which most political actors are well aware: to initiate reforms in the existing structures may result in the strengthening of those structures, thus making them even more impervious to attempts at more radical change. Conversely, to eschew piecemeal reform in favor of revolutionary overthrow is to overlook the immediate needs of individuals who must live in the present system and whose concrete needs cannot be met by promises of a better time to come. Present necessity clashes with future freedom.

This dilemma between reform and revolution, as it continues to be fought between the liberals and the Marxists, is thoroughly, perhaps even tragically, fundamental to our political experience because it is the reflection of an underlying ontological dualism in the structure of human experience. Our existence is both a "being" and a "becoming"; we are tied both to what we know, to the facticity of our present existence, with its manifold pressures and requirements, and to what we can imagine in the unknown, with its equally manifold possibilities. Ontologically, the dilemma of freedom versus necessity indicates a basic duality in human experience. We are both tied to the immediacy of the perceived present, as it is spread around us and weighted with history and need, and able to project ourselves into the future, and reconstruct our past, on the basis of imagined possibilities.

Small wonder, then, that contemporary political theory continues to be plagued by the split between liberalism and Marxism, reform and revolution. The dualism exists in the structure of our experience, and it is felt politically in the need to choose between the two paradigms of liberation, to throw one's hat into one ring or the other. Yet, perhaps this choice is premature. Although the dualism cannot be magically abolished, perhaps it can be reformulated and approached from a different perspective. While the experiences connected with the dimensions of "being" and "becoming" stand in tension with one another, they are by no means unrelated. To attempt to conceptualize them independently of one another is to ignore their essential relatedness and the extent to which one influences and defines the other. Thus, while it is probably not possible to abolish this dualism, since the tensions it represents will continue to reemerge in various forms, it is possible to reformulate it in such a way that new insights into the elusive goal of liberation are attained.

Several contemporary feminists have noted the need for a new base in political theory for the feminist critique of male-dominated institutions. [20] Feminism requires an overall theory of liberation that can enable us to understand the complex multiplicity of factors involved in sexual oppression and to integrate the policy goals that women's liberation requires. It is the very dynamic of domination that we must seek to understand, the manner in which the oppressor and the oppressed interact, the way in which power is wielded and enforced. Once this dialectic between master and slave is understood, then we can explore the possibilities of and requirements for transcending it toward relations of liberation.

There is virtually unanimous consent among the non-Marxist radical feminists that liberation theory must center on the basic process of self-definition and the nature of the obstacles that prevent it. This is because it is basic to the structure of power relations, including male/female relations, that the subordinate party is denied the opportunity, and perhaps the ability, to define her own sense of self and her own situation. A theory of liberation must address the problem of achieving self-knowledge that is not colored by the definition of self which the dominant party prefers and is willing to enforce. It must aid the subordinate party in breaking out of what one feminist has called the "sector of silence" into the realm of *sophia*—human self-knowledge.[21] Thus, it is necessary to start at the very beginning, ontologically, with a well-defined concept of the self.

The concept of the self is of central importance to any major political or social theory. Every such theory has underlying it, implicitly or explicitly, a conceptualization of the human self or, more generally, of "human nature." The reasons are readily apparent: in order to make any statements about or recommendations for human political association, one must have some notion concerning the possibilities for and limitations on such activity. In order to know these things, one must have some concept of the self, of what people are "made of," of how they "tick." Such concepts serve a number of important functions. They can be used to mark the prudential boundaries of human actions; by painting a dismal portrait of human nature, they can indicate what conditions must be overcome in order to lead "the good life"; or, by drawing a more optimistic picture of the self, they can indicate what is "good" for humanity by showing what is "natural." Depending on their content and how they are used, concepts of the self can justify some political conditions because they conform to the requirements of human nature, or they can condemn others because they violate mankind's "true nature."

A brief glance at the ideas of both the classical and modern traditions of political thought will confirm the centrality of the self in each perspective. Each of these paradigms focuses on a particular view of the human being, and the differences between them reflect the vast gulf between the two concepts of self each formulates. In the classical tradition, as represented by Plato, the concept of the "soul" is central to the understanding of politics. Plato states early in *The Republic* that one must understand political association as the individual "writ large" and that to conceive of justice within the *polis* one must first comprehend the nature of justice in the soul. The proper political society is that which meets the implicit ends of human nature; since that which is truly human is rational, the true political society is the rational *polis*. Plato posits three basic aspects of the self, paralleling the three basic aspects of the *polis*: the desire for material goods, the desire for order and activity, and the desire for knowledge. While all individuals possess all three of these traits to some extent, within any particular person one characteristic is more basic than the others, and that characteristic determines what that person's proper function within society should be. The proper ordering of each individual soul consists in the proper relation between these three traits. Similarly, the proper ordering of the *polis* consists in the harmonious relations of the appetitive, spirited, and noetic individuals. Plato posits an underlying rationality in human beings that allows them to perceive the good through the use of "right reason."

Plato provides an excellent example of the centrality of the notion of the self to political theory: the tendency within the classical world-view to unite ethics and politics, to bring together morality in the individual's life with morality in the public domain. Plato's view of the self both guides and limits his political analysis. In order to outline the proper form of political association, he endeavors first to define the self, believing that what is natural to the individual—reason—must also be natural to the *polis*. The relationship between the three basic aspects of the self, and the three basic selves, determines the proper ordering within the *polis*. His concept of the self limits his political analysis by imposing certain constraints upon what is possible. For example, while he clearly perceived the danger that material acquisition presented to the community, he believed that the desire for unlimited wealth was a basic trait of human nature, and any plan for political organization must take it into account. His political recommendations, then, are based upon a clear and well-specified concept of the self.

In contrast to the classical perspective, modern political thought has developed a view of the self that is divorced from any concern for the ethical development of the individual, or the intrinsic goodness of reason, or the relation between human fulfillment and community. The modern view originated largely in the writings of Thomas Hobbes. Hobbes' view of the self laid the groundwork for much of modern social contract theory, and in his thoughts on human motivation he can be seen as fathering the utilitarian tradition. He depicts the self as an aggregation of desires, a solitary individual who is locked with others in an unceasing struggle for power. He sees an egoistic world-view as a natural consequence of individual self-consciousness; that is, as soon as an individual becomes aware of himself, he knows and is concerned about only himself. Based on his understanding of human motivation—that we act so as to maximize our pleasure and to minimize our pain, with fear and greed as our primary motivations—Hobbes draws his conclusions concerning the social contract. His outline of the form of civil society is based, then, on his ideas about the requirements of human nature. A strong central authority, using terror and intimidation, is necessary to keep order among beings such as he describes. In Hobbes more than in most political theorists, his concept of the self clearly imposes limitations on his political recommendations. In a society of Hobbesian selves, one would do well to dispense with considerations of community or participation and cling dearly to political order imposed from above.

It can thus be seen that both the classical and the modern traditions place the concept of self at the very heart of political analysis. Recognition of this fact is particularly important when one is dealing wih a theory of liberation, for in such a case it is imperative to understand *who* is being liberated and from *what*. In order to know the requirements for liberation, one must understand how it is that people interact with one another, how such interactions can become oppressive to those involved, and how such oppression can be overcome. One must, in other words, seek to understand the principles of domination and association. When the view of the self underlying a particular theory of liberation is stated explicitly, it can be used to give clarity and direction to the analysis. Conversely, when the view of the self is "smuggled" into the theory, as an implicit, but unexamined, view of human nature, it often serves more to conceal assumptions and value choices than to explicate them.

The perspective of the social philosopher George Herbert Mead provides a useful basis from which to approach the issue of self-definition in liberation theory. Following Hegel, Mead examines the self by relating it to a broader socio-historical context. His analysis of language, communication, and consciousness is based on his view of the underlying sociality of human experience. Like Hegel, Mead regards the self, and self-other interaction, as a dialectical process. His analysis is relational, focusing on the connections between concepts and on the ways in which they influence and define one another. (Chapter 2 is devoted to a critical explication of Mead's view of the self, emphasizing the two primary characteristics of sociality and process.) Since the ideas in the following chapters are largely drawn from Mead's concept of the self, his view requires careful explanation. Proceeding from his arguments for sociality and process, one can then understand Mead's arguments concerning roles and role-taking behavior, the social act, and the generalized other.

There is a basic inconsistency in Mead's treatment of the relation between the two aspects of the self, the "I" and the "me." In some of his writings, Mead describes the "I/me" relation in such a way that his theory leads toward a version of social determinism, in which the actions of the self are ultimately determined by the standards of the community of which that self is a part. This view, which is here called "I/me" relation #1, contradicts Mead's insistence on individual creativity and undermines his analysis of emergence and process. The second definition of the "I/me" interaction that Mead provides is a more useful and more accurate one in that it avoids the pitfalls of determinism while allowing for both individual creativity and social control. His vacillation between these two views of the internal dialectic of "I" and "me" accounts for much of the ambiguity in his writings. In order to maintain an internal consistency in Mead's position, and to utilize the Meadian perspective to examine specifically political phenomena, one must adopt the second, rather than the first, view of the interaction of the "I" and the "me."

While the basic "kernel" of Mead's analysis, the social processual self, is a sound basis for further consideration of the politics of self-other interaction, there are several problems in Mead's theory that require attention. These problems emerge particularly with regard to Mead's political views and his epistemological claims. In these areas, Mead's analysis is clearly rooted in the tradition of American liberalism. Like John Dewey's, his views are strongly colored by what might be called a peculiarly American "optimism," especially as shown by his faith in science as the savior of politics, his reliance on gradualism and incrementalism in political affairs, and his faith in the ultimate progress of humanity toward moral ends. Mead, like many other analysts in the liberal tradition, fails to account adequately for conflicts. He centers on self-other interactions that take place between equals, thus omitting the kinds of interactions that might be called specifically political—that is, those that do not take place between equals. Since it is precisely these sorts of relations that characterize the interaction between oppressor and oppressed, this conceptual bias in Mead's theory and its implications for political and social analysis must be carefully scrutinized.

While Mead's conceptualization of the self as social and processual is fundamentally sound, his view of self-other interaction must be expanded and differentiated if it is to address such interactions as they take place in political situations. (Chapter 3 outlines the multiple advantages of Mead's basic conceptualization, then goes on to expand and radicalize it by including a consideration of power and conflict as an element of self-other relations.) Mead emphasizes the importance of the social act, which he defines as coordinated interactions among individuals, integrated by reference to each person's relation to the others and to the relevant social objects. But some individuals, by virtue of their ability to control these social objects, have a greater voice than others in defining the situation in the social act. The generalized other which Mead describes as an important source of socialized self-definition then assumes a particular function he did not envisage: it both expresses and reflects the distribution of power in society as it is seen in the dominant social institutions. An understanding of self-other inter-actions between persons who are not equal in their ability to define the situations within which they act must include a consideration of power and the effects of domination. Any theory of liberation must take this step if the complexity of dominance/subordinance rela-tions is to be understood. Knowledge is not the same as liberation, although it is certainly a necessary part of it; to understand one's oppression is not necessarily to be free of it. Domination has a facticity that extends beyond the individual's own understanding of it because it is institutionalized in the social structures that surround us. Thus, an analysis of the various ways in which power is exer-cised and perpetuated is a central dimension of a theory of libera-tion.

Two conditions correspond to the two primary characteristics of the self as Mead describes them. The first is the requirement that one be able to define one's own situation and enforce the definition through control of the relevant social objects. This condition corre-sponds to the process characteristic of the self, for it is essentially the demand for an area of autonomy so that one can define one's own self-process; it is the demand for freedom. The second condi-tion, which corresponds to the characteristic of sociality in the self, is the ability to apprehend and to appreciate the perspective of the other. This, essentially, is the requirement of compassion. (Chapter 4 discusses the dialectical relation between the two components of liberation, freedom and compassion, indicating the nature of their interaction.) It is here that the ever-present tension discussed above reappears and demands consideration. The conditions for achieving the two moments of liberation may not coincide. With respect to the dialectic of male/female relations, it is all too likely that they will not. For the subordinate party to take the perspective of the other, in its entirety and with compassion, is for her to risk abandoning her own definition of the situation, since it will prob-ably clash with that of the man. Similarly, to insist on the freedom to define her own situation she may be forced to violate his perspec-tive on the relation, if his perspective includes the desire to retain his dominance. This tension between the two conditions must be continually confronted. Liberation, the dialectical balance between the two conditions, is an elusive and difficult goal.

Along with the Marxist and liberal feminist analyses, the existential tradition had also offered a theory of women's liberation. Simone de Beauvoir's *The Second Sex* is unique in its attempt to ground the feminist perspective in a sound philosophical base by examining the self and self-other relations. Ultimately, the theory she proposes is inadequate to understand the entirety of the dialectic of liberation, but it has made a major contribution toward doing so, and, thus, it must not be undervalued. (The analysis in Chapter 5 seeks to integrate the contributions of Beauvoir and others while going beyond them and to explain the dynamic of women's domination and the requirements for women's liberation from within the Meadian perspective on the self.)

When asked to comment on the supposed lack of outstanding women writers, Virginia Woolf once remarked, sadly, that "Anonymous was probably a woman." Anonymity is perhaps the most signal aspect of the situation in which any dominated group finds itself. It obscures one's very existence, making for a life of shadows rather than of light. When the suppressed are in the impossible position of relying on the oppressor for their very definition of self and of their situation, then anonymity is complete. We become inarticulate about ourselves, and the masks we wear seem more real than that which underlies them. A theory of liberation for women must strive to put away the masks, allowing women to "come out into the open," so that they may seek to know who they are and what they might become.

Notes

1. For an analysis of this split from the viewpoints of the participants, see Martin Luther King, Jr., *Where Do We Go From Here?* (Boston: Beacon Press, 1967); and Stokely Carmichael and Charles V. Hamilton, *Black Power* (New York: Vintage Books, 1967).

2. For a brief analysis, along similar lines, of the ideologies of the women's movement, see William T. Blackstone, "Freedom and Women," *Ethics* 85 (April 1975): 243-8.

3. See, for example, Judith Hole and Ellen Levine, *Rebirth of Feminism* (New York: Quadrangle Books, 1971); Maren Lockwood Carden, *The New Feminist Movement* (New York: Russell Sage Foundation,

1974); Jo Freeman, "The Origins of the Women's Liberation Movement," *American Journal of Sociology* 78 (January 1973): 792-811.

4. This distinction between the two branches of feminism is by no means a new one: the "first wave" of the feminist movement, which peaked around the turn of the century, was also divided in this way. In the United States, the radicals, led by Susan B. Anthony and Elizabeth Cady Stanton, organized the National Women Suffrage Association and demanded, in addition to the vote, fundamental changes in the areas of marriage and the family, religion, sexual standards, and public ethics. The American Women Suffrage Association, which drew the more moderate, "respectable" women and was led by, among others, Lucy Stone, concentrated on the suffrage issue and eschewed the more radical issues. (See Hole and Levine, *Rebirth of Feminism* for an overview of these events and organizations.) The European women's movement was similarly split. Russian revolutionary Alexandra Kollantai divided it into "bourgeois feminist" and "proletarian." (See Barbara E. Clements, "Emancipation Through Communism: The Ideology of A. M. Kollantai," *Slavic Review* 32 (June 1973): 323-38, for a summary of Kollantai's views.)

5. Marlene Dixon, "Where Are We Going?" in Edith Hoshino Albach, ed., *From Feminism to Liberation* (Cambridge, Mass.: Schenkman Publishing Co., 1971).

6. In her otherwise excellent analysis of the women's movement, *The Politics of Women's Liberation* (New York: David McKay Co., 1975), Jo Freeman underestimates the importance of these ideological distinctions. She claims that "structure and style rather than ideology more accurately differentiate the two branches" (p. 51), and she asserts that "The terms 'reformist' and 'radical' by which the two branches are so often designated are convenient and fit into our preconceived notions about the nature of political activity, but they tell us little of relevance" (p. 50). For evidence she draws upon a survey in *Psychology Today* (Carol Tavris, "Woman and Man," *Psychology Today* 5 [March 1972]: 57-82). However, Tavris does not, for the most part, distinguish between respondents belonging to radical groups and those belonging to moderate groups. In the one table in which such a distinction is made, the data are not very revealing. The questions are closed-ended and issue-oriented. Because they do not show the reasoning behind the response, they do not provide an adequate basis for drawing conclusions about the overall ideological perspectives of the respondents. Freeman also points out that over time the members of NOW and of the liberation groups have begun to accept each other more readily and to see the importance of the different approaches to the same issues. Freeman claims that the broadening of NOW's perspective is in part a

response to the "inherent logic to feminism. Once one adopts the feminist perspective on the world, it is very easy to apply it to an ever-widening circle of issues; one can analyze all aspects of society, and easily come to the conclusion that all aspects of society must be changed. The relevant questions then become where to begin and what to do first—and these are strategic, not ideological questions " (p. 98).

However, these assertions do not convincingly make Freeman's case. The radicals and the moderates certainly do share a similar stance on specific policies and issues, and coalition-building among them is no doubt possible and desirable. This has also been the case in the black movement and the labor movement; there is enough similarity in the immediate aims of the two branches to warrant such a link. But that does not therefore demonstrate that there are no ideological differences between the two. A program that calls for the full integration of women into all social institutions, and one that demands the total reformulation of such institutions, cannot be equated ideologically. There is no "inherent logic of feminism," but rather an inherent logic to the reformist and radical perspectives. Once they are coupled to the feminist critique, they share some issue objectives, but the crucial distinctions of world-view remain. Freeman occasionally recognizes this difference. For example, she asserts that the radicalization of NOW is "largely due to the ideological pull of the younger branch. Without their influence, NOW might not be able to resist conservatization" (p. 100). She describes this branch in the following terms: "Their concepts of participatory democracy, equality, liberty and community emphasized that everyone's contribution was equally valid" (p. 105). These convictions are clearly ideological in nature, not simply "organizational." Freeman fails to see that organization, in fact, reflects ideology rather than substituting for it. While she may have been trying to ward off these criticisms by claiming to be "using ideology in the narrow sense to refer to a specifically feminist belief system rather than a general worldview on the nature of politics and society" (p. 50), this caveat will not serve. Its only contribution is to blur important distinctions rather than to clarify them.

7. In *The Feminine Mystique* (Middlesex, England: Penguin Books, 1963), Betty Friedan matter-of-factly accepts capitalism and private property as "the way our economy is organized to serve man's needs efficiently" (p. 181).

8. For representative analyses of the Marxist feminists, see Altbach, ed., *From Feminism to Liberation*; Sheila Rowbotham, *Woman's Consciousness, Man's World* (Baltimore: Penguin Books, 1973); Branka Magas et al., "Sex Politics; Class Politics," *New Left Review* 66 (March-April 1971): 69-96; Evelyn Reed, *Problems of Women's Liberation: A*

Marxist Approach (New York: Pathfinder Press, 1971); Juliet Mitchell, "Marxism and Women's Liberation," *Social Praxis* 1 (Spring/Summer 1973): 23-33

9. For representative works of the non-Marxist radicals, see Cellestine Ware, *Woman Power* (New York: Tower Publications, 1970); Shulamith Firestone, *The Dialectic of Sex* (New York: William Morrow and Co., 1970); and Kate Millet, *Sexual Politics* (New York: Avon Books, 1970).

10. C. B. Macpherson, *The Political Theory of Possessive Individualism* (London: Oxford University Press, 1962).

11. Margaret Benston, "The Political Economy of Women's Liberation," in Altbach, ed., *From Feminism to Liberation*, p. 201. One wonders if Ms. Benston is as willing to reduce herself, and her own theoretical efforts, to this level of one-dimensionality.

12. Herb Gintus, "Activism and the Counterculture: The Dialectics of Consciousness in the Corporate State," *Telos* (Summer 1972): 61.

13. Evelyn Reed, *Problems of Women's Liberation: A Marxist Approach*; and Selma Jones, "The American Family: Decay and Rebirth" in Altbach, ed., *From Feminism to Liberation*, are especially adamant on this point.

14. See Barbara Jancar, "Women Under Communism," in Jane Jaquette, ed., *Women in Politics* (New York: John Wiley and Sons, 1974); and Hilda Scott, *Does Socialism Liberate Women?* (Boston: Beacon Press, 1974), for a discussion of this point.

15. Hilda Scott, *Does Socialism Liberate Women?* pp. 210-11.

16. Peggy R. Sanday, "Toward a Theory of the Status of Women," *American Anthropologist* 75 (October 1973): 1684.

17. Freeman, *The Politics of Women's Liberation*, p. 60.

18. Hole and Levine, *Rebirth of Feminism*, p. 120.

19. See, for example, the writings of Rosa Luxemburg, whose popularity may stem in part from the attractiveness of her attempt to overcome the split within the framework of the Marxist dialectic.

20. See, for example, Hole and Levine, *Rebirth of Feminism,* p. 130; Hilda Scott, *Does Socialism Liberate Women?*, p. 212.

An interesting divergence from this trend toward calling for a new feminist theory is that by Mary Mothersill, "Notes on Feminism," *The Monist 57* (January 1973): 105-14, who argues that we in fact do not need a new theory since it is quite obvious that women are being treated unfairly:

> Nor is there any point in speaking of a "viable theoretical foundation" unless we know what a theory of feminism would be like. What problems would it solve? What data would be relevant? If what is imagined is a theory that is normative or justificatory, what is it that

needs justification? Whether or not the claim that women are and have always been oppressed by men can be made good—something that would require a more satisfactory analysis of "oppression" than is currently available—it is clear that in particular places at particular times, for example, here and now, women are treated unfairly. Once this fact is recognized, wherein lies the need of theory? (pp. 113-14).

But Ms. Mothersill, in the process of arguing against the need for a new theory, in fact makes a strong case in favor of one; in the very act of making her argument she undermines herself. How does one know that women are being treated "unfairly" without having a definition of "unfair" by which to judge? The "fact" is meaningless without some theoretical context to provide it with definition. This bias against theory in favor of a "problem-solving" approach smuggles in the theoretical stance of liberalism, with its legalistic definitions of fairness, in the guise of common sense.

21. Abigail L. Rosenthal, "Feminism Without Contradictions," *The Monist* 57 (January 1973): 41.

The Social,
Processual Self:
G. H. Mead   2

Writing in the tradition of the American pragmatist philosophers and drawing heavily on the heritage of Hegel, George Herbert Mead offers a social theory that involves an elaborate philosophical analysis of human perception and interaction. The reality with which Mead deals is a social reality, and the self as he conceptualizes it exists within this reality as a process, not a substantive thing. The process is a dialectical one in that its different aspects do not intersect in a mechanical way but rather interact with one another in a complex process of development and change. It is crucial to examine the basic concepts in Mead's theory, not as independent factors, but as relations. By virtue of this relational quality, the linkages between the concepts are intrinsic to their definition. Thus, Mead's theory of the self and of self-other relations is not so much a description of what the self *is*, at any particular moment, as an analysis of how the self *develops*.

According to Mead, the self is social and it is processual. In order to see how Mead's view of the self can be used to build a theory of liberation, it is necessary to examine these two characteristics and to analyze their relation to one another. In so doing, certain problems in Mead's theory will come to light, particularly with regard to his political and epistemological claims. Mead's theory is in no sense problem-free, but once the difficulties in his work are located and confronted, the remaining "kernel" of his analysis can contribute a sound basis for a new liberation theory.

The Primacy of Sociality

Mead's theory of the self commences with a total rejection of that tradition in liberal theory which views the self as a private, solitary, self-contained whole that consciously decides, for whatever reason, to initiate contact with other of its kind. This view of the self, which gave rise to the contract theory of human relations, overlooks the important anthropological and biological facts that human beings are born into groups, that they learn about themselves and others within the context of these groups, and that without this social context, there would be no vehicle for the development of the human self. The self arises within the community; one becomes a self by responding to the perspectives and attitudes of those around him. This relationship between the self and the community is not a simple linear, cause-and-effect relation. Rather, it is a dialectical relation, in which the individual and the social group interact with one another and are selectively and causally determinative of both each other and the environment. In Mead's words, "neither can be explained in terms of the other except as the other is determined by it. The attempt to proceed otherwise leads to an impossible solipsism or to an equally impossible determinism."[1]

Given this emphasis on the priority of the social process, communication between individuals is an interaction that arises out of the social process. Communication at the nonhuman, nonlinguistic level (that is, communication among animals other than humans) is largely a matter of direct automatic responses to stimuli. Gestures at this level serve to call out the appropriate responses in other animals, but they take place without the mediation of meaningful symbols. Mead's famous example of the dogfight is used to illustrate the process of animal communication. Each dog responds "instinctively" to the other; it does not stop and figure out what its options are and what response it will give. At the human level, individuals respond to each other on the basis of the meanings and intentions they assign to the gestures of others. This, in Mead's terminology, renders the gesture *symbolic*; it becomes a symbol to be interpreted, something which, in the understanding of the participants, stands for the entire act of which it is a part. A gesture becomes a significant symbol when it acquires a shared, common meaning, when it becomes a linguistic element. The significant symbol characterizes specifically human interaction because it establishes the basis upon which human beings are able to share each other's experiences, to respond in the same way to the same gesture. Thus, meaning is socially defined. It rests upon the recognition that others give (or have given in the past) to the individual's gesture, and it emerges in a social situation.[2]

In Mead's discussion of consciousness, he distinguishes between pure experience and consciousness of what is going on in experience. Most nonhuman animal action, as well as much human action, can proceed without the individual being aware of himself as an object in the act. In one's habitual actions, for example, in which one moves about in a familiar, unquestioned world to which one is so adjusted that no thinking is involved, there can be a certain amount of immediate experience that does not involve consciousness. As illustration, Mead cites the experiences one has when first waking up, "a bare thereness of the world."[3] In other words, there is a distinction between experiences in which the self is present only as the experiencing subject, not as the object of the experience, and those experiences in which the self can be present as both. In Mead's view, this fundamental capacity to be both subject and object differentiates human beings from other animals. By virtue of his behavior in groups, the individual is able to be an object to himself.[4] This ability to have the experience of oneself is consciousness. Mead gives the example of a man running to escape a pursuer. The man is so occupied with his running that his experience is swallowed up in the objects about him—he concentrates on avoiding the stone in the path, leaping the puddle, and so forth. He has no consciousness of the self as object; it is only later, after successfully escaping his pursuer (assuming he runs swiftly), that he reflects back on the experience of running as *his* experience. It is only in reflection that he sees in the experience his self as object. This act of seeing oneself as object is the source of self-consciousness.

Consciousness, then, is social. It exists within human experience because human beings can take the attitude of the other toward themselves. The vehicle through which the self as object arises, through which the individual develops a sense that his experience belongs to him, is the significant symbol. The individual becomes object to himself through communication directed not only at others but at himself as well. The ability to stimulate oneself verbally in the same way as one stimulates others, and to respond to one's own verbal gestures as one responds to the gestures of others, places in the individual's conduct the experience of himself as object.[5] The individual may thus act socially toward himself just as he acts toward others. One may, in different situations, praise or blame oneself, punish or encourage oneself, become disgusted with or enchanted with oneself, and so on. The conscious self arises by the process of becoming an object to itself; this process requires interaction with other human beings; therefore, all conscious experience is necessarily social in origin. In Mead's words:

Whatever may be the metaphysical impossibilities or possibilities of solipsism, psychologically it is non-existent. There must be other selves if one's own is to exist. Psychological analysis, retrospection, and the study of children and primitive people give no inkling of situations in which a self could have existed in consciousness except as the counterpart of other selves. We even can recognize that in the definition of these selves in consciousness, the child and primitive man have defined the outlines and the character of the others earlier than they have defined their own selves. We may fairly say a social group is an implication of the structure of the only consciousness that we know.[6]

In analyzing the conceptual web surrounding this notion of the self as object, the relational nature of Mead's theory becomes clear. As is shown later in this chapter, Mead's self has a multiplicity of meanings, and it can only be understood in terms of its links to other concepts. By examining each in turn, I will show that the notion of self as object is the basis for consciousness; that it is a function of language; that it is central to Mead's theory of role-taking, the generalized other, and the social act; that it gives rise to his view of knowledge; and that it provides for his account of privacy. These concepts are related dialectically, for intrinsic to each factor is its relationship to the other factors. The act of defining any one of them demands an examination of its relationship to others.

Mead tries to avoid certain traditional philosophical questions that inevitably arise when one conceives of the self as separate from the surrounding world. In other words, he wants to avoid the subject/object dualism that leads to such questions as 'Starting from my own inner experience, how can I know the world?'' or ''Starting with my knowledge of the experienced world, how can I know myself?'' The separation of subject and object, self and experience, which had plagued classical epistemologists since the days of Plato, is rejected in Mead's view of the social act. In our ''primitive phenomenological experience,'' it does not exist because we are both subject and object to ourselves and to others within the social act.[7] In Mead's process philosophy, the act is the unit of existence, and it requires both subject and object. He sees no philosophical problem inherent in the joining of the two, for they have never been separated.

The basic unit of experience, then, is the social act—that class of actions which requires the coordinated action of more than one individual and whose object is a social object. In more everyday language, social acts are events in which people coordinate their actions with those of others on the basis of their ability to anticipate the other's response and adjust to it. The ''object,'' whether material or other, that provides the common focus of this event is a social object. Social objects integrate the actions of the participants by providing a shared field for response. Social objects can be material things, such as food and money, or they can be less tangible phenomena, such as norms and rules. The fully social act consists of a process of adjustment to the other individuals involved in the act, and it is integrated by virtue of the social object to which all the individual participants in the act respond. For example, in a football game the entire activity is a social act organized by reference to the ''rules of the game,'' which have meaning for all the participants in the game and serve to integrate their activities. Each player performs his role as it is defined with reference to the rules; each player's relation to the football and to the roles of the other players is also defined by reference to the rules. Without these rules, the entire activity loses its meaning: the football ceases to be a meaningful object and becomes only a strangely shaped leather article; the players cease to be purposeful actors and become a random assortment of oddly dressed individuals. The social object, in this case the rules of the game, thus integrates the actions of all the participating individuals and allows them to adjust their acts to the actions of the others through a common anticipated response. Mead presents a somewhat abstract definition of the social act:

A social act may be defined as one in which the occasion or stimulus which sets free an impulse is found in the character or conduct of a living form that belongs to the proper environment of the living form whose impulse it is. I wish, however, to restrict the social act to the class of acts which involve the co-operation of more than one individual, and whose object as defined by the act, in the sense of Bergson, is a social object. I mean by a social object one that answers to all the parts of the complex act, though those parts are found in the conduct of different individuals. The objective of the acts is then found in the life-process of the group, not in those of the separate individuals alone.[8]

Mead's analysis of time is also fundamental to his notion of the social act. Each act has a past, present, and future. A social act takes place in the present, but it has meaning only by reference to the past (history) and the future (purpose). Each act has phases (parts or components) that exist only in relation to each other, and can be separated only through an abstraction arrived at by analysis.[9] An illustration of the intersection of the phases of the social act can be seen in Mead's analysis of eating.[10] The body and the surrounding objects (food, utensils, and so forth), when perceived solely as objects, are part of the manipulatory phase of the act; that is, they are part of the means by which the act is performed. The self, the states of consciousness, the values involved in the act, and the process of realizing these values involved are all involved in the consummatory phase of the act. If eating is simply thought of as the ingestion of nutrition into the stomach, where it is processed by the digestive organs, absorbed or expelled, then it is conceived in terms of the means and conditions of the act and answers to the manipulatory phase. But when the self enters into the act and defines certain feelings as hunger, certain objects as food, certain instruments as utensils, and certain biological sensations as satisfaction, then the act is constructed in terms of the consummatory phase. The consummatory phase of the social act is that by which the individual brings values into the world by defining certain objects as valuable in relation to chosen goals. The objects exist *as objects* prior to one's evaluation of them, but they do not exist in their capacity as values until then. Grass exists as a plant, but it does not exist as food until a grass-eating animal appears to define it as food. An individual who is hungry normally has the satisfaction of his hunger as his goal and therefore defines food as valuable. But if the individual is a political prisoner on a hunger strike, then satisfaction of hunger is not his chosen goal and food is therefore not defined as valuable. While objects can claim a prior existence in the "world that is there," they do not have value prior to human perception of them.

Thus, the relation between social objects and social acts is one of intricate dialectical interaction. Social objects do not contain their own intrinsic meaning, for they receive meaning only through human actions. At the same time, social acts are held together by the orientation of the actors toward particular social objects. Consider, for example, a funeral. The corpse is a social object in this case in that it provides the focus of the participants' actions. But the sheer presence of the body is not sufficient, for it is also surrounded by a particular cultural context that confers meaning upon it. In our society, we expect that the funeral director will appear both concerned and professionally distant, that relatives of the deceased will be aggrieved, that friends will be sympathetic, and that strangers will be respectful. The body, and the norms and rules governing its proper disposal, constitute the social object. The pattern of interactions among the participants is the social act.

By maintaining that the social act is the fundamental unit of society, Mead is saying that it cannot be broken down into the elements of common behavior on the part of all the participants. This is because each participant occupies and acts from a different position, defines the situation differently, sustains a somewhat different relation to the social object and to the other actors, and so on. The participants fit their parts of the act together by identifying the particular social act that is about to take place and by intercepting and defining each other's acts with reference to it. For example, if the act is a bank robbery, the teller, the witness, and the robber all define the act and interpret and respond to the others from different positions within the act. While it is probably not appropriate to speak of a bank robbery as having "rules," most people are sufficiently familiar with the idea (if for no other reason than their persistent appearance in television scripts) so as to be able to anticipate the behavior of the other participants and act accordingly. Because they have different perceptions of the situation, the act cannot be broken down to common behavior on the part of each individual. It must instead be viewed as a fundamental social unit within which each participant occupies an integral role.

The social act is important to Mead's theory of the self because it provides a view of society as an ongoing process of action rather than as a posited structure of relations. The social act connects the process at the individual level to the process at the social level. Social acts also give a certain stability and continuity to community life: They are

generally orderly, fixed and repetitious by virtue of a common identification or definition of the joint action that is made by its participants. The common definition supplies each participant with decisive guidance in directing his own act so as to fit into the acts of the others. Such common definitions serve, above everything else, to account for the regularity, stability, and repetitiveness of joint action in past areas of group life; they are the source of the established and regulated social behavior that is envisioned in the concept of culture.[11]

However, it is important to note that joint actions are also open to uncertainties: they must be initiated; they may be abandoned or altered; the participants may have different definitions of the process; new situations may call for new kinds of joint action; and so forth. These possibilities introduce uncertainty, contingency, and transformation as basic to the social act, and insure that social actions will not automatically follow fixed, established channels.

Mead describes the process by which individuals interact with the community by reference to the notion of the "generalized other." The generalized other is the attitude of the community or social group that gives the individual his unity of self. It is a composite role constructed from the roles of the others in one's social group, and as an internalized standard of behavior it provides a basis from which a person views himself and his behavior. It is the paradoxical function of the generalized other that it provides both for social control and for individual freedom, due to the dialectical relationship that it sustains to the other components of the social act. By organizing and then generalizing the attitudes of particular other individuals toward their social situation, and then internalizing this stance as an accepted standard of conduct, the self becomes an individual reflection of the general systematic pattern of social or group behavior in which it and the others are all involved. Through the vehicle of the generalized other, the individual takes the attitude of the other, not only toward himself, but also toward the social objects in his environment.[12]

But the element of social control which the generalized other exercises is only half the story; the other half is individual freedom. It is not despite the generalized other that the individual self is free to create new meanings and initiate new actions, but because of it. The standards of the community consist of commonly accepted ways of thinking and acting of which the individual must become cognizant in order to function socially, but, Mead maintains, these standards need not simply be accepted blindly by each individual. They can equally well serve as a basis for constructing alternatives and proposing new ways of living. Taking the attitude of the generalized other does not therefore require that one will necessarily perform the behavior required by the social group. The generalized other is likely to contain both inconsistencies and diversity, and these give rise to grounds for a critical response. In addition, the self has the capacity, through the "I," to respond to the generalized other in an innovative fashion. For example, community standards may demand that its individual members accept the sanctity of private property. Each member of the community will be taught, through the institutionalized channels of social communication, about the proper function and use of private property. But each individual has the capacity to react critically to this community standard. Thus, a person's reply might be to urge the abolition of private property in favor of a communal arrangement. The individual may reject the standards of the community in favor of other standards, but he can never learn about such standards and concepts outside of some social context.[13]

It is clear, then, that the fact that the generalized other exercises a kind of social control does not mean that the individual is therefore determined or defined solely in terms of existing social roles. Nor does it mean, in Mead's view, that society will remain static and repetitive. Creativity and initiative are equally intrinsic aspects of the self, both because of the function that the ''I'' performs and because within the generalized other itself there is likely to be a certain amount of diversity with respect to community standards. Mead says that ''the self, then, would inevitably be organized about the patterns of the group activities *in so far as they are unitary.*''[14] The word ''unitary'' is important here; in all but the most homogeneous of societies, it is likely that most political, economic, and social issues will not be unitary. That is, it is likely that the generalized other will itself contain differing viewpoints on such issues, so that the individual will learn early in life that there is precedent for dissent. There is no reason to assume that in complex societies the generalized other will be homogeneous or consistent. The existence of different, and perhaps conflicting, standards of conduct within the generalized other broadens the grounds that are available for a critical response.[15]

The generalized other, then, both makes freedom possible and limits the scope of things that the individual, in his freedom, can challenge. One cannot question one's whole world all at once; rather, the world that is there, with its past and its future, provides the background against which different aspects of its structure are brought into question. For Mead, freedom is a social phenomenon, and it is neither necessary nor possible to escape the social world in order to be free. The world imposes certain boundaries on the individual's actions, but it is not a prison. It is the setting within which creative reconstruction of different aspects of the social structure can take place.

Mead analyzes the role-taking activity, as it goes on within each individual, in terms of two different moments of the self, the ''I'' and the ''me.'' The ''I'' is the initial, spontaneous, unorganized aspect of human experience. The ''me'' is the social organization of attitudes within the individual self, the internalization of the attitudes of others in the form of the community's norms and rules. One takes the attitudes of others through the ''me'' and responds to them through the ''I.'' The social act is the result of the interplay between the "I," which initiates and propels the act, and the "me," which reflects back upon the act in a regulatory manner and disposes the self toward community-sanctioned activity. Those critics of Mead who maintain that he sees the self as determined by the social group have neglected to consider the importance of the "I" in his account of the self.[16] Mead clearly emphasizes that the "I" is as important as, if not more important than, the "me." It is because of the "I" that one can never completely know oneself or predict one's own actions; the response of the "I" is uncertain; it is movement into the future and cannot be strictly anticipated or determined. It is because of the creative "I" that one is able to surprise oneself by one's own action. The "I" both calls out and responds to the "me"; the self is a social process of interaction between the two dialectically complementary elements of the self:

The "I," then, in this relation of the "I" and the "me," is something that is, so to speak, responding to a social situation which is within the experience of the individual. It is the answer which the individual makes to the attitudes which others take toward him when he assumes the attitudes toward them. Now, the attitudes he is taking toward them are present in his own experience, but his response to them will contain a novel element. The "I" gives the sense of freedom, of initiative.[17]

Mead's separation of the "I" and the "me" as different aspects of the human self is made only for analytic purposes. He does not claim that the two are empirically separate parts of the psyche; on the contrary, they are dialectically related in such a way that each can only be defined in terms of the other. Both the "I" and the "me" are essential to the full expression of the self. The "me" is that which connects the individual to the social world; by providing for and making necessary the taking of the attitudes of others, the "me" makes community possible. By the same token, the "I" is that which provides for novelty and change; by virtue of the "I" the individual has creative possibilities and is more than simply a reflection of the social group. The "I," as the source of change within the community, is that which makes freedom possible.

Mead's major accomplishment is that he has proposed a view of the self that allows for both freedom and community, and he has done so by defining the self as a dynamic, ongoing dialectical process rather than a substantive thing. However, in doing so he has tried to unite two disparate views of the "I/me" relation that do not lend themselves to a conceptual merger. Both the "I" and the "me" in Mead's analysis operate at dual levels of meaning.[18] The "me" is both (1) the internalization of the norms and rules of the community; and (2) the memories of the experiences of the individual, the totality of the content of one's past actions, as they are constantly being added to in the process of experience. This second aspect of the "me" introduces the idea of temporality into the self and gives it the quality of permanence and continuity. Because of the temporal relatedness of the contents of the "me," one's known past experiences and anticipated future experiences can be thought of as belonging to oneself, as being one's own.

The "I" can also be seen as functioning at two levels. First, the "I" is that which calls forth the "me" into the social act. The "me," as the individual's internalization of the community's norms, is propelled into the social act by the initiative of the "I." The temporal dimension of this bringing forth of the "me" by the "I" is such that the "I" can only be grasped in the form of the "me" of the past action:

The "me" as an apperceptive mass can be elicited, can be brought forward to meet a problem only through the services of an "I" that acts as liaison between the self and the object situation facing the self in choice. The "me," then, is continually being called forth through the "I." The intimate nexus between "me" and "I" consists of the fact that the "I" is always grasped through the "me," becoming a part of the "me" as the temporal process unfolds in experience. This becomes clear when we seek to experience the "I" directly: we are unable to grasp it in its immediacy for the very reason that the "I" makes itself known, manifests its presence only in its performed acts. The "I," then, in so far as it can be grasped experientially, is always an "I" that was the novel emergent of a past action which became and is now part of the "me." To inspect this "I" of last year or of last week or of last minute, we must understand it as the "me" derived from the past "I" and now seen from the standpoint of the present "I."[19]

Second, Mead portrays the "I" as an independent source of individual uniqueness and creativity. By maintaining that the "I" is that which allows the individual to reconstruct creatively his environment and to react critically to the standards of the generalized other, Mead asserts an independent existence of the "I" at this level. The "I" is not simply the byproduct of the social setting, nor is it the "essence" of the human personality, since Mead's view does not deal in the realm of immutable essences. Rather, it is the capacity within each individual for creative self-expression, a capacity that each self possesses by virtue of the process of self-definition. The "I" here is the source of originality and invention.

But Mead's attempt to combine these dual functions is not successful; the two levels do not mesh. [20] The first function of the "me" is as the internalized generalized other; the "me" in this case applies the standards of the community to the actions of the "I." At this level, the "I" acts and the "me" judges. As noted in Chapter 1, this level of the "I/me" interaction will be referred to in the present work as "I/me" relation #1. The second function of the "me" is what Justus Buchler in *Toward a General Theory of Human Judgment* refers to as the "summed-up self"; the totality of past experiences belonging to the individual by virtue of one's memory of them. Here the "I" both acts *and* judges the act; the "me" is the repository of acts and memories which the "I" may draw upon to make its judgments, but the "me" in this case does not judge. This level of the interaction will be referred to here as "I/me" relation #2. The first view of the "I/me" interaction is one of a spatial relationship between the two, in which there is a seesaw action and reaction between them. The "I" acts, then it must pause while the "me" brings the generalized other to bear in judging the act. In this view, the ongoing process of expression and reflection is blocked. The second view unifies the self and allows the process to continue by positing a temporal relationship between the two. The "I" both acts and judges its act, while the "me" provides the context within which this judgment takes place.

Mead attempts to maintain both of these "I/me" relationships simultaneously and does not see that the second is hostile to the first. It is true that the "me" can have both levels of meaning in the sense that the memories of past experience which constitute the "summed-up self" can *include* the norms and rules learned from the community. Certainly, the generalized other is part of one's past experience, although it is not the whole of it. But to say that the "me" as generalized other is the judge of experience is to say that one automatically judges one's experience by the standards of community acceptability. There is a contradiction between Mead's claims for the creative abilities of the "I" and his insistence that the generalized other provides the standards by which acts are judged. At times, Mead describes the "I/me" relationship as one in which the "I" acts by calling forth the "me," defined as the internalized generalized other, into experience to judge the "I's" acts. At other times, he is equally insistent that the "I" is the individual's unde- termined, creative abilities and that the "I" both acts and judges its acts within the context set by the "me." In his most often read work, *Mind, Self and Society*, the overall tone of the argument places the "I" in a secondary position: "The 'I' reacts to the self which arises through taking the attitudes of others. Through taking these attitudes, we have introduced the 'me' and we react to it as an 'I.' "[21] And again: "The 'I' is the response of the organism to the attitudes of others. . . ."[22] Here the emphasis is on the passivity of the "I," relative to the "me"; the emphasis is on its "reactive" function. The notion of the "I" as the source of novelty is still present, but the novelty is a response to the community's norms. Here our capacity to surprise ourselves is rooted in the process of responding rather than initiating.

This nuance of interpretation, dominant throughout *Mind, Self and Society*, is largely abandoned in Mead's too frequently ignored manuscript *The Philosophy of the Present*. The emphasis in this work is on the reality of emergence, the primacy of the unique in experience. Even the past is continually rewritten because of the persistent appearance of novelty; Mead speaks, in a representative phrase, of the "constant appearance of the novel from whose standpoint our experience calls for a reconstruction which includes the past."[23] Here the emphasis is on the "I" as the individual's spontaneous, unique capacities, and the implication is that the "I" both acts and judges its acts within the context set by the "me."

But Mead cannot have it both ways. If, as in the first case, the "me" judges the actions of the "I" by reference to the community's standards, then the range of possible actions open to the "I" is limited by the range of these standards. Such a limitation is clearly not consistent with the "I" as it is pictured in the second case. This

inconsistency plagues Mead throughout his writings and is responsible for his inability to account for the existence of power relations
in society. Mead assumes that the act of demonstrating how individuals internalize the content of the generalized other is sufficient
for showing why they in fact obey it. He assumes that people
internalize and then act on the generalized other because they are
naturally social beings. He sees the internalization as a kind of
self-evident control, which needs no further justification or explanation. But this assertion is not satisfactory; one must explain
why people accept this generalized other, and not simply state *that*
they do. The "I/me" relation #2 reintroduces a version of the
self/society dualism, despite Mead's efforts to eliminate it, because
in this view it is possible that the "I," although it acts within a
context set by the "me," may act in ways contrary to the generalized other. This makes rebellion possible and requires that conformity be explained. In this respect, Mead's argument, while
presented in theoretical terms, does not go beyond description.
One must also allow for the fact that, in complex heterogeneous
societies, the content of the generalized other is often characterized
by inconsistencies and discontinuities, and that the individual, in
internalizing these standards, may internalize conflicting rules and
norms. Mead's account of the individual self does not allow for the
kinds of conflict and cognitive dissonance that may go on *within* the
self as it attempts to deal with such conflicting and competing
claims. [24]

A further aspect of sociality that is central to Mead's description
of self-development is his view of knowledge as the process of
coordinating the shifting social perspectives that result from taking
different roles. In this light, role-taking is a process of passing from
one perspective to another. Many such perspectives are involved in
this process, none of which is all-inclusive or absolutely true. One
acquires information in part by assimilating the experience of
others into one's own experience. This process requires that one
relativize one's experience, that one view the situation at hand from
different perspectives. Mead is said to have introduced action
into knowledge: he maintains that thinking is a process of passing
from one perspective to another and, within this process, seizing
upon that which best answers to the hypothesis in question. [25]

A perspective, then, is what one acquires when one takes the role of another. A perspective is the ordering and organization of events by an individual with reference to a part of the person's environment, sharing perspectives is fundamental to Mead's view of the self and of knowledge. One becomes a self by sharing perspectives with others, by evoking in oneself, by one's own gesture, the same response that one evokes in another. In order to think, to acquire knowledge, to solve problems, and to make adjustments in the world, one must be conscious of alternative ways of manipulating objects. That is, one must be conscious of different perspectives.

If knowledge is defined as the sharing of perspectives, then Mead needs a criterion to judge the adequacy of different perspectives. Like other pragmatists before him, Mead appeals to the criterion of workability: knowledge is a process in conduct that so organizes the field of action that otherwise delayed responses can take place. The success of this project is the test of truth. Mead defends this claim by demonstrating the similarity between the scientific method and the everyday procedures through which individuals know the world. The experimental method is involved in all knowing; it is the way people know the world. Science has systematized it, but it is not qualitatively different from the way in which all knowledge proceeds. Mead substitutes the generalized other, as the standard by which social knowledge is judged, for the scientific paradigm, which performs the same function within the scientific community. In each case, some body of socially defined knowledge provides the context from which individual perspectives emerge and against which they are tested. Thus, Mead sees a parallel between change in the everyday world of social knowledge and change in the scientific community. Each involves a process of considering hypotheses raised by individual members, comparing those hypotheses to the standards of the generalized other (or scientific paradigm), and accepting or rejecting the hypothesis based on its ability to be incorporated into the community perspective.

To Mead's credit he abandons the fruitless attempt to "prove" absolutes and allows knowledge to refer to a criterion that arises from the community. His view also dispenses with the myths that surround the endeavors of science by demonstrating that the scientific method is simply a systematized and rule-governed application of the experimental approach that is involved in all knowledge. But certain problems in Mead's view of knowledge must be confronted before his view of the self and self-other relations can be used as a base for a theory of liberation. Briefly, one problem is that, by equating change in the social world with change in the scientific world, Mead has both idealized the processes of science and over-looked the many social, political, and economic forces that intervene to prevent such change from taking place. Another problem is his conceptual error in attempting to apply the methods of science to answer questions of values. Before exploring these problems in greater detail, however, it is necessary to examine the other major characteristic of Mead's self—temporality.

The Primacy of Process

The second major characteristic of the self in Mead's analysis is that it is processual. These two qualities—social-ness and process-ness—are not two distinct characteristics or aspects of the self, for each is fundamentally a part of the other. The process by which the self develops is thoroughly social, while at the same time the social interaction at the heart of the self is by its nature a process. As the starting point of his analysis, Mead presupposes social experience as a process of communication out of which selves develop. The human infant is not born with a self in the same way that it is born with a body; it develops a self through the conversation of gestures within the social process. The self is not a substance. It is not a definable, circumscribed thing that first exists and then processes experience as a computer processes information. In Mead's words,

The self is something which has a development; it is not initially there, at birth, but arises in the process of social experience and activity, that is, develops in the given individual as a result of his relations to that process as a whole and to other individuals within that process.[26]

Any theory that attempts to erect a structure for the self misses the crucial point that the human self is characterized by a reflexive process that enables it to act upon and respond to itself. If it is not able to do so, then it is simply reduced to an organization of characteristics awaiting activation and release, without the ability to exercise any influence upon itself or its environment. Mead shows how this fundamental characteristic of being able to act upon itself changes the nature and the status of the self. The self of yesterday or of last week may not be the same as the self of today because the experiences that took place in the intervening time may have contributed to a redefinition. Self-interaction, and interaction with others, are processes that imply development. The self changes, expands, grows; it is not static. Thus, Mead rejects all psychological theories that seek to delineate a structure for the self, including those theories that view the self as an ego, or a hierarchy of needs, or an organization of attitudes, or a structure of internalized norms and values.[27] Each of these theories omits the crucial element of process and is thereby unable to view the self as an acting, creative agent, as one who must "construct his action instead of merely releasing it."[28]

In much the same way as the self is processual, Mead describes mind, or mental activity, as processual and social. Mind is identified with reflexiveness, the turning back of the experience of the individual upon himself. Through reflexiveness the whole social process is brought into the experience of the individual, and the individual becomes aware of his relations to that process and to the other individuals participating in it. It is through this capacity to incorporate the experience of others and of the process as a whole into one's own experience that one is able consciously to adjust oneself to that process and modify the result of the process with regard to particular social acts.

Mead's view of the self is in direct opposition to the traditional liberal view of the self as an object separate from other objects, and of knowledge of self and of immediate personal experience as prior to knowledge of the world. In such a psychological atomism, Mead says, "Each self is an island, and each self is sure only of its own island, for who knows what mirages may arise above this analogical sea."[29] He explicitly criticizes contract theory for its reversal of the relationship between the individual and society:

Thus, the contract theory of society assumes that the individuals are first all there as intelligent individuals, as selves, and that these individuals get together and form society. On this view of societies have arisen like business corporations, by the deliberate coming-together of a group of investors, who elect their officers and constitute themselves a society. The individuals come first and the societies arise out of the mastery of certain individuals. The theory is an old one and in some of its phases is still current. If, however, the position to which I have been referring is a correct one, if the individual reaches his self only through communication with others, only through the elaboration of social processes by means of significant communication, then the self could not antedate the social organism. The latter would have to be there first.[30]

Mead's view of the ''me'' as the internalization of the generalized other within the self blurs the distinction between selves. Part of what each individual is exists in the others around him, and vice versa. The fact that interaction *among* selves is an integral part of the content of any *one* self makes the distinction between selves a hazy and ill-defined one. Mead states that

No hard-and-fast line can be drawn between our own selves and the selves of others, since our own selves exist and enter as such into our experience only in so far as the selves of others exist and enter as such into our experience also. The individual possesses a self only in relation to the selves of the other members of his social group; and the structure of his self expresses or reflects the general behavior pattern of this social group to which he belongs, just as does the structure of the self of every other individual belonging to this social group.[31]

Similarly, Mead explicitly rejects the stimulus/response account of human activity that characterizes much of psychological behaviorism. He views the mental process as one in which the self organizes the data from the environment and selects a response to the stimuli coming from the environment. One *constructs* one's act and does not simply respond in some predetermined or preestablished way. The distinctive characteristic of human interaction consists in the fact that human beings can define or interpret each other's actions instead of merely responding to them, and that they can base this interpretation on the meaning they attach to each other's action, and not merely on the fact of the action itself. The method by which individuals ascertain the meaning of one another's actions is communication based on the use of symbols. This mediation has the effect of inserting an act of interpretation between the stimulus and the response.[32] Watsonian behaviorism[33] is oversimplified and conceptually faulty because it looks only at the stimulus and response aspects of the act and ignores the human self that intervenes between the two by its selective attention to stimuli and its choice of response.

Mead's objection to Watsonian behaviorism, then, is based on Mead's differing notions about how perception takes place. According to Mead, perception is a complex activity in which selected stimuli from the environment are responded to during the course of acts and are interpreted symbolically and with reference to the self. Perception is selective, and it is active; it involves the symbolic interpretation of stimuli by the actor. This is why identical stimuli are perceived differently by different individuals and by the same individual at different times and during different acts. Human beings are not simply passive agents who receive and react to stimuli. Because of their ability to point out to themselves that an action has a certain meaning, human beings can insert the act of interpretation into the stimulus/response procedure. To indicate something to oneself is to extricate it from its setting, give it a meaning, and make it an object. An object, then, is different from a simple stimulus. Instead of having an intrinsic character that stands apart from the individual and acts upon him, its meaning is conferred upon it by the individual during the process of the act. Similarly, one's actions back onto the object are constructed responses to it, not simply releases or reactions.

Mead's view of the active mediation between stimulus and response also implies a view of the environment as process. The environment is not fixed because individuals select from it what is important to them and they act on their selection. Perception is an activity that involves selective attention to certain aspects of the environment. Mead draws on the general principles of evolution to stress the reality of change and the genuineness of emergence in the environment. The setting within which social acts take place is not fixed or static because that very setting is given its shape by the perceptions of the actors. This does not mean that individuals create the outside world they experience. Mead recognizes that the world of physical objects is real and has a prior existence. But this is not a static, unchanging existence; rather, the environment must be characterized as part of an ongoing process of interaction with the organism.

Thus, there is an element of process in the environment in two related ways. First, the physical environment itself is one that undergoes change; Mead's affinity with Darwinism leads him to stress the importance of emergence in the physical surroundings. Secondly, and more importantly for a theory of the self, human beings interact with their environment in such a way as to introduce variation and change into it. Human beings do not create the environment in the sense that they bring it physically into being, but they do create it in the sense that they define it and give it meaning. A physical thing becomes an object when a human being comes into contact with it and gives it a definition, and this bestows meaning on it:

The relations in which the environment stands to our reactions are its meanings. To respond to such meanings, to treat them, rather than mere immediate data, as the stimuli for behavior, is to have imported into the world as experienced the promise of the future and the lesson of the past. Meanings are now the very essence of what an object really is, and in seeing it in terms of its meanings, in reacting to what it can do to us under crucial or standard conditions, we are bringing organic sensations into a new and emergent context.[34]

Through his emphasis on evolution, Mead views every existing entity as involved in a continuous process of adjustment. History is not a static account of the past because it, too, partakes of this continuous emergent process. When he claims that the past and the future are not real, he means that they are not fixed. Human beings rewrite their past and direct their future on the basis of present perspectives, and when these perspectives change, the interpretations of the past and anticipations of the future also change. Mead does not deny the factual existence of objects and events in the past, but he maintains that the significance and meaning of those events and objects can and do change. For example, the fact that Trotsky led the Red Army against the

Kronstadt sailors in 1921 and that the Red Army was militarily victorious is not in dispute. But the significance and meaning of this action change according to the perspective of the person viewing the act. For Lenin, it was a necessary action to save the revolution from counterrevolutionary subversion; for the anarchists, it was the last gasp of revolutionary freedom against the Bolshevik tyranny; for modern liberal historians, it is still another example of the internal disputes among leftist forces. That this event occurred is an irrevocable fact; what the event signified, and how it influences present action, is open to dispute. The present, then, does not simply flow logically from an irrevocable past; the past is redefined with respect to every present. Mead places emergence and novelty at the heart of experience. The real is not fixed; it is process.

The future also sustains a particular relationship to the present. Because human action is purposeful, because it is projected toward future goals, the future is that which directs the present; that is, present actions are projected into the future for definition. Process, as the temporal spread that extends over a series of acts and events and lends unity to them, requires that past, present, and future all be included in the meaning of present phenomena. Mead is denying the view that time is simply a linear progression from past, to present, to future, in which each temporal phase is separate from the other and each leads directly into the other. He posits a dialectical interaction among the temporal phases, each of which affects the other as the process moves toward its projected future, based on its redefined past.

In his concept of emergence, Mead tries to capture the temporal side of experience. The emergent form arises in a process that is projected toward a future, and it relates itself to the previous condition by reconciling itself to the past. Mead draws heavily on Henri Bergson for his analysis of experience as a continual temporal process. The organism is never in a state of equilibrium but is always striving toward a future and reconstituting a past. This movement is creative because it does not admit of repetitions—it does not have ''parts'' that can be shifted, replaced, or repeated but has a continuous emergent content. Our common categorizations of experience into discrete quantities and stages are, in fact, arbitrary abstractions from the unbroken stream of change. Bergson cap-

tures the experience of passage in his concept of duration. In his
words:

What is duration within us? A qualitative multiplicity, with no likeness to
number; an organic evolution which is not yet an increasing quantity; a
pure heterogeneity within which there are no distinct qualities. In a word,
the moments of inner duration are not external to one another.[35]

Mead contrasts this world of passage and ongoing experience
with the world of science. Science, with its requirements of preci-
sion in measurement, has reduced the experienced temporal extension to an abstract series of moments that follow statically one
after another. The abstractions that science has made in its treatment of time have become so embedded in our way of thinking that
it has become difficult to see beyond them to the world of passage.
Mead insists nevertheless that a dialectical temporal unity is inti-
mately connected to the self as process:

The future that is there is a part of the process that is just taking place, in so
far as it controls the whole process going on. The past projected into the
future, hypothetically, is justified by the result, but the future into which it is
projected is an extension of the future that is actually there in the act. The
present is the combination of the future and the past in the process that is
going on. The future is the control of the process, and the past is that which
is there as an irrevocable condition of the on-going of the process.[36]

The importance of Mead's view of temporality and emergence
for his overall theory is further indicated in its relation to the
concept of sociality. Sociality is that characteristic which enables
the organism to exist in more than one system (perspective) at a
time. In other words, it is the capacity for emergence. There are two
dimensions to this sociality: the temporal dimension, which refers
to the passage from one perspective to another within the mind of
the individual; and the structural dimension, which refers to the
overall organization of perspectives within the society.[37] The
mutual influence which the components within a perspective exert
upon one another is one aspect of sociality; the second aspect is the
influence of what something is within one perspective on what that
same thing is within another perspective. We are who we are by

virtue of the perspectives into which we move. We have no "essence" or "nature" outside of these multiple intersecting perspectives, nor are our possibilities exhausted by them, since there is potential novelty in our movement into new perspectival situations.[38]

Emergence, then, is the key to sociality. The emergent organism, the individual, has the ability to occupy different perspectives at the same time and to move from one to another in such a way that one takes something of the old into the new. This means that one has the ability to relativize one's perspective; that one need not be trapped within a set perspective that one acquired during childhood, or in school, or during professional training. One can become cognizant of and participate in the different perspectives by which individuals in different social situations view their world. Because of the emergent capacities of the self, new perspectives on ourselves and the world are always potentially available to the inquiring self.

Critique

As thus far presented, there is much value in Mead's view of the self. By showing the dynamic nature of the social process that underlies the development of the human self, Mead has overcome the mechanistic, deterministic aspects of more conventional behaviorism. By demonstrating the dialectical nature of the relations between the different components of the developmental process, he had gone far beyond the linear, static view of human action inherent in the stimulus/response models. Perhaps most important of all, he has shown that freedom and community are complementary aspects of the development of the self and that one does not necessarily exclude the other. These achievements recommend his theory of the self as a sound basis for further analysis of self-other relations.

But as noted earlier in this chapter, certain problems arise in Mead's theory with regard to his political and epistemological claims. These problems can be seen most clearly in his views on the nature and source of values, his claims concerning the role of science, and his analysis of the nature and functions of institutions in society. It is important to confront these limitations and analyze their source, so that the parts of his perspective that are valuable to a theory of liberation may be differentiated from those that are not.

The empiricism that Mead inherited from the pragmatic tradition and the biological emphasis that accompanies his evolutionary views make strange bedfellows, particularly with regard to his standards of truth and value. The pragmatist's definition of truth, taken from James, is that of workability: the meaning of a statement is verified by the appearance of that which was meant. The biological view, on the other hand, defines meaning as that which allows the expression of behavioral impulses in conduct.[39] In Mead's discussion of the self, his leanings toward empiricism are for the most part dominant, but in his discussion of values he clearly is an advocate of ethical naturalism. Although he often states that he rejects any appeal to an absolute moral order, and instead refers to experience as the source of moral values, in the end he appeals to a naturalistic standard that stands above the process of experience, i.e., the imperative that the process must continue. One of the implications of his view of human creativity and freedom is that human beings bring value into the world by bestowing meaning upon objects. In his discussion of eating, for example, Mead makes clear that a physical thing becomes a social object by virtue of some human being directing his action toward it and defining it in relation to his project. For example, a potato is only a physical thing until someone defines it with reference to that person's actions. To a hungry person, it becomes food; to a child it may be a toy; to a gardener it is the fruits of hard labor; to a person under attack it may be a weapon. If it is human action that brings value into the world, then by implication the range of values is limited only by the versatility of human imagination. Whatever people value by definition becomes valuable. There is no standard outside of this process by which values can be judged to be right or wrong, good or bad. If experience is truly the source of value, then anything within the realm of human experience is a potential candidate.

The logic of this position must lead to an ethical relativism, but Mead does not accept the logic of his position. Instead he wants to find a middle ground between moral absolutism and moral relativism. He wants to affirm that the individual is free to create moral values, and at the same time he wants to endorse a moral imperative that would impose a limit on this creativity. This moral imperative has two aspects: it holds that all relevant values must be considered whenever a decision is made, and that the process of interaction between self and environment that gives rise to such decisions—that is, life—must go on. As Mead maintains:

> That process of continuing reconstruction is the process of value, and the only essential imperative I can see is that this essential process has got to go on—the community, on the one hand, and the selves that make up the community. It has to be continued not so much because the happiness of all is worth more than the happiness of the individual but, being what we are, we have to continue being social beings, and society is essential to the individual just as the individual is essential to society. That relationship has to be kept up, and the problem is how the essential social values involved can be maintained. . . . We have no more right to neglect a real value than we have a right to neglect a fact in a scientific problem. In the solution of the problem we must take all relevant values into account . . . in problems in which values come in conflict with one another, we want to reconstruct our lives so as to take in all the values involved. It is conceivable that we may have to surrender values entirely for the present, but we ought to recognize them and fashion our lives in such a way that we can realize them if we possibly can. [40]

Mead's moral imperative, then, has two parts: one must consider all relevant values when deciding upon an action; and one must act so as to maintain both the individual and the social order, so that the social process can continue.

Mead does not anticipate the problems that immediately arise with his attempt to resurrect the moral imperative. What are "real" values? Where do they come from? Why does the fact that the social process exists give rise to the moral rule that it ought to exist? He does not see that acting so as to take all values into account is in itself a value choice; there is nothing self-evident or obvious about this claim. Moreover, it may not be possible to take all values into account in particular, concrete situations. How does one know what constitutes all possible relevant values? Mead sounds as though he has a list of all possible values that he can check when making a moral decision, but this obviously contradicts his view that human beings have the capacity to create new values and reconstruct old ones. Lastly, he does not adequately recognize that values may be mutually exclusive, so that to realize one is to forfeit another. His examples of conflicting values are benign. As a case of conflicting values, he offers the example of a person who wants to go to college but needs to work because he has two people to support. Mead's resolution is that the person should go ahead and support the people by working, while at the same time find another way to get an education. He says that "You must take into account all values; you are morally wrong if you refuse to consider certain ones."[41] He wants to make room for all alternatives at once and does not recognize that moral dilemmas often present us with an "either/or" choice. He urges that all interests be considered in making moral decisions, but he does not recognize that they may be conflicting, especially in the political and economic realms. Thus, Mead would advise that the interests of the capitalist and the worker be brought together and harmonized. He feels that inadequate judgments are made in these regards because not all social interests are included. He says "Every such problem is the inevitable indication of what had been left undone; of impulses checked, or interest overlooked."[42] In not recognizing that the interests of the workers and the capitalists may be mutually exclusive, he refuses to recognize the irreconcilable nature of some social conflict. He has faith that all social problems can be solved by reconstructing the objective situation to allow for the accommodation of all relevant values and interests: "The test of the reconstruction is found in the fact that all the personal interests are adequately recognized in a new social situation. . . .Solution is reached by the construction of a new world harmonizing the conflicting interests into which enters the new self."[43] This is a blandly consensual view of public life, overlooking those tragic arenas of conflict in which clashing interests cannot be reconciled so as to satisfy all parties.

Mead maintains that wants or impulses are good to the degree that they reinforce themselves and give rise to other wants and impulses. His imperative is based on his biological analysis of impulses, which he defines as tendencies to action. His moral rule is that one ought to act so as to allow action to continue, which means act so as to maintain the life process:

The process of adjustment of living forms consists in the selection of the characters in the environment which will set free the impulses which maintain the life process, together with such spatiotemporal organizai: n of these characters as answer to the pattern of the act that arise out of impulses when the opportunity arises for its expression.[44]

He does not see that he is attempting to bridge an unbridgeable conceptual gulf in this argument. The fact that there is a life process does not lead to the conclusion that one ought to act to maintain it. Mead's description of the adjustment process may describe how, in fact, most organisms respond to their environment, but it cannot *prescribe* what an organism should do. Similarly, "act to maintain the social order" does not follow from the statement "there is a social order." One cannot deduce a prescriptive statement from a descriptive one, as Mead has tried to do. The rules of logic make such a move impossible, since the "ought" of conclusion is not contained within the "is" of the premises.

Mead's naturalistic imperative contradicts his previous state- ments concerning the freedom of individuals to construct their moral choices as they interact creatively with each other and their environment. If human beings are truly free to choose their own values, then it is possible for one to choose to reject the life process itself. Indeed, many people choose suicide, not only out of per- sonal unhappiness or desperation but for other reasons as well. The political martyr is a good example of one who chooses to terminate the life process in order to pursue a crucial value. Mead's analysis cannot account for such a choice because he assumes that the life process must continue. He appeals to nature for his criteria: the life process exists in nature; therefore it is natural; therefore it is good. Mead does not take his relativism seriously. In the final analysis, it is to a naturalistic imperative that he appeals.

Reflecting a perspective on science and experience common to many American theorists of his era, Mead attempts to ground his moral imperative on the authority of science by the application of the scientific method to questions of value. Thus, he makes no qualitative distinction between facts and values with regard to their respective methods of inquiry. He does not see that values are not like data, that one cannot simply go out and observe a value. One may obscure a person who *holds* a value, and this observation may give the observer a great deal of information about the consequences and implications of holding such a value in certain situations, but this procedure cannot then tell the observer whether he should also hold that value. Furthermore, Mead does not see that to choose to take all values into account is itself a value choice, not a scientific one. Mead tries to bridge the gap between "is" and "ought" with science:

But it would be a mistake to assume that scientific method is applicable only in the fashioning and selection of means, and may not be used where the problem involves conflicting social ends or values. The advance of scientific medicine in dealing with public health amply substantiates this. [45]

But Mead's example of public health services is a false one. Science cannot tell us that we *ought* to be concerned with public health; it only tells us how, if we choose, we could go about maintaining public health. The methods and procedures of the public health services could be used to subvert public health rather than maintain it; one could use scientific procedures to put LSD in the drinking water as well as fluoride.

Mead's attempt to treat values as data is further illustrated with reference to the role of the generalized other. It is true that taking the role of the other can give the individual some insight into the values that the other holds and his reasons for holding them; it can allow the individual to empathize with the plight of the other; and it can furnish, through the process of socialization, the source and legitimation of values. But it cannot tell one what one *ought* to believe, and as soon as the individual acquires the capacity for reflective thought, he is able to see that the fact that others do hold certain values does not therefore mean he also ought to hold those values.

Mead attempts to find a middle ground between absolutism and relativism upon which to rest his uneasy merger of science and ethics. But such an effort is doomed. To describe, as Mead has, the process by which values do *in fact* arise within the social process is not the same as showing which values *ought* to arise within that process. Mead's description of the process through which values appear is brilliant, but this does not then constitute a prescription of which values ought to appear. The choice between absolutism and relativism is an either/or dilemma, and Mead, in the final analysis, appeals to nature for his absolute.

Mead's reliance on science also affects his analysis of institutions and of the process of social change. He sees political and economic change as taking place through much the same process as does change within the scientific community. Problems arise within a generally accepted context or paradigm, and individuals address themselves to these problems. They solve them either by reconciling the problem to the existing paradigm or by demonstrating to everyone's satisfaction that the paradigm must be altered to accommodate the new issue. However, Mead's account of the process of change is wrong on several counts. Not only does he idealize and misrepresent the procedures involved in scientific endeavor, but he also overlooks factors within the political and economic realms that are barriers to change. Since any account of liberation must involve an analysis of the nature of social change, it is important to look at this problem and see clearly its implications for a theory of liberation. In order to substantiate my claim to "radicalize" Mead's perspective, it is first necessary to demonstrate the existence of problems that make such a move desirable.

The history of scientific pursuits shows the inaccuracy of Mead's description. First of all, scientific experimentation is guided by a body of theory that defines what the world is like and orients the scientist toward the selection of certain phenomena that are defined as significant facts. The scientist selects data that are relevant to the theory at hand in order to test the theory, and this choice of certain data out of the available universe of phenomena is based on the highly selective criteria required by the theory. "What a man sees depends both on what he looks at and also upon what his previous visual-perceptual experience has taught him to see. In the absence of such training there can only be, in William James' phrase, a 'bloomin' buzzin' confusion.' "[46] Contrary to Mead, the scientist is not able to take all interests (data) into account. The very fact that one is guided by an already established theoretical definition of the subject matter imposes important restrictions on the selection of relevant data.

Second, the process of change within science is uneven and discontinuous. Major change is usually initiated by an extraordinary, tradition-shattering set of innovations that constitute a radical break with the past.[47] Mead's description of the progress of science as a methodical, incremental, cumulative process of gradual change does not square with historical accounts of major innovations. In *The Structure of Scientific Revolutions*, Thomas Kuhn points out that changes in the theoretical perspective by which research is ordered generally come through a relatively sudden and unstructured experience that resembles a gestalt switch. This description had little in common with Mead's idea of a gradual and orderly process of problem-solving, through which a unified body of scientific theory is reconciled with "the facts."

Third, the history of scientific endeavor further shows that the scientific community is not as open to change as Mead indicates. Once a particular world-view is accepted as the proper theoretical guide to research, individuals who attempt to challenge it make themselves heard only with the greatest difficulty. According to Kuhn, anomalies and novelties that are subversive of the basic commitments underlying the prevalent paradigm are often ignored or suppressed. He cites numerous examples of the resistance to challenge that often accompanies the acceptance of a dominant paradigm.

In addition to this tendency to idealize the procedures of scientific investigation, Mead's account of change also suffers from his naive view of conflict within the political and economic realms. He sees conflict as arising only when the practices of the community are inadequate to solve a particular problem. The individual then proposes a solution to the problem, which, if tested and shown valid, is accepted by the community and becomes a part of the generalized other. This smooth and simple procedure does not, however, describe the reality of political change. Challenges to the dominant political system do not simply rise and fall around certain specific problems. There may be challenges to the entire political system, not simply to some part of it, and these kinds of challenges are often suppressed or ignored by the dominant community. A new approach is not likely to be tested and judged openly if it challenges the vested interests of certain members of the ruling group. Furthermore, the criteria for what constitutes an adequate and successful test of a political proposal are not likely to be as universally shared as are scientific criteria. Mead does not recognize that there may be organizations of individuals within the community who, because of their vested interest in the status quo, will not permit certain questions to be raised. These groups may value the present arrangement enough to resist any contribution that could lead toward change. Especially if one is working within the marketplace, or within mass institutions and bureaucracies, challenges to the present structue may go unmet, even unheard.

Mead defines institutions as organized manifestations of general social life processes, or as social habits and attitudes assumed under certain situations. He maintains that institutions arise when there is an identical response by the whole community toward an individual under certain circumstances. To use Mead's example, a person who steals is a thief in the eyes of the whole community, and the behavior of others toward him is patterned by this common response. They may imprison him, cut off his hand, or hold a feast in his honor, but their response takes an institutional form because of their common perception of the meaning of "thief."[48] But Mead overlooks the tendency in complex society for other institutions to intervene and render this result inconsistent. For example, in a society based on corporate capitalism, a high-level executive who steals is guilty of white-collar crime and, if caught, is not likely to suffer the same consequences, either legally or socially, as is the unemployed black who robs a white storekeeper. In each case, the economic and social status of the individual intervenes between the act and the community's response to the act. Mead's analysis of institutions overlooks the fact that vested interests may exercise power which will intrude into the social process and affect the interaction of the individuals and groups within it. Because he fails to consider the role of entrenched power in society, he posits that all conflict can be rationalized, and thus he tries to replace politics with science.

These problems in Mead's theory reveal the extent to which he relies on an exclusively cognitive theory of society. The difficulty, as discussed above, of pinning down the "I/me" relationship also revolves around this notion that the relation between self and society is purely an intellectual one. Mead states clearly that the cognitive self is dominant in his theory:

Emphasis should be laid on the central position of thinking when considering the nature of the self. Self-consciousness, rather than affective experience within its motor accompaniments, provides the core and primary structure of the self, which is thus essentially a cognitive rather than an emotional phenomenon. The thinking or intellectual process—the internalization and inner dramatization, by the individual, of the external conversation of significant gestures which constitutes his chief mode of interaction with other individuals belonging to the same society—is the earliest experiential phase in the genesis and development of the self. . . . The essence of the self, as we have said, is cognitive: it lies in the internalized conversation of gestures which constitutes thinking, or in terms of which thought or reflection proceed.[49]

But a purely conceptual theory of self and society is not sufficient, because knowledge does not necessarily lead to action. It is not enough simply to say, as Mead does, that people obey the generalized other simply because they have internalized it. One must demonstrate why this takes place by exposing the sanctions that accompany it. Otherwise, the generalized other would not exercise any stronger influence on the individual than does any other context of the experiential "me." The norms and rules of the community would then be simply one more aspect of the general experiential context within which the "I" acts. But this is obviously not the case. Mead's psychological theory shows that the socialization process is one of the strongest single influences on individual development, but it does not demonstrate *how* or *why* this influence take place. It is understandable, then, that certain of Mead's critics have attempted to identify Mead's generalized other with God.[50] Although this was certainly not Mead's intent, identifying the generalized other with divine authority is one way of bestowing upon it the sanctions for which Mead has neglected to account.

From this perspective the conservatism of the generalized other becomes clear. Mead incorporates it into his theory as a self-evident kind of control, thereby dispensing with any need to justify its effects. Mead's naive view of political institutions and his over-simplified concept of change stem from his denial of any need to investigate the source of the influence of the generalized other. The generalized other has *power* on its side; it is the incorporation within the individual of the distribution of power within society, in the form of the norms and rules generated by the dominant institutions. Institutions are not neutral settings within which each individual takes the role of the other in an egalitarian manner. Rather, institutions represent the distribution of values within the society. Once social acts are organized into a social setting, that setting imposes certain restrictions on further social acts. The element of social control intervenes, allowing certain individuals and groups more power than others to define the situation and to control the interaction. The example of the bank robbery can again be used. Each individual involved (the robber, the teller, and the witness) is an integral component of the act in that each is consciously and meaningfully interacting with the others, but this does not mean that they are on an equal footing. The armed robber obviously has more power to define the situation; the teller, who presumably wishes to avoid being killed, must take the role of the other in order to anticipate what the robber will do and comply with his demands. The robber is under no such pressure since the distribution of power in the situation is such that he can enforce his demands without doing so. Because Mead overlooks social control, in this example he only sees individuals interacting together within the social act.

A further consequence of Mead's cognitive theory of the self is that it makes no allowances for concrete emotions and tends to swallow up the individual within an abstract morality. Mead deals only briefly with the role of emotions, stating that they have a different status than do cognitions in that they do not arouse in the self the same response they arouse in others:

There is, of course, a great deal in one's conversation with others that does not arouse in oneself the same response it arouses in others. That is particularly true in the case of emotional attitudes. One tries to bully someone else; he is not trying to bully himself. . . .We do not normally use language stimuli to call out in ourselves the emotional response which we are calling out in others. One does, of course, have sympathy in emotional situations; but what one is seeking for there is something which is, after all, that in the other which supports the individual in his own experience. In the case of the poet and actor, the stimulus calls out in the artist that which it calls out in the other, but this is not the natural function of language; we do not assume that the person who is angry is calling out the fear in himself that he is calling out in someone else. The emotional part of our act does not directly call out in us the response it calls out in the other. [51]

For Mead, taking the role of the other is natural because people are social by nature, and it is good because it provides the basis for morality. He does not allow for situations in which one takes the role of the other in order to be either loving and sympathetic or hateful and cruel. He does not make room for choices about *who* or *what* the individual chooses to value. The concrete individual is lost within Mead's society of abstract rational social beings interacting indiscriminately within a neutral social context.

As stated earlier, Mead's theory of self and society is by no means free of problems and limitations. In particular, his view of change is simplistic and inaccurate, and as it stands, it contributes little to a theory of liberation. But the basic kernel of his view, the social, processual self, is sound and can provide an adequate base for further analysis.

Notes

1. George Herbert Mead, *The Philosophy of the Act* (Chicago: University of Chicago Press, 1938), p. 153.

2. Mead states that "It is only through the response that consciousness of meaning appears, a response which involves the consciousness of another self as the presupposition of the meaning in one's own attitude. Other selves in a social environment logically antedate the consciousness of self which introspection analyzes" ("What Social Objects Must Psychology Presuppose?" *Journal of Philosophy* 7 [March 16, 1910]: 178).

3. Mead, *Mind, Self and Society* (Chicago: University of Chicago Press, 1934), p. 135. Mead's idea here is parallel to William James' description of "pure experience," an undifferentiated process of sensation

without reflection. The immediate flux of experience surrounds us with a plain and unqualified field of life, a *that* which is not yet any particular *what*. It is, as James indicates, "as yet undifferentiated into thing and thought" (William James, *Essays in Radical Empiricism and a Pluralistic Universe* [New York: E. P. Dutton and Co., 1971], pp. 40-41).

4. The analysis of the self that is presented here is clearly applicable to both women and men. Accordingly, I have tried to avoid sexist language whenever possible. However, when it is necessary, in order to avoid awkwardness or confusion, I have begrudgingly made some limited concessions to the domain of common usage.

5. Mead, "Social Mechanism of Social Consciousness," *Journal of Philosophy* 9 (July 18, 1912): 405.

6. Mead, "Social Psychology and Counterpart to Physiological Psychology," *Psychological Bulletin* 6 (December 15, 1909): 407.

7. David L. Miller, *George Herbert Mead: Self, Language and the World* (Austin, Tex.: University of Texas Press, 1973), pp. 114-15.

8. Mead, *Mind, Self and Society*, p. 7, quoting Mead, "The Genesis of Self and Social Control," *International Journal of Ethics* 35 (April 1925): 263-64.

9. Miller, *George Herbert Mead: Self, Language and the World*, pp. 30-31.

10. Mead, *The Philosophy of the Act*, pp. 451-52.

11. Herbert Blumer, "Sociological Implications of the Thought of George Herbert Mead," *American Journal of Sociology* 71 (March 1966): 541.

12. Mead states that

It is in the form of the generalized other that the social process influences the behavior of the individuals involved in it and carrying it on, i.e., that the community exercises control over the conduct of its individual members; for it is in this form that the social process or community enters as a determining factor into the individual's thinking. In abstract thought the individual takes the attitudes of the generalized other toward himself, without reference to its expression in any particular other individuals; and in concrete thought he takes that attitude toward his behavior of those other individuals with whom he is involved in the given social situation or act. But only by taking the attitude of the generalized other toward himself, in one or another of these ways, can he think at all; for only thus can thinking—or the internalized conversation of gestures which constitutes thinking— occur. And only through the taking by individuals of the attitude or attitudes of the generalized other toward themselves is a universe of

discourse, as that system of common or social meanings which thinking presupposes as its context, rendered possible (Mead, *Mind, Self
and Society*, pp. 155-56).

13. Mead's defense of individual freedom is couched, typically, in the
language of cognitive choice:

> The only way in which we can react against the disapproval of the
> entire community is by setting up a higher sort of community which in
> a certain sense outvotes the ones we find. A person may reach a point
> of going against the whole world about him; he may stand out by
> himself over against it. But to do that he has to speak with the voice of
> reason to himself. He has to comprehend the voices of the past and of
> the future. That is the only way in which the self can get a voice which
> is more than the voice of the community. . . .We must not forget this
> other capacity, that of replying to the community and insisting on the
> gesture of the community changing. We can reform the order of
> things; we can insist on making the community standards better
> standards. . . .The process of conversation is one in which the individ-
> ual has not only the right but the duty of talking to the community of
> which he is a part, and bringing about those changes which take place
> through the interaction of individuals. That is the way, of course, in
> which society gets ahead, by just such interactions, as those in which
> some person thinks a thing out. We are continually changing our
> social system in some respects, and we are able to do that intelligently
> because we can think (ibid., p. 168).

14. Mead, *The Philosophy of the Act*, p. 449. (Italics mine.)

15. This argument had been called into question by some social critics,
who argue that contemporary society had become so standardized into
bureaucratically administered technologically rational units that it has
become "one-dimensional." The most well-known advocate of this position is, of course, Herbert Marcuse, whose neo-Marxian analysis of contemporary society in *One-Dimensional Man* (Boston: Beacon Press,
1964), is based on this contention. However, it is possible to grant these
critics their point concerning the danger of administrative fascism while still
maintaining that in large and complex societies there is genuine pluralism
in the generalized other. Even Marcuse states that "there are large areas
within and without these societies where the described tendencies do not
prevail" (p. xvii), thus recognizing some cultural diversity. The continued
existence of ethnic and cultural subgroups, and the appearance of various
political and social critiques of mass society, are indicators of such pluralism.

16. For example, Charles T. Gillen labels Mead a "social determinist,"
claiming that "the 'I' is not a logically integral and clearly demonstrated

part of Mead's theory," and that "in the Meadian perspective the self is entirely dependent upon the socially determined 'me' " (Charles T. Gillen, "Freedom and the Limits of Social Behaviorism: A Comparison of Selected Themes from the Work of G. H. Mead and Martin Buber," *Sociology* 9 [January 1975]: 37). However, Gillen admits that he bases his analysis only on the ideas in *Mind, Self and Society* and on a few of Mead's essays. Through this sloppy scholarship Gillen has allowed himself to overlook the impact of the ideas in *The Philosophy of the Present*, wherein Mead discusses the importance of the unique and novel individual. The same omission is found in Richard Lichtman's analysis ("Symbolic Interaction and Social Reality: Some Marxist Queries," *Berkeley Journal of Sociology* 15 [1970]: 73-93), in which he makes reference to "Mead's extreme social behaviorism." These analyses err because they fail to recognize the complexity of Mead's "I" and "me" concepts, and the multidimensionality of the relation between them. As I argue later in this chapter, there is a problem with Mead's formulation of the "I/me" relation, but this criticism does not adequately capture it.

17. Mead, *Mind, Self and Society*, p. 177.

18. This idea is also proposed by Maurice Natanson in *The Social Dynamics of George Herbert Mead* (Washington, D.C.: Public Affairs Press, 1956), p. 15, which is one of the most suggestive analyses available of Mead's view of the "I/me" relation. Taking a phenomenological perspective, Natanson argues that Mead has emphasized the social base of individual self-consciousness at the expense of an adequate account of the subjective "I." Much of my own critique parallels Natanson's insight. However, Natanson argues that it is necessary to posit a transcendent ego that stands above experience and orders it definitively. This means abandoning the processual view and substituting a substantial self that puts the stamp of ownership onto one's experiences and differentiates them from the experiences of others. I argue, however, that this function can be accounted for adequately within the framework of the processual self. It is the function of the "me," in addition to internalizing the attitudes of the generalized other, to provide temporal continuity to one's experiences. This aspect of the "me" refers to the total content of the individual's experience, including one's memories of the past and one's expectations for the future. The "me" provides for continuity and permanence in experience. It gives the self the unity that is necessary to define one's experiences as belonging to oneself, without denying the importance of interactions between selves and without erecting a transcendent self outside of experience. William James provides a similar, and characteristically

eloquent, explanation of the manner in which one can identify experiences as one's own without taking refuge in the substantial self:

> My experiences and your experiences are "with" each other in various external ways, but mine pass into mine and yours pass into yours in a way which yours and mine never pass into one another. Within each of our personal histories, subject, object, interest, and purpose *are continuous or may be continuous*. Personal histories are processes of change in time, and the change itself is one the things immediately experienced (William James, *Essays in Radical Empiricism and a Pluralistic Universe*, pp. 27-28).

19. Mead, "The Social Self," *Journal of Philosophy* 10 (July 3, 1913): 374.

20. I am grateful to Dr. Michael Weinstein, Department of Political Science, Purdue University, for pointing out to me the consequences and implications of this dual level of "I/me" interaction.

21. Mead, *Mind, Self and Society*, p. 174.

22. Ibid., p. 175.

23. Mead, *The Philosophy of the Present* (Chicago: Open Court Publishing Co., 1932), p. 27.

24. My thanks to Dr. Edwin Fogelman, Department of Political Science, University of Minnesota, for pointing out to me the importance of this omission in Mead's account of the self.

25. In Mead's discussion of action and knowledge, he clearly emphasizes the importance of this point. He states that

> reflective thinking consists in communication, in role-taking, wherein the individual form assumes the attitudes of the group, a generalized other, and it is this common perspective, common attitudes, which is the universal in the philosophy of the act. The forms of knowledge consist, then, not of static subsisting relations or of Platonic eternal objects but rather of tested hypotheses. The testing of a hypothesis consists of an act which unifies the various perspectives of which statement is given in the hypothesis itself. Perspectives are united through action, and action is essential to the scientific verification (Mead, *The Philosophy of the Act*, p. xlix).

26. Mead, *Mind, Self and Society*, p. 9.

27. Even the most open and flexible of the "substantial self" theories are incompatible with Mead's nonessentialist process view. For example, Harry Stack Sullivan tries to integrate some of the Meadian insights into a neo-Freudian framework, emphasizing the extent to which selves are constituted through interaction. However, Sullivan sees human inter-

action as guided by certain basic psychological drives—the pursuit of gratification and of security. These are basic structural components of the self in the sense that they hold true under all circumstances and do not vary with social context. From the Meadian perspective, even this qualified neo-Freudianism imposes an unacceptable structure onto the ongoing temporal process of experience.

For a good brief introduction to Sullivan's ideas, see J. A. C. Brown, *Freud and the Neo-Freudians* (London: Cassell and Co., 1961).

28. Blumer, "Sociological Implications of the Thought of George Herbert Mead," p. 536.

29. Mead, "What Social Objects Must Psychology Presuppose? " p. 176.

30. Mead, *Mind, Self and Society*, p. 233.

31. Ibid., p. 164.

32. Jerome G. Manis and Bernard N. Meltzer, eds., *Symbolic Interaction* (Boston: Allyn and Bacon, 1972), p. 145.

33. John Watson, the founder of the school of behaviorism in psychology, was a frequent target of Mead's criticism for his reductionist, linear approach to human behavior.

34. Mead, *The Philosophy of the Present*, p. xxxiii.

35. Henri Bergson, *Time and Free Will* (London: George Allen and Unwin, 1910), p. 226. One finds a parallel concept in William James' notion of "fringed" experience, extended and indeterminate: "Our fields of experience have no more definite boundaries than have our fields of view. Both are fringed by a *more* that continuously develops, and that continuously supercedes them as life proceeds" (William James, *Essays in Radical Empiricism and a Pluralistic Universe*, p. 39).

36. Mead, *The Philosophy of the Act*, pp. 347-48.

37. Frank M. Doan, "Notations of George Herbert Mead's Principle of Sociality with Special Reference to Transformations," *Journal of Philosophy* 53 (September 27, 1956): 609.

38. Charles Morris, *The Pragmatic Movement in American Philosophy* (New York: George Braziller, 1970), pp. 129-30.

39. Mead, *The Philosophy of the Act*, p. xii.

40. Ibid., pp. 460-61.

41. Ibid., p. 18.

42. Mead, "The Philosophical Basis of Ethics," *International Journal of Ethics* 18 (April 1908): 318-19.

43. Mead, "The Social Self," p. 379.

44. Mead, *The Philosophy of the Act*, p. 450.

45. Mead, "Scientific Method and the Moral Sciences," *International Journal of Ethics* 33 (April 1923): 235.

46. Thomas Kuhn, *The Structure of Scientific Revolutions* (Chicago: University of Chicago Press, 1962), p. 113.

47. Ibid., p. 96.

48. Mead, *Mind, Self and Society*, p. 167.

49. Ibid., p. 173.

50. Paul E. Pfeutze, *The Social Self* (New York: Bookman Associates, 1954).

51. Mead, *Mind, Self and Society*, pp. 147-48.

Power and Domination in Self-Other Relations 3

Despite the difficulties that surround Mead's discussion of certain political and epistemological issues, his analysis is basically sound and can be taken as the starting point for an expanded theory of the self. The key insight in his analysis lies with his insistence that the self is social and that it is processual. By viewing these two interrelated characteristics as primary, Mead dispenses with many problems that plague competing theories that start from an individualistic rather than a social perspective and that view the self as a substantive thing rather than an ongoing process of experience. Mead's emphasis on process recognizes the basic temporality of experience and integrates the self into this temporal flow rather than trying to "fix" it outside of time. It is often difficult for individuals who are accustomed to conceiving of time as a linear progression of identical, evenly spaced units, from past to present to future, to grasp the impact of this radically different view of temporality. Mead conceives of time in terms of change, in terms of the duration of a particular event or activity. [1]

Mead locates the self squarely within the flow of experience rather than hypothesizing some Archimedian point from which the self looks down upon and organizes experience. For Mead, as for Bergson before him, time is not the spatially defined units of minutes or hours as they are depicted by the clock but the duration that extends over a series of actions and events and lends unity to them by incorporating them into the ongoing process of experience. To use Bergson's metaphor, time is the relation between human actions in the same way that a melody is the *relation* between the notes, not simply the notes themselves.[2]

Mead's emphasis on the processual nature of the self also preserves his analysis from the necessity of positing any nonempirical prior consciousness at the base of the self. This further avoids the unhappy problem of specifying any substantive content to human nature. Mead's analysis is not concerned with the pursuit of the elusive spectre of "human nature" but with the process of human experience. In Mead's analysis of the relation between the "I" and the "me" (what has here been called "I/me" relation #2), he accounts for the manner in which the self unifies its own experience, and he distinguishes that experience from the experience of other selves. He does so without appealing to any transcendental ego or substantive self that would have to stand apart from the temporal flow of experience in order to organize it. Mead's view is not an "essentialist" one, in that he does not search for some single set of traits that constitute the basic substance of the self. He views the self not as a thing that develops but as the very process of development itself.

Another merit of Mead's analysis is that he provides for individual creativity and uniqueness as well as for coordinated social interaction. The internal dynamic of the self as described in the "I/me" relation #2 sees individuals as constructing their activity, not simply as responding to external stimuli. Mead recognizes that meaning and value in the world are not intrinsic to things, nor are they a coalescence of psychological elements in the minds of individuals; rather, they are created in and through social interaction. The view that individuals create meaning in their world through the process of interaction with other selves is one that makes individual selves the authors of their world.

A further advantage of Mead's view is his account of the nature of consciousness. The process of self-expression, which is the realm of the creative "I," and of reflections back upon the expressive activity, which is also the function of the "I" as it is set within the context of social experience provided by the "me," is one that still further integrates individual uniqueness with social continuity. The dialectic of expression and reflection, which parallels Mead's account of consciousness and of self-consciousness, integrates the ability of the self to be both the subject and the object of its actions. Moreover, the complex dialectical interaction which takes place on multiple levels simultaneously—within each self, among selves, and between selves and the environment—brings out the relational character of Mead's analysis. The different aspects of self-other relations are actually interconnected moments that can be separated only artificially for purposes of analysis. In reality, each factor can be defined only in relation to the other factors because basic to each is its relation to the others. For example, the expressive-reflective activity of the "I" can only be understood with reference to the accompanying function of the "me," of the generalized other, of language, of the social act, and so forth. Each aspect of self-other relations is bound to every other aspect, so that basic to each one is the interaction between them. [3]

A final merit of Mead's analysis is that he explains behavior by reference to the interaction that takes place among acting selves, and not by reference to some factor that is attributed to these selves, such as roles and attitudes. Mead recognizes that it is human beings who act, not some abstracted psychological or sociological characteristic that observers have attributed to human beings. In this manner, Mead demystifies both collective and psychological categories. Collectivities such as class or party are revealed as being abstract classifications made up of individuals fitting their actions together and taking joint action through the process of making meaningful indications to themselves and others. Similarly, psychological classifications such as roles and attitudes are seen as partial characterizations of concrete selves, not as the whole of any acting self. [4]

The multiple advantages to Mead's view of the self can, then, be traced to the implications that follow from adopting a theory of the self that emphasizes sociality and process. The major problems of Mead's analysis can likewise be traced to a primary characteristic of his theory: his insistence on an exclusively cognitive theory of self and society. These problems, as discussed in the preceding chapter, are largely a result of Mead's total emphasis on cognition, on individuals as thinking beings, interacting rationally and instrumentally with one another. This emphasis leads to his failure to consider the effects of social structures and to his inability to account for relations involving power and domination.

In his analysis of self/society relations, Mead's primary emphasis on cognition as the basis for interaction leads him to be satisfied with an analysis of *how* people internalize the content of the generalized other. He neglects to demonstrate *why* in fact they obey it. He assumes that knowledge leads to action, that because the norms and rules of the generalized other are available as a framework for organizing self-other interaction, they will automatically be accepted as such. This view is a result of Mead's inconsistent treatment of the "I/me" relation. In the view that has here been called "I/me" relation #1, in which the "I" acts and the "me" judges the act by bringing to bear on it the standards of the generalized other, there is no problem in explaining why people obey the generalized other because by definition they are limited to the range of its standards in judging the actions of the "I." If every act of the "I" is judged and guided by the rules and norms of the generalized other as applied by the "me," then there is no alternative but to conform to the community standards. In such a case, knowledge and action would indeed coincide. But this way of viewing the "I/me" interaction is plagued with internal problems. It cannot account for why anyone ever could reject the standards of the generalized other, even though it is clear that historically this has often been the case. The relationship of the "I/me" #1 is a dualistic one in that every action of the impulsive "I" is limited by the implacable, inflexible "me." Thus, the ongoing nature of the temporal flow of experience is interrupted, and the emphasis on process is lost.

In order to preserve the important kernel of Mead's view of the self as process, it is necessary to reject this view in favor of the more adequate view of the self captured in the "I/me" relation #2. When Mead stresses this aspect of the internal dynamic of the self, as he does most clearly in *The Philosophy of the Present*, the creative spontaneous "I" both acts and judges the results of its acts and does so within the context that is set by the "me." In this case, the content of the "me" is determined partially, *but not exclusively*, by the standards of the generalized other. The "me" also contains the individual's memories of past actions and anticipations of future actions, and these broaden the context within which the "I" acts, allowing the "I" a field of action that is not strictly limited by the definition of acceptable conduct that is established by the generalized other. The dialectic of expression and reflection is thus broadened and made more inclusive of different possibilities for individual action. By expression, the self takes action in the world; by reflection, the self turns its experience back upon itself, becoming the object as well as the subject of its actions. Part of this action involves the taking of the attitude of the other toward oneself. Mead assumes that the individual then acts to adjust himself to the ongoing social process and to coordinate his activities with the actions of others within the social act. But one could also use the expression/reflection process to reject the generalized other and disrupt the social act. The expressive/reflective (subject-object, "I/me") interaction is indeed primary, but the direction it will take in any given instance is not so easily established.

It is from the perspective of the "I/me" relation #2 that one is led to question the role of the generalized other in regulating individual conduct. Mead has demonstrated that the socialization process is one of the most dominant single influences on the actions of the self, but he had not shown *why* this is the case. In order to explain why as well as how the generalized other plays such a dominant role in guiding individual action, it is necessary to go back to Mead's discussion of the social act and to redirect this discussion toward a more adequate account of the function of institutions in society.

Mead defines the social act as the coordinated interactions among individuals in which each adjusts to the other involved in the act from the standpoint of their different perspectives. Each individual occupies and acts from a different position with respect to the social object and the other actors, and each individual acts from a somewhat different perspective, so that the social act must stand as the most basic element of self-other interaction.[5] Mead recognizes the link between social acts and institutions. He sees that institutions are organized sets of social acts structured with reference to the generalized other. Mead maintains that

the complex cooperative processes and activities and institutional functionings of organized human society are also possible only in so far as every individual involved in them or belonging to that society can take the general attitudes of all other such individuals with reference to these processes and activities and institutional functionings, and to the organized social whole of experiential relations and interactions thereby constituted —and can direct his own behavior accordingly.[6]

And again:

Thus the institutions of society are organized forms of groups or social activity—forms so organized that the individual members of society can act adequately and socially by taking the attitudes of others toward these activities.[7]

Thus, Mead recognizes the incipient link between social acts and institutions, but he does not provide an analysis of the nature of this link. Certainly, social acts can be thought of as coordinated interactions among individuals, integrated by reference to each individual's relations to the others and to the social object. But some people have different relations to the social object than do others, and these people, who *control* social objects, are thereby able to control, or at least influence, the activities of others. These people can define the situation within which others act and can enforce their definition of the situation because they have control over the particular social objects at hand. These people can be said to have *power*. Power, defined as the ability to establish and enforce the definition of the situation within which the other participants must act, radically alters the nature of the self-other interaction taking place. Mead is correct in pointing to social interaction as the source of human meaning, but most social interaction does not take place between equals. Those actors who control the appropriate social objects can establish and maintain their definition of the situation, often at the expense of the other actors involved. The powerless may cling to their own perspective on the interaction, but they lack the means to insist that others recognize it. The persons who have the power to define the situation are not under the same pressure to adjust their actions to the behavior of the others as are those without this power because they are capable of directing the social act without making such adjustments. On the other hand, the individuals lacking power to define the situation are left with little alternative but to adjust their behavior to the behavior of the powerful. In other words, the dominant person or group does not need to take the role of the other, while the subordinate must do so.

This definition of power includes, but goes beyond, the conventional view of power as the ability to make a person do something that he would not otherwise have done.[8] One aspect of power is the ability to direct the actions of others. The policeman who arrests me for illegal possession of marijuana and who causes me to appear in court and pay a fine has exercised power over me and has caused me to do something I would not have done otherwise. However, power is a broader and more multidimensional phenomenon than this conventional view indicates. Powerful individuals or groups can affect my actions without directly causing me to take a particular action because they can effectively constrain the alternatives available to me and attach stringent sanctions to them. The policeman in the above example cannot directly force me to pay the fine in question, but he can constrain my choices severely —I can either pay the fine or go to prison. Similarly, my employer cannot literally force me to do a particular task, but he can structure the situation so that the consequences of acting otherwise are undesirable; i.e., I can follow orders or be fired. An armed robber can force me *either* to hand over my money *or* to be killed (robbers seem to have given de facto recognition to this situation through the phrase "your money or your life,") and so on. Power more often appears as the ability to manipulate available alternatives than as the ability to cause specific actions.

This perspective also provides a contextual approach to the study of power. This point, which will be elaborated below, is important because it takes into account the multidimensionality of power relations in contemporary society. Power is a characteristic that emerges within relationships where certain individuals or groups are able to define the situation and control the social objects. It does not accrue directly to the people or objects themselves, but to the context in which they appear. A working-class black may find himself in a position of power in his role as a policeman, but still be powerless during his confrontations with racist landlords or hostile bureaucrats. Power, then, is seldom absolute since even the most abject slave has suicide as an option, and it is contextual, residing in relationships rather than in objects or individuals.

The link between social acts and institutions now becomes more explicit. An institution exists when a social act arises and arrangements are made to perpetuate it. An institution provides the context within which individual members of society take the attitude of the generalized other toward their own activity in order to direct it socially. Once particular social acts are institutionalized, the power relationships within them are also institutionalized; that is, the ability of particular persons or groups to define the situation within which others must act is perpetuated. Power then resides in the institutional arrangements that give rise to and are in turn justified by the generalized other. Hence, it becomes clear why the generalized other exercises such influence over the behavior of individuals. The generalized other represents the distribution of power in society by embodying the norms and rules of the dominant institutions. People tend to conform to the behavioral guidelines of the generalized other because it embodies *power*. It both expresses and reflects organized power relations. These institutions mediate between the individual and society in a way that Mead was not able to address because he did not clearly perceive their function as agents of social control.

With this in mind, the stability that social acts provide in society can be seen in a different light. As symbolic interactionist Herbert Blumer maintains, social acts are

generally orderly, fixed and repetitious by virtue of a common identification of definition of the joint action that is made by its participants. The common definition supplies each participant with decisive guidance in directing his own act so as to fit into the acts of the others. Such common definitions serve, above everything else, to account for the regularity, stability, and repetitiveness of joint action in past areas of group life; they are the source of the established and regulated social behavior that is envisioned in the concept of culture. [9]

But what both Mead and Blumer neglect to consider is that social acts provide this stability because they are organized into institutional settings that reflect a relatively fixed distribution of power in society. The stability provided by organized social acts both reflects and perpetuates the position of the "haves" and the "have-nots," that is, of those who are able to define the situation and those who are forced to operate within a situation that is defined by others. And once institutions arise around particular organizations of social acts, the power resides within the institution itself, thus further perpetuating the inequality. Once a particular distribution of power has become institutionalized, people come to have power through the position they occupy within the institutional setting. They have power because of the way in which the situation *is defined*. They have access to already established points of power and they can generally be expected to use that access so as to secure and perpetuate it for themselves, thus further ensuring the continuation of the situation.

Of course, some social acts—those that take place between equals—are not subject to this analysis. A friendship, for example, may be a relation in which both individuals have equal capacities to define the situation and control the social objects. If this friendship is institutionalized in some way—for example, into a club or society —then the power dialectic might be avoided, providing that all the actors have equal capacities to affect the organization. To continue the example given in Chapter 1, a football game may be a social act that does not entail the exercise of power. If the game is entered into voluntarily by individuals who have substantial bargaining power (that is, they could quite easily quit the game, join another team, and so on), then no power is exercised because no one individual or group has control over the relevant social objects. (One might, however, argue that in the highly competitive and organized world of professional sports, owners, managers, and trainers do have power because they control important social objects—the salaries of the players and the "rules of the game," including both the playing procedures and the informal norms governing the players' behavior.) Unfortunately, examples of social acts based on voluntary and spontaneous camaraderie with others, such as friendships and games, are the exception rather than the rule in our society. Social acts more frequently take place within institutional settings that both express and reflect existing power relations.

Thus, the key to incorporating a consideration of the role of social structure into Mead's theory of the self lies in the role of social acts. Social acts, for the most part, are not neutral settings within which interactions among equals take place. They are settings within which certain individuals or groups, by virtue of their control over social objects, can impose their definition of the situation upon the other participants. Social acts, which connect the individual to society, are organized into institutional settings, which then impose continuing restrictions upon further acts. This implies that not all characteristics are equally important in their effect on the inter-actions between individuals. In a complex industrial society, social acts take place within an institutionalized setting that defines certain characteristics as more important than others with reference to a particular individual's ability to define the situation he is in. The fact of being a woman, or black, or poor, or a student is not simply one further factor that must be taken into account in the social inter-action. Such factors are likely to be decisive in determining the performance of the individuals involved[10] because the institutional arrangement within which social acts take place are such that these characteristics place the individual who possesses them at an initial disadvantage. Such individuals lack the control over social objects which is the source of the ability to define the situation within which they must act. Such factors define individuals as members of a common group, and that group membership may well be the single most important characteristic placing those individuals within their social setting.

In his book *Asylums*, Erving Goffman gives a further illustration of the ways in which the claims of the generalized other are enforced. Goffman describes social interaction within total institu-tions (i.e., institutions that exercise total control over their partici-pants, such as mental hospitals and prisons) as a process through which the dominant parties (i.e., the hospital staff or the prison wardens) define the situation of the subordinates (patients or prisoners), by virtue of the ability of the dominant to control the relevant social objects (the hospital or prison facilities and the norms and rules that govern their operation). Through their posi-tion of power, the dominant group provides and controls the con-tent of the generalized other that is dominant in that setting, so that the patients' and prisoners' views of themselves are mediated through the eyes of the powerful.

This perspective on the source and function of power allows mutiple bases of power to exist within society. It does not reduce the field of dominance/subordinance relations to any one axis of self-other interaction: Instead, it broadens the theory to take account of differing sources of power. By refusing to define any particular characteristic of human behavior as the "essence" of "human nature," by referring instead to a continuing temporal process of experience for a definition of self, this perspective refrains from singling out any one aspect of the broad field of human action as more basic than the rest. By proposing a definition of power that rests on the ability of persons or groups to define the situation within which others must act, this view also addresses all different kinds of dominance/subordinance relations without reducing them to any one particular common denominator, whether it be class, or race, or sex. Thus, within contemporary American society, one could say that, on the whole, men have power over women, whites over blacks, employers over employees, social workers over poor people, teachers over students, and public officials and bureaucrats over citizens. These broad generalizations refer to the contemporary dynamics of dominant institutions in society and to the generalized other that reflects and legitimizes them. The institutions of marriage and the family, of capitalist economic arrangements, of welfare bureaucracies, of educational institutions, and of the government, plus the ubiquity of ideas concerning sexual and racial inferiority, provide the settings within which these power relations take place. The interlocking nature of the relationship among institutions, and between the institutions and the generalized other, becomes clear. The links between them are such that each tends to act to support and reinforce the others. So, for example, the institution of marriage, by defining the woman as dependent economically on her husband and as inferior to him in terms of her capacities and activities, creates a dominance/subordinance relation that has further implications for the woman's relation to other institutional settings. If she is poor, she is likely to become the recipient of welfare aid and thus become a subordinate party with reference to the welfare bureaucracy; if she enters a traditional educational institution, she is likely to be defined by similar ideas concerning the inferiority of her capacities and activities; if she enters the public work force, she will probably discover that her labor is not as highly valued as that of men. The individuals or groups who have power in one institutional setting are thus not unlikely to have it in others as well. One reason is the linkages between institutions. Another is that the norms and rules of the generalized other that serve to reflect and legitimize such relations within one realm are likely to operate in a similar way in other realms as well.

This perspective on the nature of power accounts for multiple bases of power and points out the possibility, and, indeed, the likelihood of interconnecting links between these bases, but it does not posit any one source as more fundamental than the rest. In this way, relations of dominance and subordination become one possibility for human interaction within any particular sphere, without it being determined in advance that any particular set of interactions will be relations of dominance and subordination. Thus empirical examination is required to establish in any one case that a power relation exists because one must establish which party or parties can define the situation within which others must act, and which party or parties has control over the relevant social objects.[11] This approach demystifies power by refusing to attribute it to any one particular collectivity or principle, and by refusing to erect any abstraction standing outside the concrete interaction of individuals in order to account for the relations between them. Power relations become the subject of empirical investigation. The above generalizations can be taken as providing general guidelines for discerning the existence of relations of dominance and subordination, inasmuch as the dominant institutions and the fundamental norms and rules of the generalized other do seem to operate in such a manner, but they cannot be taken as overall laws regarding such relations. Human interaction is so complex that there will always be exceptions to and variations on such generalizations. It is therefore necessary to insist that in each particular case the existence of a power relationship must be demonstrated empirically rather than simply assumed.

This way of viewing power focuses on the process by which relations of dominance and subordinance take place rather than on the historical origin of such relations. Anthropological evidence regarding the origin of power is not conclusive and in any case is open to differing interpretations. Theoretical assertions that attribute power relations to economic factors, biological instincts, or psychic drives, are in the end forced to appeal to some static concept of "human nature" in order to support these claims. Such concepts of "human nature" are ultimately unverifiable, for they rest on the assertion that some primitive quality underlies and motivates all behavior. Behavior that is contrary to this quality or characteristic must then be explained away, often through some elaborate and contorted theoretical argument. For instance, if it is asserted (as it has often been) that people act to maximize pleasure and minimize pain, then it becomes difficult to explain a deliberate act of self-sacrifice—for example, the self-torture that some Indian holy men inflict upon themselves, or the self-immolation of certain political and religious martyrs. To explain such acts by asserting that they constitute the pleasure of the individuals involved, and are thus consistent with the specified principle of human activity, is to engage in circular argument. It is to assert that whatever one does is by definition pleasurable. It reduces to the statement that "people do what they do, and don't do what they don't do," and thus becomes tautological. Such concepts of human nature are in direct opposition to Mead's concept of the social, processual self, which does not attempt to single out any dimension of experience as more basic than the rest. Thus, an explanation of power based on Mead's view of the self can account for the *perpetuation* of domination, not its origin.

This view of power is clearly a contextual approach in that it locates power relations with reference to certain contexts of human interaction. The types of interaction that are the most significant arenas for self-other interactions and that involve the most important social acts and the most crucial social objects are the contexts within which power is exercised. Consequently, the locus of dominance/subordinance relations is likely to vary across cultures and through time. Moreover, within a particular social setting, the importance of certain contexts is likely to vary from person to person. Therefore, while one can make generalizations about dominance/subordinance relations, based on observations of the particular institutional ordering at hand, there are no hard and fast laws that can be said to govern the exercise of power.

Other social theorists have recognized that Mead's theory lacks a viable concept of social structure, and they have suggested various ways in which this inadequacy might be remedied. In his book *Rethinking Sociology*, Irving Zeitlin recommends a theoretical merger of Mead, Marx, and Freud (à la Marcuse) in order to develop the idea of repression that he claims is implicit in Mead's writings. Zeitlin maintains that

Mead's "me" and "generalized other," and their impact upon the "biologic I," do not sufficiently recognize the element of domination in the process of taking the role of the other and in internalization. To use Freud's terms as modified by Marcuse, Mead recognizes repression (although not as explicitly as Freud and without the focus on sexuality) but not surplus repression. In other words, he fails to take systematic account of the very condition that Marx placed at the center of his investigation. Just as we are able to extrapolate from Freud's concepts, so are we able to extrapolate from Mead's. Everything in Mead's work suggests that surplus repression is wholly compatible with his theory. Indeed, by building this concept into his framework, we enhance greatly the compatibility of his dialectical conceptions with Marx's.[12]

Zeitlin thus argues that Mead's inadequate account of social structure can be supplemented satisfactorily by incorporating into the "I/me" relationship the notion of surplus repression, defined as restrictions, above and beyond those necessary to perpetuate society, that are placed on individual instincts by social rules.

Zeitlin is correct in his observation that Mead does not deal adequately with the effect of domination and coercion on the individual, with the "price" that one must pay in obeying the generalized other. He is also correct in asserting that Mead's conceptual scheme is sufficiently flexible to allow for the insertion of such supplementary insights in order to deal with these inadequacies. But Zeitlin's analysis suffers from a misinterpretation of Mead and from a failure to recognize a basic incompatibility between Mead and Freud that makes a merger of their two theories of the self unlikely.

First, Zeitlen views Mead's "I" as an impulsive biologic unit, similar in nature to Freud's "id." He emphasizes the organic references in Mead's writings and Mead's reliance on Darwinian concepts to support this view of the biological "I." It is undeniable that Mead does indeed make such references and utilize such conceptual language, but to emphasize this as primary is to overlook the basic priority that Mead gives to the cognitive functions of the self. In fact, as indicated in Chapter 2, the major difficulties in Mead's theory can be traced to this exclusive reliance on the cognitive, intellectual aspect of the self. Mead defines thinking, the internalization of the conversation of significant gestures, as the primary experiential phase in the genesis of the self: "The essence of the self, as we have said, is cognitive: it lies in the internalized conversation of gestures which constitutes thinking, or in terms of which thought or reflection proceeds."[13]

Second, Zeitlin's attempt to merge Mead and Freud suffers from a failure to recognize that the basic emphasis on process and sociality in Mead is incompatible with Freud's view of an instinctual, substantive self. As has been shown, Mead rejects the idea that there is a primary content to the human self. He opts instead for the notion that the self is characterized by an ongoing temporal process that is fundamentally social in character. Mead does make reference to certain naturalistic aspects of the self, but I have argued that these are inconsistent with his emphasis on process and that they give rise to two divergent views of the relationship between the "I" and the "me." It is the second view of the "I/me" relationship, as is argued above, that is consistent with the social, processual self and that resolves the contradiction between Mead's biologism and empiricism. Freud, on the other hand, sees certain specific innate instincts as the most basic determinants of human behavior, and he relegates social interaction to a position of secondary importance. Clearly, then, the attempt to synthesize Mead and Freud founders on the basic incompatibility of the social, processual self versus the instinctive, substantial self. This accounts for Zeitlin's inability to do more than merely "add' the concepts of Marx, Mead, and Freud, rather than actually integrating their analyses. The project fails because of this basic divergence between the two theories of the self. The shortcomings in Mead's view of social structures are not adequately addressed by a merger with Freud.

A second attempt to broaden Mead's conception of the self in order to include a more adequate account of social structure is that proposed by Peter L. Berger and Thomas Luckmann in *The Social Construction of Reality*. Their argument is extremely suggestive, and as an analysis of institutionalization it has much to offer, but it, too, is ultimately unsatisfactory as a revision of the Meadian perspective. Berger and Luckmann rely heavily on Mead (along with Schutz and others) for their analysis. They argue that, while contemporary Marxists have been seeking liaison with Freud in order to develop the psychological side of Marx's theory, these theorists should instead look to Mead for such assistance. Berger and Luckmann's analysis of the sociology of knowledge is concerned with the relation between human thought and the social context within which it arises. They tie this analysis to Mead's theory by virtue of the common emphasis on the relativization of perspectives, which Mead calls taking the role of the other. In addressing the issue of the relation between human beings and their environment, Berger and Luckmann, like Mead before them, maintain that human beings produce their environment through a process of specifically social activity: "As soon as one observes phenomena that are specifically human, one enters the realm of the social. Man's specific humanity and his sociality are inextricably intertwined. *Homo sapiens* is always, and in the same measure, *homo socius.*"[14] Berger and Luckmann contend that human beings produce their social order, that it is not a part of the "nature of things," or derived from some "laws of nature." On the contrary, it arises as a result of human activity and continues because human activity maintains it.

The basic question, then, is to explain why the social order often appears to be so remote from and independent of human activity. If the connection between human action and the social setting is so intimate, then why does society often appear so stable and unwieldy, so difficult to change? The answer, according to Berger and Luckmann, lies in an analysis of the nature of institutionalization.

Like Mead, Berger and Luckmann posit a convergence between the habitualization of individual actions and the institutional setting in society. In *Movements of Thought in the Nineteenth Century*, Mead argues that institutions are "congealed" habits: "Now these institutions are, after all, the habits of individuals in their interrelation with each other, the type of habit that is handed down from one generation to another." And further, "If institutions are social habits, they represent certain definite attitudes that people assume under certain given social conditions."[15] Berger and Luckmann expand on this connection between habits and institutions. All human action, they maintain, is subject to habitualization; that is, it becomes cast into a pattern, defined in a series of steps that can be reproduced with an economy of effort. Common, everyday actions become habitualized so that one performs them automatically. They become the basis for making decisions about action but are not themselves the subject of decisions. For example, one does not have to decide every morning whether and how to brush one's teeth because the action has become habitualized. This habitualization makes it unnecessary for each situation to be defined anew, and it allows for a large variety of activities to be subsumed and anticipated under the predefinitions of habit. When certain kinds of activities become habitualized in a common way for a group of people, those activities can be said to be institutionalized. The actors share a common definition of the situation and of their actions, a "reciprocity of institutional typifications," based on a common history and a shared pattern of conduct.[16]

Thus, Berger and Luckmann conclude that institutions arise out of habitualization and operate as organizers, controllers, and perpetuators of certain social relationships. This process of institutionalization has multiple effects upon the individuals within it. Since actions have become routinized and structured, it becomes possible to predict other people's behavior. Social interaction becomes stabilized and patterned because the actions relevant to all the actors within a given situation have also become routinized. As a result of existing over time, institutions gain an historicity and are seen as possessing a reality of their own, above and beyond those individuals who are taking part in them at a particular time. Institutions become objectified and crystallized, and they appear to possess an objective reality of their own. Individuals born into a situation in which powerful institutional structures already exist must confront them as historical and objective facticities, as external realities possessing a coercive power. These institutions were produced by human action, but they take on a facticity of their own and their power does not rely on the acknowledgment of particular persons operating within them. It is paradoxically true that human beings are capable of producing a world that we then experience as something other than a human product. Like Marx and Hegel, Berger and Luckmann see that the objectification of the social world can easily lead to its reification, that is, that human beings are capable of producing a reality that denies them:

Reification is the apprehension of human phenomena as if they were things, that is, in non-human or possibly supra-human terms. Another way of saying this is that reification is the apprehension of the products of human activity *as if* they were something else than human products—such as facts of nature, results of cosmic laws, or manifestations of divine will. Reification implies that man is capable of forgetting his own authorship of the human world, and further, that the dialectic between man, the producer, and his products is lost to consciousness. The reified world is, by definition, a dehumanized world. It is experienced by man as a strange facticity, an *opus alienum* over which he has no control rather than as the *opus proprium* of his own productive activity. [17]

The relation between the producer and the product is a dialectical one; self and society interact through a complex process of externalization, objectification, and internalization. Through externalization, society is established as a human product; through objectification, society is established as an objective reality, apart from the individuals within it; and through internalization, the objectified world reenters consciousness through socialization, and human beings are seen as social products as well as social producers. Berger and Luckmann emphasize that this process takes place at both the macro and the micro levels. It is an account of how society as a whole is formed, as well as of how each individual within society is shaped.

As can readily be seen, Berger and Luckmann draw heavily on Mead for their analysis of institutionalization. They have expanded and made more explicit Mead's analysis of the dialectic of self-society interaction by discussing in detail the complex interconnections between habitualization, objectification, and institutionalization. But the heritage of Mead can be a disadvantage as well as an advantage: Berger and Luckmann have incorporated from Mead much that is problematic as well as much that is insightful. Certainly, many of the more routine, tedious, and repetitive activities that human beings perform are subject to the habitualization-institutionalization dialectic that Berger and Luckmann describe. But to maintain that *all* human activity can be so organized is to deny the creative, indeterminate aspect of the human self; it is to center on the "me" and ignore the "I." It seems that Berger and Luckmann's view of the self centers on the "I/me" relation #1, in which the "me," defined solely as the internalized generalized other, dominates and guides the activities of the "I." They do not account for the actions of the creative "I" as depicted in the "I/me" relation #2, in which the "I" both acts and judges its acts in a way that allows it to go beyond the constrictions of the generalized other. The activities of such a creative "I" cannot be subjected to the habitualization process without losing their creative force. Habit is that which is routine, repetitive, and fixed, while the "I" is always capable of unpredicted, indeterminant action. This view also overlooks the fact that activities that have become routinized and structured for some individuals may still be spontaneous and unstructured for others. For example, sexual activity between two long-married individuals may well become routinized, predictable, even boring, while sexual interaction between two (or more) newly acquainted individuals is likely to be anything but routinized or boring.

Berger and Luckmann go on to maintain that institutionalization can take place around any collective action and that there is no *a priori* reason for institutions to hang together in an integrated fashion. The fact that institutions *do* seem to hang together in such a fashion is explained by reference to a "strain toward consistency" on the part of individuals within the institutions:

> But while performances can be segregated, meanings tend toward at least minimal consistency. As the individual reflects about the successive moments of his experience, he tries to fit their meanings into a consistent biographical framework. . . .Great care is required in any statement one makes about the "logic" of institutions. The logic does not reside in the institutions and their external functionalities, but in the way these are treated in reflection about them. Put differently, reflective consciousness superimposes the quality of logic on the institutional order.[18]

Berger and Luckmann rest their explanation on the reciprocity of institutionalization; that is, institutions are integrated and take their meaning from the way people define them. This may well be the case, but it is not the whole story. Some people or groups have greater ability to define institutional settings than do others, and these people or groups have *power*. Institutions do not hang together by accident or by a fortuitous reciprocity of definitions, but because dominant groups structure the institutional settings according to their own definition of the situation. The interaction between the generalized other and the various institutions, as indicated by the internalized generalized other within individuals who are acting in those institutional settings, serves to guide and integrate the functions that institutions perform. The dominant norms and rules of the society come to be reflected more or less consistently in the dominant institutions, as a result of the pervasiveness of the generalized other as both the expression and the reflection of the distribution of power. Like Mead, Berger and Luckmann have neglected to account for power relationships in society. Their analysis of the self-society interaction that leads to institutionalization is a necessary clarification of Mead's self-society dialectic, but their failure to account either for the activities of the creative "I" or for the existence of relations of dominance and subordination are crucial defects in their analysis. Like Zeitlin, Berger and Luckmann also have failed to incorporate an adequate consideration of power into the Meadian perspective.

Other social theorists have attempted to deal with Mead's inadequate conception of social structure by constructing a theoretical merger of Marx and Mead. As indicated earlier, this merger was recommended by Berger and Luckmann and also has been discussed briefly by others.[19] The most explicit attempt to effect such a merger is that proposed by Richard Ropers in his article "Mead, Marx, and Social Psychology." Ropers proposes to fit Mead into a Marxian framework in order to provide an account of subjectivity that he observes to be lacking in Marx. After indicating certain common themes in both Marx and Mead (both have an evolutionary frame of reference and both emphasize the social origin of the individual), Ropers states that

while Mead's social psychology, in itself, is insufficient for a complete sociological understanding of social reality, if it is relieved of its Idealist philosophical baggage and is incorporated into the structural-historical framework of Marxism, then, even its value as a social psychology would be greatly enhanced. Such an incorporation would provide a foundation for a continued development of a social psychology based on Marxist principles.[20]

Ropers proposes that Mead's social psychology be used to establish certain "mediating links" between the psychological processes of individuals and the social structures in society. While Mead's analysis of the subjective factor is insightful, Ropers maintains, it is grossly inadequate when compared to the "scientific" treatment that Marx provides. He intends to incorporate Mead's "unsystematic" insights into the overall "scientific" framework of Marxism.[21] Ropers claims that Mead's theories of self-other interaction, once incorporated into the Marxist paradigm, can explain the nature of the socialization process, can elaborate the social psychology of class consciousness and false consciousness, and can specify the link between macro- and micro-level phenomena, or what Marx called the substructure and the super-structure. Ropers emphasizes the complexity of the Marxian dialectic as it relates the economic substructure to the various aspects of the superstructure, and he hopes to insert Mead's self-other relationship into the Marxian picture in order to clarify this relation further.

Ropers' attempt to merge Marx and Mead is in part a response to the same inadequacy in Mead that has already been noted: his failure to take adequate account of the working of social structures. But, like Zeitlin's attempt to merge Mead and Freud, Ropers' effort is unsuccessful because it ignores certain basic tenets of Mead's view of the self that make a merger with Marx impossible on any but a very superficial level. Both theorists emphasize the social origin of the individual, and both have an evolutionary notion of change, but beyond these very general common characteristics the two theorists diverge in a fundamental way. Marx, for all his emphasis on sociality, ultimately relies on a concept of human nature that is inconsistent with Mead's denial of such an essence. In addition, Marx's idea of a scientifically based praxis is inconsistent with Mead's notion of the self as process. In order to explicate these two basic disagreements between the two theorists and to demonstrate that they fatally undermine the merger that Ropers proposes, it is necessary to proceed to a more detailed consideration of Marx.

To the extent that Marx can be said to have a psychology, it is based on the idea of needs. The link with Hegel is apparent here; in *The Philosophy of Right*, Hegel discusses the nature of needs as an element in civil society. [22] In *The German Ideology*, Marx elaborates on his view of human beings as the makers of history on the basis of their economic needs. He lists four characteristics of "man's" economic history: (1) people must satisfy their primary material needs in order to survive; (2) when old needs are satisfied, new needs simultaneously emerge; (3) the act of reproduction, of people propagating themselves, leads to the social relationship of the family; and (4) the fulfillment of general material needs leads to the establishment of social relations as modes of cooperation for purposes of production. Marx's analysis of the division of labor, of class structure, of the substructure/superstructure relation, and of alienation are all based on this view of human beings as primarily and fundamentally creatures of needs. [23]

Although Marx is highly critical of other theories that depend upon some particular concept of human nature or the human essence, and while he tries to avoid specifying any particular content to human nature by insisting that it is something that unfolds through history rather than something that is fixed, in the final analysis he appeals to material, physical needs as establishing the content of human nature. Starting from the observation that human beings must meet their physical needs in order to exist, he concludes that all other kinds, and, in fact, all other human characteristics, are manifestations of the need to labor. He claims that

Empirical observations must in each separate instance bring out empirically, and without any mystification and speculation, the connection of the social and political structure with production. The social structure and the State are continually evolving out of the life-process of definite individuals, but individuals, not as they may appear in their own or other people's imagination, but as they *really* are, i.e., as they operate, produce materially, and hence as they work under definite material limits, presuppositions and conditions independent of their will. [24]

For Marx, the ontological foundation of all human activity lies in the sphere of material production, the specific expression of human interchange with nature in the process of satisfying needs.[25] By describing human beings as natural beings, that is, as beings with needs and with the powers to satisfy those needs, Marx, in spite of his disclaimers, indicates a particular direction that human nature must take. Human fulfillment becomes the proper gratification of need through productive activity:

Thus if man is a natural being with a multiplicity of needs, human fulfill-ment—the realization of human freedom—cannot be conceived as an abnegation or subjugation of these needs, but only as their properly human gratification. The only proviso is that they must be inherently human needs. . . .Productive activity, imposed upon man by natural necessity, as the fundamental condition of human survival and develop-ment thus becomes identical to human fulfillment, i.e., the realization of human freedom.[26]

The difficulties with this view become clear in the above restate-ment of Marx's position. Who determines which needs are "human" and which ones are manufactured or artificial? What about people who find fulfillment in denying or subjugating their material needs —for example, monks, aesthetes, and holy persons? Marx's claim that human beings have no nature, *except* for that which flows from their natural needs and powers, allows for a rather large "except." He seems to be maintaining that, because people have needs, they *must* and *ought* to gratify these needs. There is, however, no reason to assume that this is always the case since people are quite capable of choosing to deny their "needs" in particular circum-stances. The observation that people must meet certain physical needs in order to survive is an empirically accurate one, but it does not thereby follow that they ought to do so. Nor does it follow that all other needs and all other human activities are simply manifesta-tions of the need to labor. Marx denies any independent source of human motivation or inclination apart from the activity of labor and the need to labor.

Ropers' attempt to synthesize Marx and Mead founders on the incompatibility of the concepts of human nature in the two theories. Marx, by starting from the assertion that material needs are natural and basic to human activity, builds his theory on the image of the *producing* individual. Mead, on the other hand, in his analysis of the self as a temporal process, denies any particular content to human nature. Mead's emphasis on process is inconsistent with any attempt to attribute a substantive content to the self. Ropers is unable to effect a merger between Marx and Mead for the same reason that Zeitlin was unable to synthesize Mead and Freud. Mead's analysis of the social, processual self cannot be fixed with reference to the image of the *producing* individual. It is, rather, concerned with the entire *experiencing* individual. A theory that denies the existence of any substantive human nature, and one that locates the essence of human nature in the productive activity, are not capable of being combined at this level. To attempt to insert Mead's psychological perspective into the Marxist framework would be to deny the vital element of process in Mead's theory of the self.

It is true that there are certain similarities between Marx and Mead in their discussions of nature. In Marx's view, nature, as that which provides the raw material for labor, is a bond between people. It provides the framework within which social activity takes place. Through their labor, human beings as producers are united with nature, which provides the materials of production. In the *Economical and Philosophical Manuscripts*, Marx maintains that

the human significance of nature only exists for *social* man, because only in this case is nature a *bond* with other *men*, the basis of his existence for others and of their existence for him. Only then is nature the basis of his own *human* experience and a vital element of human reality. The *natural* existence of man has here become his *human* existence, and nature itself has become human for him. Thus *society* is the accomplished union of man with nature, the veritable resurrection of nature, the realized naturalism of man and the realized humanism of nature.[27]

This argument in Marx is quite similar to Mead's statements concerning the self as part of nature and to Mead's reliance on an ethical naturalism to support his moral claims. But, as is argued in Chapter 2, it is precisely this naturalism in Mead that is inconsistent with his process view of the self and with his emphasis on empiricism. So, while it is true that both Marx and Mead share a naturalistic bias, to attempt to use this commonality as the basis for a merger of the two analyses is to forfeit the kernel of Mead's view that is primary in the analysis at hand—the social, processual self.

Ropers' attempt to merge Marx and Mead is in reality an effort to incorporate Mead's idea of self-other interaction into the Marxist body of "scientific truth." Ropers asserts the Marxist claim to scientific status without dealing with the problems that arise with regard to this claim. He chastises Mead for not adhering to the body of truth that Marx supposedly discovered: "For Marxism truth is *discovered* in practice, for Pragmatism truth is *created* in practice."[28] In this sentence, Ropers reveals the basic difference between Mead's view of process and the Marxist concept of praxis. The process that Mead describes is one in which meaning is *created* by the interactions of human beings with each other and the environment. The Marxist notion of praxis refers to the *discovery* of truth through the interaction of human beings with their environment, that is, through productive activity, through labor. On this perennial philosophical question Marx and Mead are at loggerheads, and Ropers cannot bring them together. Ropers notes with regret that "though Mead concurs with Marx on the social origins and functions of the mind and its prerequisites, as far as I know, Mead makes no acknowledgement of the specific social relationship, labor, which is central to the *Weltanschauung* of Marx."[29] The Marxist notion of praxis as the process through which a specific historical truth is revealed is incompatible with Mead's notion of process as the open-ended emergence of socially created meaning.

Drawing on Mead's theory of the self, Ropers tries to show how it is that people mediate between the substructure and the superstructure. He claims that "it is the real living people, who have selves, and take various roles, who are the mediations between macro- and micro-social phenomena and who are the links between substructures and superstructures."[30] He thus urges us to view the concrete, existing individual as the mediating link between the micro-level abstractions (such as roles, attitudes, and motives), and the macro-level abstractions (such as class and society). Ropers' suggestion is dangerous because it is reductionist; micro-level abstractions are fragments of living individuals, not the whole of them. It may be useful for analytic purposes to look at roles, attitudes, postures, and so on, as though they were independent phenomena, but ultimately it must be remembered that these are only partial characterizations of real human beings. Similarly, macro-level abstractions such as groups and classes are conglomerates of real persons who coordinate their activities in particular ways. Neither level actually apprehends the experiencing individual in all of his complexity; both reduce us either to parts of ourselves or to parts of our relations with others. Ropers apparently fails to perceive the irony in his suggestion, for he has essentially turned Mead on his head (to use a well-worn metaphor). Mead locates the concrete, acting individual at the base of his theory, and he points out the hazards of reifying abstract concepts into independent forces, while Ropers wants to relegate the real living individual to the secondary status of mediating between two levels of abstraction. Instead of viewing institutions as mediating forces between individuals, Ropers reduces people to the mediating force between institutions. In his analysis, human beings are the missing link between the substructure and the superstructure.

Mead, by ignoring the influence of power, views all social interactions as equal[31]; Marx, by identifying labor as the most basic form of human activity, singles out economic relations as the sole source of power and ignores or subsumes all others. Neither extreme offers a satisfactory account of self-other relations in contemporary society. A complete account of self-other interactions must deal with *all* forms of dominance/subordinance relations in society, without reducing them to any one axis of activity.

It must be made clear that, while claiming that there are multiple bases of power in society, I am not ignoring or oversimplifying the Marxist case. It is true that, as many Marxists claim, many forms of conflict can be seen as a "cover" for economic domination, or as attempts to draw attention from basic to peripheral issues. For example, Andrew Hacker points out that many recent studies of ethnicity, by focusing on the distinctions between and among ethnic groups, actually obscure the economic status which these groups share.[32] And certainly economic domination remains *one of* the basic and forceful expressions of power in contemporary society. But there are other kinds of power as well. The kind of power that men are able to exercise over women, or white people over black people, or bureaucrats over citizens, cannot be reduced to these individuals' relations to the mode of production. A male blue-collar worker who is married to a female white-collar worker may well be able to dominate his wife in their personal relationships; the politics of the family is not limited to economics. No supposed economic relationship would prohibit a working-class male from raping a middle-class female, and rape is certainly an example of the exercise of power. A group of white working-class families can successfully prohibit a black middle-class family from moving into their neighborhood; the politics of racial prejudice is not limited to economics. Similarly, a petty university official can wreak havoc on the lives of university professors, regardless of the economic differences between them. In the final analysis, the issue of the source of power, of the ability of some persons or groups to define the situation within which others must act, must be an empirical question. It cannot be answered by theoretical fiat; it requires continued empirical investigation. The bases for the exercise of power vary across historical epochs and across cultures, and are multi-dimensional within cultures and epochs. As C. Wright Mills points out, to search for the one exclusive base of power in society is to engage in a form of metaphysics.[33] In order to analyze self-other relations adequately, one must view this question of power as a proper subject for empirical investigation rather than as a target for dogmatic pronouncement about "historical laws."

There are four major sources for the exercise of power in contemporary American society: class, sex, race, and hierarchy (bureaucracy). The Marxists have thoroughly documented the ubiquity of economic domination; Max Weber, among others, has indicated the importance of the bureaucratization of industrial societies; and countless contemporary studies document the dimensions of racial and sexual domination. These four sources of power are not determined in any historical or natural sense; one can imagine societies in which such factors are not salient bases for the exercise of power. In addition, contemporary conflicts such as those in Northern Ireland, Canada, and Lebanon, indicate that religious and linguistic differences can equally serve as bases for social conflict. But in our society at this point in time class, sex, race, and hierarchy can be observed to be the most prominent bases for the exercise of power. Most radical theorists readily recognize the ubiquity of the first three forms of domination in contemporary social relations, and the increasing power of administrative bureaucracies in the post-World War II industrial world makes it incumbent upon us to recognize the fourth as well.[34] The fact that these different types of dominance/subordinance relations often overlap does not therefore mean that they are reducible to a common element. The often lampooned stereotype of the WASP businessman is a telling example precisely because it represents the overlap of sexual, racial, economic, and hierarchical groupings, but that does not mean that any one of them is more basic than the others.

From this perspective, it is possible to reach what might be called a middle point between Mead and Marx: to avoid reducing power relations to a single social dimension, while at the same time indicating which characteristics of selves are more important in determining whether a particular individual is or is not in a position to define the situation in which others must act. For Mead, all characteristics are of equal importance in their effect on the interactions between individuals, and all types of interactions are put on the same plane. All involve acting individuals making meaningful indications to each other and themselves and adjusting their behavior to the behavior of others in order to continue the social act. From this perspective, cooperation cannot be distinguished from conflict. A rape or an embrace, a brawl or a party, a riot or a parade, all have the common characteristic of being social interactions among individuals. By introducing the idea of power into the account of social acts, one can begin to distinguish between and among social acts based on an analysis of the ability of the participants to define the situation within which they must act. These four dimensions of power—class, sex, race, and hierarchy—can then be seen as defining which characteristics are more important in indicating an individual's role in power relations. The fact of being wealthy, or being white, or being male, or exercising administrative authority are characteristics that are more relevant to one's ability to define the situation and control social objects than are other personal characteristics. The more overlap there is between these characteristics with regard to particular individuals or groups, the more likely they are to be able to exercise power.

A word of caution is in order here. These characteristics are only *potential* indicators of power. Every particular situation must be investigated in order to establish whether or not power is in fact being exercised by specific individuals or groups. These are tentative indicators rather than definitive statements; there are always exceptions to such generalizations about self-other relations. Women are often able to manipulate men, and workers can successfully coerce employers. Minority groups can sometimes overpower racial majorities, and bureaucratic hierarchies can be undermined. Here it is necessary to avoid oversimplification. The fact that a male factory worker abuses his wife and children does not therefore warrant the conclusion that this man occupies an overall position of power in society. The exercise of power in a particular social interaction is relative to the status of the participants in the social act. This man in all likelihood occupies subordinate, powerless roles in most of his social interactions, due to his subordinate economic status. He certainly exercises no power with respect to his overall position in society. But in his family relations he is able to define the situation within which others must act; within the institution of marriage and the family, he does wield power. A person can be powerful in some social interactions and powerless in others or one's status within the same social act can alter over time. There is no exclusive categorical definition to rely upon when analyzing dominance/subordinance relations in society.

The means by which the dominant definition of the situation is enforced also needs some clarification. In *The Philosophy of the Present*, Mead recognizes the link between social objects and social control:

Social control depends, then, upon the degree to which the individuals in society are able to assume the attitudes of the others who are involved with them in common endeavor. For the social object will always answer to the act developing itself in self-consciousness. Besides property, all of the institutions are such objects, and serve to control individuals who find in them the organization of their own social responses. [35]

The enforcement of power is thus a function of control over the relevant social objects. For example, within the economic realm, these social objects would be those involved in the means of production. In the political realm, public office, law enforcement, the courts, and the like would constitute the relevant social objects. As Mead's statement indicates, however, social objects also include less tangible phenomena, since anything that serves to organize the individual's social response qualifies as a social object. This would include the "rules of the game," the norms governing institutional and interpersonal interaction, as well as behavioral mechanisms such as intimidation, ridicule, bribery, praise, and manipulation. [36] There are many ways in which the dominant parties can enforce their definition of the situation, and these must all be taken into account in an analysis of power.

Another way of analyzing the kinds of interactions involved in power relations is to examine the way in which selves take the role of the other. Mead indicates that individuals take the role of the other indiscriminately in order to perpetuate social acts and that taking the role of the other is always both necessary and beneficial. But once a consideration of unequal power is introduced into the analysis of social acts, this view must be altered. In the initial development of consciousness and self-consciousness, through infancy and childhood, it is necessary to take the role of the other in order to communicate and to develop a concept of self. But in interactions between self-conscious adults the situation changes. The subordinate individual or group must always take the role of the other in order to anticipate the other's demands and to avoid negative sanctions. The stereotype of the "Uncle Tom," the shuffling Negro who answers anxiously to the beck and call of his master, is an example of the ways in which the subordinate party must anticipate the demands of the dominant party and comply with them in order to avoid punishment. But the dominant individual or group is not under the same constraint. The capacity to define the situation and control the relevant social objects removes the necessity of taking the role of the other, since the dominant party is able to continue its part in the social act without doing so.

A further question to be addressed concerns the dynamic of institutionalization: how are social acts coordinated, and what causes them to be perpetuated? It has already been shown that Berger and Luckmann, in their analysis of the dialectic of habitualization-objectification-institutionalization, provide a partial answer to this inquiry. But because they neglect to consider the intrusion of power into social acts, they, too, are unable to account for this aspect of institutional relations. Here it is argued that, in social acts between unequals, power is a fundamental characteristic of the interaction. When such social acts are institutionalized, the power relations that characterize them are also institutionalized. Social acts that, for example, involve the dominance of male over female are established in the institution of marriage and the family; social acts that involve the dominance of the owners of capital over the owners of labor are established in the institutions of capitalism; and so on.

From this perspective, an institution involves much more than simply a common definition of the situation or recognition of reciprocal roles on the part of the participants, as Berger and Luckmann maintain. Rather, institutions express and maintain the distribution of power in society. Contrary to Berger and Luckmann, the interlocking nature of institutional arrangements does indicate a "logic" to their relations, and that is the "logic" of reciprocal power relations in society. Institutions do not hang together simply because the participants in them agree to it or because of a fortuitous convergence of roles. They hang together because dominant institutions and the dominant norms and rules that are both the expression and the reflection of these institutions (the generalized other) indicate the distribution of power in society.

The overlapping dimensions of power that characterize social acts also characterize institutions. The economic, sexual, racial, and hierarchical bases of power unify the institutional settings within which they are expressed. It is not an accident, or the result of a happy convergence of role definitions, that the dominant institutions within contemporary Western society support and bolster each other. It is evidence of mutually supporting power relations. For example, the sexual roles that are instilled into most children at an early age, and that are further enforced through the schools, serve well the needs of a capitalist economic system that still defines ocupational roles according to sex.[37] The attitudes of obedience to authority and acceptance of compulsory tasks, as they are taught within the schools and the factories, also fit well with a political system based on minimal participation and with a proliferation of institutions based on bureaucratized hierarchy. One need not reduce all forms of domination to economic exploitation in order to see that the major institutions in society, and the accompanying norms and rules of the generalized other, operate so as to mutually reinforce one another and thus to maintain the existing distribution of power.

Notes

1. As one theorist paraphrased Mead:
Time is a qualitative and not a quantitative feature of the universe. Thus, when I am having a "good" time, the period is different than when I am having a "bad" time, although both have taken place within the quantitative period which we call "one hour" (John W. Petras, "George Herbert Mead's Theory of Self: A Study in the Origin and Convergence of Ideas," *Canadian Review of Anthropology and Sociology* 10 [May 1973]: 154).

2. Notes taken by George N. Pappas in a course given by Mead at the University of California, 1927, University of Chicago Archives, George Herbert Mead File.

3. From this perspective, it becomes clear that much of the quantitative research in sociology that attempts to operationalize Mead's concepts in self-inventory tests has missed the fundamental importance of relation and of process. As John Petras points out:
The interpretation made of oneself at any particular point in time is contingent upon the realities given, by the individual, to his imagined pasts and projected futures. In this sense, the self is not the individual's response to the question "Who Am I?" but might be more fully measured by his response to the questions "Who Was I?" "Who Am I?" and "Who Am I Going to Be?" given periodically over a number of years. In this way, salience of responses may become predictable on the basis of past and future projections, and the important role assigned, by Mead, to retrospection and projection in human behavior might become more fully understandable (Petras, "George Herbert Mead's Theory of Self," pp. 156-57).

4. With this in mind, it becomes clear that the research efforts of symbolic interactionist Manford Kuhn, which involve conceptualizing the self as a set of attitudes, are a regression from Mead's original conceptualization of the self. Kuhn is looking at a particular factor which he attributes to the self rather than at the concrete self as actor. (Manford H. Kuhn and Thomas S. McPortland, "An Empirical Investigation of Self-Attitude," in Jerome G. Manis and Bernard N. Meltzer, eds., *Symbolic Interaction* [Boston: Allyn and Bacon, 1972], pp. 280-304.)

5. In his commentary on Mead, David Miller succinctly outlines this difference between Meadian and Watsonian behaviorism:

The social process out of which the self arises cannot be built up from stimuli and responses. Each by itself is an abstraction. Although one can analyze the social act into gesture (stimulus) and response to it (its meaning), and although in overt behavior the gesture is temporally prior to the response, we cannot state the nature of either without bringing in the other and without including the individual and its environment (David L. Miller, *George Herbert Mead: Self, Language and the World* [Austin Tex.: University of Texas Press, 1973], p. 52).

6. George Herbert Mead, *Mind, Self and Society* (Chicago: University of Chicago Press, 1934), p. 155.

7. Ibid., pp. 261-62.

8. For the standard analysis and critique of this view of power within the political science literature, see Roderick Bell, David V. Edwards, and R. Harrison Wagner, eds., *Political Power* (New York: The Free Press, 1969).

9. Herbert Blumer, "Sociological Implications of the Thought of George Herbert Mead," *American Journal of Sociology* 71 (March 1966): 541.

10. Leon Shaskolsky, "The Development of Sociological Theory in America—A Sociology of Knowledge Interpretation," in Larry T. Reynolds and Jane M. Reynolds, eds., *The Sociology of Sociology* (New York: David McKay Co., 1970), p. 20.

11. The distinction between power and authority also becomes an empirical question in this view. If the persons over whom power is being exercised freely agree to the arrangements, then the powerful also have authority; that is, their power is recognized as legitimate by those over whom it is exercised. If the subordinate parties do not freely consent to the arrangement, then the dominant parties do not have authority, but they still have power.

12. Irving Zeitlin, *Rethinking Sociology* (New York: Appleton, Century, Crofts, 1973), p. 255.

13. Mead, *Mind, Self and Society*, p. 173.

14. Peter L. Berger and Thomas Luckmann, *The Social Construction of Reality* (New York: Doubleday and Co., 1966), p. 49.

15. George Herbert Mead, *Movements of Thought in the Nineteenth Century*, Merritt M. Moore, ed., (Chicago: University of Chicago Press, 1936), pp. 366, 376.

16 Berger and Luckmann, *The Social Construction of Reality*, pp. 51-52.

17. Ibid., pp. 82-83.

18. Ibid., pp. 60-61.

19. See, for example, Adam Schaff, *Marxism and the Human Individual* (New York: McGraw-Hill Co., 1970); and Richard Lichtman, "Symbolic Interaction and Social Reality: Some Marxist Queries," *Berkeley Journal of* Sociology 15 (1970): 73-93.

20. Richard Ropers, "Mead, Marx, and Social Psychology," *Catalyst* 7 (Winter 1973): 57.

21. Ropers' understanding of the inadequacy of Mead's analysis is couched in the language of Marxist "scientific" mystification:

> Mead's concepts of the nature of man as a subject-object, while more elaborate and social psychological than Marx's when dealing with the subjective aspect of human existence, fall far short of Marx's scientific analysis of the factors which make man an object (ibid., p. 47).

22. G. W. F. Hegel, *The Philosophy of Right* (London: Oxford University Press, 1967), Part II, Section 2.

23. Marx states the relation between history, society, and need as follows:

> The production of life, both of one's own in labor and of fresh life in procreation, now appears as a double relationship; on the one hand as a natural, on the other as a social relationship. By social we understand the cooperation of several individuals, no matter under what conditions, in what manner and to what end.
>
> It follows from this that a certain mode of production or industrial stage is always combined with a certain mode of cooperation, or social stage, and this mode of cooperation is itself a "productive force." Further that the multitude of productive forces accessible to men determines the nature of society, hence that the "history of humanity" must always be studied and treated in relation to the history of industry and exchange. . . .Thus it is quite obvious from the start that there exists a materialistic connection of men with one another, which is determined by their needs and their mode of production and which is as old as men themselves. This connection is ever taking on new forms and thus presents a "history" independently of the existence of any political or religious nonsense which would hold men together on its own (Karl Marx and Frederick Engels, *Marx and Engels*, Louis Feuer, ed. [New York: Doubleday and Co., 1959], p. 251).

24. Karl Marx and Frederick Engels, *The German Ideology*, C. J. Arthur, ed. (New York: International Publishers, 1970), pp. 46-47.

25. In his book *Alienation*, Bertell Ollman makes clear the importance of this primacy of needs in Marx's analysis of human nature:

> Contrary to widely accepted opinion, Marx has such a conception of man "outside of history." "Power" (*Kraft*) and "need" (*Bedürfnis*),

the terms most frequently employed in expressing this view, are also the keys for opening up what might be labeled Marx's conception of "human nature in general." Marx believes that every man simply because he is a man possesses certain powers and needs, some of which he calls "natural" and the other "species." Man's natural powers and needs are those he shares with every living entity. Species powers and needs, on the other hand, are those man alone possesses. They are what make him unique in nature, what set him apart as a "species being" (an expression Marx took over from Feuerbach) from the rest of the animal world. This distinction between natural and species man is the generally unrecognized foundation on which Marx erects his entire conception of human nature (Bertell Ollman, *Alienation* [London: Univerisity of Cambridge Press, 1971], p. 96).

26. István Mészáros, *Marx's Theory of Alienation* (New York: Harper and Row, 1970), p. 167.

27. Karl Marx, *Early Writings*, T. B. Bottomore, trans. (New York: McGraw-Hill Co., 1963), p. 157.

28. Ropers, "Mead, Marx, and Social Psychology," p. 49. (Italics mine.)

29. Ibid., p. 50.

30. Ibid., p. 61.

31. In his book *Symbols and Social Theory* (New York: Oxford University Press, 1969), Hugh Dalziel Duncan briefly notes the assumption of equality that underlies Mead's view of the social act:

"Taking the role of the other," the means whereby we internalize the meanings of the symbolic expression of the other, meant for Mead taking the role of an other who is equal. . . .Time and time again Mead returned to play, the game, and art, in his discussion of the act as a social act. The basis of integration in the game, the quality which gives it what Mead called structure, is rules. And in Mead's development of his concept of rules, we discover that rules can exist only among equals since our obedience to rules is determined by voluntary agreement, not by commands of superiors and certainly not by "sacred" commandments (p. 285).

In his very suggestive comparative analysis of Schutz, Mead, and Cooley, R. S. Perinbanayagam also notes, in passing, that the generalized other is often a field of contention rather than a consensus arrived at "effortlessly, unambiguously, and peacefully" (R. S. Perinbanayagam, "The Significance of Others in the Thought of Alfred Schutz, G. H. Mead, and C. H. Cooley," *Sociological Quarterly* 16[Autumn 1975]: 500-21).

32. Andrew Hacker, "Cutting Classes," *New York Review of Books* 23 (March 4, 1976): 18.

33. In his argument for empirical investigation rather than *a priori* theoretical categorization, Mills states that

> the settlement of the sociological question of how men interact, immediately and directly entails research into questions of superordination and subordination, elites and masses, rulers and ruled, ingroups and out-groups, and members and non-members (C. Wright Mills, *Power, Politics and People* [London: University of Oxford Press, 1939], p. 9).

It might be argued that the analysis at hand would be more "powerful" theoretically if it could specify some underlying cause of domination that generates all other forms of power relations. However, the entire weight of the Meadian social, processual self points in the opposite direction. To take the process perspective seriously is to abandon efforts to locate one uniform and cross-contextual cause of social behavior. The source of power, following Mills, must become an empirical question.

34. For example, in her recent and generally insightful analysis of contemporary power relations, Zillah Eisenstein recognizes three independent sources of power relations—patriarchy, racism, and capitalism. She subsumes hierarchy under racial and sexual oppression. However, the power of bureaucratic hierarchies is often independent of these other categories because it rests on a purely administrative authority—the ability to define and evoke "the rules." The power of welfare bureaucracies over poor people, educational bureaucracies over students and professors, or governmental bureaucracies over citizens must be considered as distinct from (though, of course, related to) the others. Marxists have often been insensitive to this form of power (as anarchists are quick to note) because they lack the analytic tools to address it. Even Eisenstein's more flexible socialist perspective fails to analyze it adequately. See Zillah Eisenstein, "Developing a Theory of Capitalist Patriarchy and Socialist Feminism," in Zillah Eisenstein, ed., *Capitalist Patriarchy and the Case for Socialist Feminism* (New York: Monthly Review Press, 1979), pp. 5-40.

35. George Herbert Mead, *The Philosophy of the Present* (Chicago: Open Court Publishing Co., 1932), p. 193.

36. The tendency for many symbolic interactionists to consider power only in its most benign forms, as symbol management or manipulation of impressions, demonstrates a failure to understand the multiple methods through which power is enforced. As one critic points out:

> Symbolic manipulation is a relatively mild political weapon compared to some. Power politics also involves the use of force, the bringing to bear of great financial resources, the withholding of resources or decisions, or the invoking of legitimized authority to control others. Negotiating, bargaining, and impression management give way quickly

to guns, bombs, and huge sums of money. A Howard Hughes or a Rothschild does not gain or lose influence by the kind of impression he makes or the symbols he invokes. If a policeman points a gun at a Black Panther, that weapon is more than a symbol and certainly takes precedence over any other "definition of the situation." Bureaucrats can control and sanction welfare mothers not by symbolically manipulating them or bargaining with them but by invoking the "rules" to prevent them from obtaining their payments; sanitation inspectors, similarly, can close communes, merely by utilizing their legitimate authority, and without any negotiations (Rosabeth Moss Kanter, "Symbolic Interactionism and Politics in Systemic Perspective," in Andrew Effrat, ed., *Perspectives in Political Sociology* [New York: Bobbs-Merrill Co., 1974], pp. 86-87).

37. One study that examines sex and race as indicators of economic position in capitalist society found that capitalism does not draw women into the mass working-class labor pool to create a homogeneous labor force. Instead, it perpetuates existing sexual distinctions regarding appropriate labor for each gender. The study concludes that corporate structures have vested interest in perpetuating sexism:

> The corporations have a major stake in perpetuating the masculine/feminine distinction, i.e., in encouraging meekness and subordination in women, while encouraging virility in at least many categories of male workers. As a result, there appear to be at least two major causes of the continuing sexism in the society: 1) the traditional need in men to compensate for their subordinate economic position; and 2) the need of the corporations to generate certain character traits in its women and men workers.... The structured treatment of women white collar workers (as well as virtually all other types of women workers) as subhuman adjuncts to male management during their working hours reinforces and strengthens sexism. As a result, the individual male's oppression of women is being replaced by the socialized oppression of the corporations whose need for a particular kind of labor force may be becoming the major generating force of sexism in the society (Albert Szymanski, "Race, Sex and the U.S. Working Class," *Social Problems* 21 [June 1974]: 725).

A further analysis by Heidi Hartmann of the function of sexism in the marketplace emphasizes the contribution of male workers in maintaining job segregation. See Heidi Hartmann, "Capitalism, Patriarchy, and Job-Segregation by Sex," in Eisenstein, ed., *Capitalist Patriarchy and the Case for Socialist Feminism*, pp. 206-47.

The Conditions
for Liberation

4

The argument thus far has analyzed and expanded upon Mead's original theory of the self and self-other relations by incorporating into it an analysis of power. I have argued that Mead is able to demonstrate *how* it is that people tend to obey the norms and rules of the generalized other, but that he does not explain *why* they do so. Mead does not consider the exercise of power in self-other relations because he considers only interactions among equals. For him, "taking the role of the other," the process by which we internalize the meaning of symbolic expressions, is a process of taking the role of one who is equal in his ability to define the situation within which the participants act. Mead neglects to consider those situations in which the social act takes place between individuals who do not have equal power, i.e., those involving some individuals or groups who are able to define the situation and control the relevant social objects and others who are not (or, at the least, involving some who can define the situation more often and more effectively than others). Because Mead assumes that interactions among selves and between the self and the generalized other take place on a strictly intellectual, rational level, he is unable to account for the existence of domination or to analyze its effects. The cognitive emphasis in Mead's theory leads him to make an immediate association between knowledge and action. His is a blandly consensual view in which conformity is taken for granted. This view overlooks the fact that conformity is *enforced*. The preceding chapter was devoted to demonstrating how an account of domination can be incorporated into Mead's analysis of self-other interaction.

To define the self solely in terms of its cognitive processes is to define people as *thinking* beings rather than as *acting* beings. By this view we are human insofar as we internalize and act upon the same information in the same manner. The problem, of course, is that whole areas of human experience, most notably those areas dealing with the emotions, are omitted from consideration. Mead makes no allowance for the realm of concrete emotion. When he does deal briefly with the emotions, he indicates that they are different from cognitions in that they do not arouse the same response in the self as they arouse in others:

There is, of course, a great deal in one's conversation with others that does not arouse in oneself the same response it arouses in others. That is particularly true in the case of emotional attitudes. . . . We do not normally use language stimuli to call out in ourselves the emotional response which we are calling out in others. One does, of course, have sympathy in emotional situations; but what one is seeking for there is something which is, after all, that in the other which supports the individual in his experience. [1]

This view of emotional interaction is on a purely manipulative, indiscriminate level. Mead would have us take the role of the other instrumentally, and only for the purpose of furthering social acts. He does not allow for situations in which one might take the role of the other in order to extend sympathy and affection, or to manipulate and oppress. Mead reduces sympathy to a form of selfishness by describing it as the definition of the other in terms of myself, rather than as the extension of myself into the experience of the other. Mead describes the emotions as arising from cognitive confusion, from conflicting tendencies to act. Since the self is primarily a role-taker, thinking is a conversation between the self and the generalized other in which conflicting attitudes, or tendencies to act, are reconciled so that action can continue. [2] Feelings of love, hate, fear, or greed arise out of inhibited action, and consciousness of them presupposes a self built up out of attitudes and roles as it acquires them in the process of adjustment. In Mead's analysis of abstract cognitive interactions between selves, the role of emotion is minimized and the concrete acting and feeling individual is sometimes lost.

A further consequence of Mead's cognitive bias is his failure to consider adequately the effects that obedience to the generalized other may have on the individual. Mead's view of individuals internalizing and acting on the norms and rules of the generalized other lacks any consideration of the personal conflicts and dilemmas that often characterize the interaction between individuals and their social groups. In the first place, the generalized other is not likely to be a single, homogeneous force; it is more likely that any given individual will be exposed to different, competing, and often conflicting generalized others. The clash of conflicting loyalties, the dilemmas involved in trying to honor opposing claims and meet contradictory responsibilities, are elements of personal experience that Mead does not address. For example, a young woman entering college is likely to be the subject of competing claims from multiple reference groups. There are the claims of familial ties and responsibilities from her parents, versus the image of woman as wife and mother as transmitted by the media, versus the image of professional career woman as offered by the university, and perhaps even versus the demands from some of her college peers for a commitment to radical political and social change. These conflicting roles and models are not simply a few more elements of the generalized other to be internalized and acted upon, as Mead would have it. They represent radically different and often mutually exclusive life possibilities, and the dilemmas involved in trying to reconcile them, to choose between them, or to create new alternatives are the stuff of which personal crises are made.

Because Mead does not perceive any distinction between internalizing the attitudes of the generalized other and acting upon them, he does not attempt to account for the effects of domination and suppression upon the individuals involved. He does not attempt to account for, justify, or criticize the effects of obeying the generalized other because he views it as a kind of self-evident social control. Mead demonstrates that the basis for joint action is the establishment, through interpretive interaction, of common definitions of the situation by the different participants involved. This being the case, one must then explain why it is that some kinds of joint action are more firmly grounded than others. In order to address this question, it is necessary to consider the effect that the exercise of power has on the individuals involved.

The psychological dimensions of power relations are a complex and multidimensional aspect of self-other relations. For example, in the *Wretched of the Earth*, Frantz Fanon examines the response to colonial oppression among Algerian rebels and discovers a heartrending dialectic of hatred, violence, and self-hatred, of rage so deeply rooted that it turns inward and consumes the rebel as well. Continued exploitation breeds an enormous ferocity among those whose despair leads them to prefer victory to survival. Such ferocity is not easily controlled. It breaks out of "rational" channels and turns against the rebel himself, so that he becomes his own victim. Fanon's case studies of various psychological disorders among war casualities demonstrate the complex dialectic of destruction and self-destruction that relations of domination can engender.[3] Individuals who are involved in relations of dominance and subordination may act upon any of several different possibilities in attempting to deal with their situation. They may acquiesce; they may justify their own oppression by embracing an ideological perspective which brands them as inferior; they may become schizophrenic; they may become alienated; or they may rebel. Mead's cognitive approach, which sees only individuals interacting rationally and instrumentally within neutral social contexts, fails either to account for power or to analyze its effects. The limitations of Mead's theory are the limitations of his cognitive, rationalist approach.

What Mead's theory can do is to provide an analysis of the self, based on the two main elements of sociality and process, which has concrete implications for a theory of liberation. To develop these implications, one must consider the possible responses to the exercise of power. Given Mead's analysis of the social, processual self, and given the view of power as the ability to define the situation within which others must act, what are the conditions for liberation?

Mead's theory of the self emphasizes the *emergent*: the self is seen as a creative, temporal process that projects itself into the future and redefines its past with regard to every new present. The self is not a static, preexisting entity that moves unscathed through time. It *is* time, in the sense that its own unique duration is constituted by projecting itself toward a future and redefining its past. The relational character of Mead's conceptualization is evident here, for process is precisely the dialectical relation between temporal moments, each of which affects the others as the self moves toward its projected future based on its redefined past.

The second major characteristic of Mead's self, its sociality, is dialectically related to the first; process and sociality are two sides of the same coin. Social interaction is the source of self-definition. We exist relationally with multiple others simultaneously, and through these relations we internalize images of others into ourselves. Social bonds are not merely external ties between autonomous units. They are internal parts of each individual, and the closer the social bond (such as that with lovers, parents, or friends), the more fundamental is the relation to the individual's self-definition. There are, indeed, multiple voices within us. Sociality is the capacity of selves to exist in more than one perspective at a time, or, stated temporally, it is the capacity for emergence. Emergence, then, is the key to the dialectical relation between process and sociality. The emergent self is able to occupy different perspectives simultaneously and to move from one perspective to another in such a way as to integrate parts of each with the others. Through the capacity for emergence, the self is capable of understanding, appreciating, and participating in the different perspectives by which other individuals define their social situation.

The conditions for liberation correspond to sociality and process. To be dominated is to be in a situation that has been defined by another person or group and to be forced to operate within this situation without being able to effect one's own definition of it. The first condition for liberation requires that one be able to define one's own situation and to control the relevant social objects in order to insure that this definition is not encroached upon by others.

This first condition for liberation corresponds to the process characteristic of the self. To demand the power to define one's own social acts is to demand the power to define one's own process, to create oneself as a being emerging over time. This condition of liberation might well be called freedom since it corresponds to the demand for autonomy and self-definition. This first condition, then, is the ability to affirm oneself without interference from others, by being able to define the situations within which one acts.

The second condition for liberation is the ability to take the role of the other in order to appreciate the perspective of the other; it corresponds to the social characteristic of the self. To take the role of the other is to affirm the other as a unique durational being and at the same time to affirm oneself as a social being. This second condition might well be called compassion, for it involves taking the perspective of the other in order to understand and appreciate him.

The two conditions for the liberation of the social, processual self from the domain of domination are, then, freedom and compassion—freedom to create oneself and compassion to appreciate the other. Just as the characteristics of sociality and process are dialectically related, so the two conditions for liberation are also dialectically related. In order to define one's own situation, one must first have attained a self through the process of taking the role of the other. In order to be able to relativize one's perspective by taking the perspectives of others, one must be able to define oneself and recreate the perspective of the other within the self. Neither of the two conditions is alone sufficient, for either by itself would result in a one-sided, incomplete response to domination. The ability to define the situation within which one acts characterizes the situation of those with power. Dominant parties are able (or at least more able) to define their own situation and that of others as well. By itself, the ability to define the situation within which one acts is an instrument of domination, not a condition of liberation, because other people are undoubtedly acting in that situation as well. The same is true of the second condition. Taking the role of the other is the act that characterizes the powerless in their relation to the powerful; the dominated party must take the role of the other in order to anticipate the commands of the powerful and to avoid punishment. Taken by itself, the ability to relativize one's perspective by taking the role of the other might be a defense against domination, but it would not by itself be a condition for liberation. The two conditions must come together in order to be liberating since each is the dialectical complement of the other.

Another way of conceptualizing the relation between the two conditions is to examine them in light of Hegel's description of the master-slave dialectic. The master possesses the ability to define the situation within which both are acting; thus, the master has the freedom which results from this ability. The slave can take the perspective of the other in order to anticipate the master's demands and comply with them; thus, the slave can relativize his perspective, while the master often cannot. But the delicate and subtle dialectic that Hegel outlines to characterize their relation shows the complementarity of the two components. Marx and Hegel located the possibility for liberation within the slave class, due to its labor; Stirner and Nietzsche, on the other hand, rejected the slave (cleric) as being hopelessly entangled in the morality of domination, and they believed that the hope for liberation resided in the master (egoist).[4] Relations of dominance and subordination require two parties in order to operate: one to claim the power and the other to submit to it. The dialectical relation between them is such that each grows out of and reinforces the other. It is overly simplistic to locate the key to domination exclusively with one side or the other since it is the *relation* between the two parties that constitutes the domination. If the slave were simply to ignore the claims of the master, the master's power would not disappear. As long as the master still possessed the means of enforcing his will, the consequences for the slave would be harsh. Power does not simply go away when it is ignored. By the same token, if all the slaves were simultaneously to ignore the claims of the master, and in so doing could eliminate his ability to enforce his will, then the master's power would no doubt be destroyed. In most cases, it is probably true that the ability to define the situation is not totally in the hands of one party or the other. The slave can influence the situation to some extent by choosing to kill himself rather than submit, and thus his freedom to say "no" is a kind of limitation on the master's power.[5] But the slave still cannot define the situation as he would prefer it to be, and clearly, the greater part of the power lies with the master. The dominant individual or group can define the situation more effectively, more efficiently, and more frequently than the subordinate individual or group can.

The dialectical complexity of the master/slave relationship illustrates the multidimensionality of the quest for liberation. Once Mead's view of the self is taken seriously, it becomes abundantly clear that from its very inception each individual's self-consciousness is already bound up with that of others. We are born into relationships and situations, and our own self-identity must be hammered out of the contexts within which we are thrust. As Hegel demonstrates in his description of the master/slave relation, the other is a primary constituent of my own identity, and I need the other in order that I might be recognized as a self. The dialectical tensions here are manifold: to be self-conscious I must have my own self-identity, which I can only get in relation to the other. But is that identity really my own if it is provided for me by another?[6] The dependence on others which sociality entails establishes the uneasy but incontrovertible link between freedom and community.

This tension is further compounded when the relation, as in the master/slave situation, is based on domination and power. In any case, the individual must reckon from the very beginning with the reality of the other's influence on his own determinedness. If the other is one who seeks equality, then these mutual dependencies can provide liberated self-recognition that is at the same time recognition of the other. Relations of friendship, affection, and collegiality offer such possibilities of egalitarian mutuality. But if one party wished to dominate, to enforce his definition of the situation at the expense of the other, then the limitations the other places on one's self-definition are immediate and debilitating. In such a case, the self is both close to and far away from the other; I simultaneously need the other, in order to confirm my identity through recognition, and must reject the other because he or she offers a recognition rooted in subordination. In such a situation, the potentials for tragedy are manifold.

The tension within the liberation dialectic cannot be eliminated by choosing to pursue one condition and ignore the other. Freedom and compassion are equally important aspects of the liberation process. The ability to define one's own situation by controlling the crucial social objects is central to liberation; to opt for compassion without freedom is simply to embrace our chains. Appreciation of the other that is rooted in subordination rather than autonomy is merely a guise for continued domination.

The pursuit of liberation through the elimination of compassion in favor of freedom is also one-sided. Because we are social beings, we define ourselves by recreating the perspective of the other within ourselves. Liberation is a social process in which interaction with others multiplies and deepens our experience. The ability to relativize one's perspective, to take the world of the other and appreciate the other as a unique durational being, is crucial to liberation because it opens us to the possibilities that others offer. I confirm my sociality by the extension of myself into the experience of another.

In relations of friendship and mutuality, these conditions might be harmonious, and no tension between them would emerge. In power relations, however, the opposition between the two is such that, while they are equally necessary for liberation, they are also mutually contradictory. For the slave to have compassion for the master and take the perspective of the master onto himself is for him to embrace his slavery. But for the slave to seek liberation solely by eliminating the master is for the slave to diminish himself, to damage the sociality of his life. The goal of liberation is not to destroy the master, but to destroy the relation of domination. The agony, of course, is that the master may well cling to his power, requiring the slave to abandon compassion in order to seek freedom. [7]

Different kinds of dominance/subordinance relations would give rise to different formulations of this tension. If the slave is necessary to the master in some crucial way, then the means by which domination is exercised are more limited in that it would be counterproductive to totally eliminate the slave. However, if the continued existence of the dominated group is not necessary for the powerful, then there are no limitations on the exercise of power. Most contemporary relations of domination are of the first type—women are necessary to men, and young people to older people, because the continuance of the society requires their participation. Similarly, workers are necessary to capitalists since the system cannot function without a work force. But relations of total opposition are different in that the total elimination of the subordinate group is possible and genocide then becomes an option. The Nazis aimed at eliminating the Jews, and the whites at eliminating the Indians. The continued existence of these groups was not necessary to the masters, and the power used against them was total.

Given this distinction, which is admittedly a crucial one, it is still valid to speak of domination and liberation as general processes that are common to both situations. In both types of situations, power is still the ability to define the situation within which the other acts by controlling the relevant social objects. Freedom is still the ability to define one's own situation and enforce this definition. While there is a crucial distinction to be made between total oppression, as in genocide, and partial oppression, as in sexism, there is still a shared *process* of domination. It is that underlying process that is the focus of this analysis. For that reason, I have used the Hegelian language of master/slave relations to describe many different kinds of domination. I am arguing not that there are no differences among them but that they share a common dynamic.

It is also possible to recognize the importance of these differences and still speak of liberation as a general process having common dimensions in both cases. Even in the case of the Jew facing Nazi genocide, or the Indian facing white genocide, liberation is not found solely in killing the master. As Fanon points out in his case studies of Algerian rebels, violence against the oppressor carries certain costs for the oppressed as well.[8] Because we are social beings, defined through our relations with others, violence against others diminishes us. The slave risks becoming like the master instead of eliminating his slavery. Violence and hatred have their own chains.

This is not to suggest that the Jew or the Indian ought to have "turned the other cheek" or to have "loved his enemies." Indeed, often the only option available to those suffering total domination is the total elimination of the oppressor. The point is that the only option is a tragically partial one. The two moments of the dialectic of liberation are separated from one another, and compassion is sacrificed to freedom.

Liberation, as conceived in response to Mead's theory of the self, requires the abolition of both the master and the slave. To attain the status of master is not sufficient since this would entail freedom without compassion, and to retain the status of slave would be even more one-sided. Freedom without compassion would result simply in mutual tyranny in that all would be masters. Compassion without freedom would result in mute subservience, for taking the role of the other would be accompanied by sacrifice rather than autonomy.

The specific content of the two conditions for liberation undoubtedly varies with different historical and cultural settings. Within contemporary society, however, some fairly specific proposals can be made to describe them and to indicate how they might be achieved.

The ability to define the situation within which one acts is essentially the ability to command a realm of autonomy for one's actions and choices. Most political analysts, including both Marxists and anarchists, have most consistently been concerned with this aspect of liberation. In order to achieve the capacity to define one's own situation, one must be able first to analyze what that situation is and, second, to assert and defend one's own definition of it. The first step of this process is not as self-evident as it may sound. The exercise of domination can be effectively hidden by burying it within the morass of paper-shuffling and bookkeeping that characterizes the complex bureaucratic structure of contemporary society. In *The Grapes of Wrath*, John Steinbeck's tenant farmers, being driven from their land, confront the bulldozers with shotguns. The driver, also a displaced farmer, answers that he is not responsible for the decision but is only the last person in an unfathomable chain of command. The tenant's reply is the statement of one whose oppression is even more keenly felt because he cannot locate its source: "But where does it stop; who can we shoot? I don't aim to starve to death before I kill the man that's starving me."[9]

In order to analyze the causes of domination within one's own situation, one must exercise what C. Wright Mills has called the "sociological imagination"—one must link the larger historical framework within which domination is exercised to the concrete lives of specific individuals. One's personal experience with domination only becomes intelligible when it is seen as part of a larger pattern of social interactions. The sociological imagination connects "personal troubles of milieu" with "public issues of social structures."[10] It helps the individual to understand his own experience by locating it within its historical and social context. This aspect of defining one's own situation again reveals the dialectical unity between the two conditions of liberation. In order to analyze one's own situation, one must become aware of other individuals who share the same situation and locate oneself in relation to them. In other words, one must take the perspective of the other. "The sociological imagination . . . in considerable part consists of the capacity to shift from one perspective to another, and in the process to build up an adequate view of total society and of its components."[11] Part of defining one's own situation, then, is to locate the nexus between personal troubles and public issues. In fact, one of the disguised aspects of domination is that which masks the link between troubles and issues, thus convincing the individual that his problems are the result of some personal inadequacy rather than of social, structural abuses. For instance, in *The Feminine Mystique*, Betty Friedan discusses the dilemma of the discontented housewife, who is told by her psychoanalyst that her unhappiness is an indication of personal failures rather than the result of the limitations imposed upon her by her social role.[12] It is not possible to achieve a private solution to personal troubles if they are a result or a reflection of a particular institutional setting and its impositions on the individuals involved.

To assert and defend one's own definition of one's situation is to demand a realm of freedom within which to make and carry out choices and actions. To protect one's own definition of the situation from incursions by others attempting to dominate it, one must be able to control the relevant social objects. This is where Marxist analysis becomes relevant. The Marxists maintain that, within capitalist economic systems, the capitalists can enforce their definition of the situation and maintain their economic dominance over the workers precisely because they control the relevant social objects—the mode of production and the norms and rules that govern its operation (the relations of production). In order for the workers to assert their own definition of their situation, they must be able to seize control of these social objects and direct them in such a way as to redefine the economic situation according to their own standards.[13] Similarly, for a woman who is dominated by her husband to be able to assert and defend her definition of the situation, she must have control over the relevant social objects. In this case, they would include the accepted norms and rules governing sex roles and the relations between the sexes (the "rules of the game") as well as her share of the family resources. The ability to define one's own situation includes both the freedom *from* outside interference and the freedom *to* pursue one's own projects and choices.

It is important to note the nature of the relation between the structures of human experience as discussed in Chapters 2 and 3 and the values of liberation endorsed in this and the following chapters. The relation of ontology—the structure of existence—to axiology—the theory of values guiding existence—has historically been one of the thorniest problems confronting political philosophers. It has always been tempting to rest one's recommendations for "the good life" on some claim to have grounded them in the established facts of human existence. This provides a potent "propaganda club" for convincing others, but it is ultimately unsatisfactory. Ontology does not determine axiology because the existence of certain structures of experience does not thereby recommend those structures as desirable. One might choose to value a particular aspect of experience and prescribe ways to maximize it—but not simply "because it's there." Value commitments ultimately rest on choices, not on ontological conditions. People cannot choose ontological structures; the process by which the self develops is a universal aspect of the human condition. But people must and do choose values. We *are* social beings; we *can* choose compassion. We *are* temporal beings; we *can* choose freedom. These values can be clarified and defended by demonstrating that they enhance or diminish particular aspects of experience but they cannot be shown to be more "real" or "natural" than any other table of values.[14]

Compassion can be endorsed on the grounds that it enriches our experience by bringing in and making available the perspectives of others, thus expanding our experience and making us more aware of our dependence on others for our concepts of the world. Relativization can provide a way of experiencing more "first-hand worlds.'' The ability to place oneself in multiple perspectives, and to organize and direct one's activity with regard to these perspectives, makes available a dimension of experience that would otherwise remain closed. But compassion does not necessarily follow from sociality. One could deal with the sociality of existence by taking the perspective of the other in order to violate, abuse, or control the other.

In like manner, freedom can be defended because the ability to define one's own situation and control important social objects allows us to engage in multiple independent projects. Freedom enriches our experience by expanding and diversifying the possibilities for self-development. But one can certainly choose to avoid defining one's own situation and instead embrace the definition of the situation that others supply. People can choose to deny freedom and affirm subordination, and they can also define their situation in many different ways. The fact that we are temporal beings, that we continually project ourselves into the future and recreate the past, does not require us to be autonomous. We might choose to capitulate to the will of others.

The social and temporal process of self-development is, then, a universal condition; and interest in liberation is not. It is possible, for example, that a woman might evaluate her options and consciously decide to choose her traditional role. She might take as her own definition of her situation that which is supplied by the patriarchal system in which she lives. But such decisions must be examined closely because in many cases a woman may be claiming to choose that which she in fact never seriously questioned. Given the immense power of socialization and the strength of those forces that channel women into seeing themselves and their possibilities in conventional terms, it is important to distinguish between choosing and rationalizing. Admittedly, it may be impossible to specify the precise boundaries that distinguish embracing a value from merely accepting it as the given order of things, but in an exploitative society, claims to have freely chosen that which one is in fact expected to choose must be closely scrutinized.

Given this distinction between ontology and axiology, it follows that an interest in liberation need not be a universal aspect of the human condition. If people choose to seek liberation, then this analysis can provide a way of conceptualizing it. The reasons why some people embrace such an interest and others do not are undoubtedly many-faceted and complex. To the extent that one can ever determine the source of an interest in liberation, such determinations lie outside of this analysis. But I can at least point to the conditions that make the development of a commitment to liberation likely.

In order to assert one's own definition of the situation, one must acquire the capacity to reject the dominant definition, that which is expressed through the generalized other and enforced by those in power. Mead has demonstrated the importance of the generalized other for each individual, in that the process of acquiring the self is the process of interaction of the self and the other, the "I" and the generalized other as incorporated within the "me." Therefore, the subordinate party must somehow acquire the ability to reject the terms of the generalized other and establish his own. Since the generalized other is internalized within each individual as part of the "me," one must reject a part of oneself. Indeed, rebellion would be far simpler if it were only a case of the self shaking loose from external chains. But when the chains are interiorized, rooted in one's very conception of oneself, then the individual is somehow called upon to thrust away an integral part of that which he has thought himself to be. To the extent that this is possible, it is never easy; the terms of liberation can be harsh.

How, then, is such a thing possible at all? The key to understanding the capacity of the slave to reject the master's definition of the situation lies with the "I/me" relation. As discussed in Chapter 2, Mead is not consistent in his treatment of the nature of this relation. In some cases, he states that the "I," the capacity for autonomous choices, is directed by the "me," the internalized generalized other. In this case, it would be difficult to imagine how the subordinate self could acquire the capacity to reject the generalized other. Thus, in the "I/me" relation #1, in which the "I" acts and the "me" judges the act, social conformity is assured, and the generalized other, the expression of the interests of the powerful, is not threatened.

In other cases, however, Mead is equally insistent that the creative capacities of the "I" are not annulled by the generalized other.

In what has here been called "I/me" relation #2, the "I" both acts *and* judges its acts. The "me," the summed-up past experience of the self, provides the context within which such judgments are made, but it does not itself judge the acts. The "me" in this case includes the generalized other, but it is not restricted solely to it since the past experience of the individual, as stored in the memory, is likely to include more than the internalized standards of the community. In some very restrictive caste or slave systems, where social control is total, this may not be the case. But most dominance/subordinance relations are not so enclosed as to totally eliminate all diversity. Even the slave may have parents who remember freedom and describe it, or friends who have seen and reported on other ways of life, thus introducing diversity into the "me." Without recognizing this fact, it would be difficult to account for either disobedience or rebellion. In the second view of the "I/me" interaction, the slave possesses the capacity to reject the master's definition of the situation because the slave's view of the world is not limited solely to the master's perspective.

Given the notion of the "I/me" interaction in the second relation, one must explain why some subordinate parties reject the dominant definition of the situation, while others do not—why some slaves rebel and others remain in, or even embrace, their slavery. The more homogeneous the experience of the individual is and has been, the more likely it is that the person will be circumscribed by and limited to the standards of the generalized other. The greater the variety and scope of one's past and continuing experiences, the more likely one is to have multiple sources of experience from which to draw when making decisions. When the "me" contains many different role models and standards of behavior, then the context within which the "I" makes decisions and choices is broadened. The availability of alternative roles greatly increases the chances that the slave will be able to reject the master's definition of the situation and assert his own.

It follows then that the more heterogeneous the social setting, the more likely it is that subordinate individuals or groups will be able to reject the dominant definition of the situation because there will be more competing roles available for them to draw upon. Complex heterogeneous societies present multiple and competing reference groups, so that even a person leading the most sheltered of lives is likely to be aware that there are alternatives. For example, for a little girl raised in a conventional middle-class American family, the most dominant role available to her is that of wife and mother. Since the media content (for example, television programs, commercials, and children's books) she is exposed to is also primarily directed toward women in this role, the influence of the generalized other will lead her to this traditional role. However, early in life she is likely to become aware of other alternatives. Perhaps she has an older sister in college, or a female cousin who joined the military, or her mother works outside the home, or an older friend becomes a prostitute. The presence of competing and conflicting role models provides multiple reference groups that serve to broaden and diversify the content of the "me." In fact, one measure of the power of dominant individuals or groups would be their ability to prohibit alternative role models from becoming available, or from appearing viable, to the dominated. Parents who prohibit their children from playing with children of another racial or ethnic background, husbands who forbid their wives to work, slave owners who deny education to their slaves—all obstruct another's experience by prohibiting other models of experience and behavior from becoming available.

The presence of competing, conflicting roles as different models of behavior gives rise to internal dissonance within individuals who try to utilize these models as guides for decision-making. In Mead's terms, an individual whose "me" contains many different models of behavior will have a broader and more varied context for making decisions and judging actions than will a person whose "me" is more strictly limited to the standards set by the generalized other. The broader context may well lead to internal conflict and suffering, to competing motives and desires, and, in extreme cases, to schizophrenia, as an individual tries to reconcile, choose between, or go beyond the available alternatives. But without these conflicting role models to provide variation to the experiences of the "me," it is less likely that one would be able to reject the dominant definition of the situation. This explains why historically slave societies have prohibited extensive education of slaves since education is in part a process of acquiring knowledge of alternatives. The introduction of education for slaves undermines the institution of slavery. Similarly, the education of the working class and of women was and is feared because it undermines patriarchal capitalism. Educational reform, then, is a potentially radical change: it acquaints the oppressed with alternatives and provides the incentive to reject the master's definition of the situation and assert their own.

The role of the "I" is no less fundamental than that of the "me" in understanding how subordinate individuals are able to reject the definition of the situation imposed by those who are dominant. The "I" is the capacity within each individual for uniqueness and autonomy; it is the irreducible element of creativity within the self. Because the "I" is not circumscribed within any particular definition of "human nature" or "human essence," it can project itself outside of past behavior and adopt untried courses of action. The ability to create oneself over time is a capacity that the self has by virtue of the innovative and imaginative "I," which cannot be reduced to the sum of social interactions but which arises out of social interactions. Since the "I" acts and judges its acts within the context set by the "me," the self who has a broader and more varied content within the "me" is more likely to be able to exercise its creative capacities, to extend itself beyond the structures of the generalized other, than one who has more uniformity and homogeneity to its experience. The dialectic between "I" and "me" is such that it is the *relation* between them that constitutes the key to the ability to reject the dominant definition of the situation. Without the creative "I," the self would be condemned to repetition of the experiences and activities of those before him; he would be trapped within the generalized other. No matter how much variation was available within the generalized other, creativity would be eliminated and experience would be reduced to imitation. Without the "I," one can explain neither rebellion nor diversity.

Without the "me," the "I" is left floundering outside of any social context. To neglect the "me" is to neglect the important effect of history upon biography. Without multiple reference groups or competing role models, it would require an acute imagination and an enormous act of will to project oneself outside of the limitations of the generalized other. The "I" without the "me" is left without social context; the "me" without the "I" is left without imagination. Neither by itself adequately represents the possibilities and realities of the self. The capacity for liberation, like the capacity for conformity, is rooted in the dialectical development of the social self.

According to this view, one acquires knowledge by assimilating the experience of others into one's own experience, by looking both at oneself and at the external world from the perspective of the other. A perspective, a particular way of viewing oneself and the world, is that which locates the individual within space and time. But perspectives are also emergent, as the self is emergent, so that the process of passing from one perspective to another is a process of passing from one emerging world-view to another. Each of us is at the center of our own perceived reality, and we are able to move into the perspectives of others through the powers of emergence, of passage.

The apprehension of the role of the other is the act of "taking over" his perspective, sharing his definition of the situation. By this act, the self can participate in the perspective of the other; shifting perspectives makes it possible for one to relativize one's experience by adopting other perspectives on it. Mead's adage "with each new present a new past" refers precisely to this ability to reinterpret and reevaluate one's past from a different perspective. As an aspect of liberation, taking the role of the other enables one to break through the boundaries of past consciousness by taking on multiple and constantly intersecting perspectives. Individual self-development could be defined as the process of taking on different time dimensions and occupying different perspectives through the interaction of other selves within the social act. [15]

Taking the role of the other hinges on apprehending the *context* of the other, on taking the concrete world of the other in its particularity. To take the role of the other does not mean to define the other in terms of some abstract category, such as one of the "the working class" or "the female sex" or "the poor." Rather, it means seeking the other as a concrete existing individual living within a social context that contains specific relations to various institutions and social settings. The characteristic of being a worker, or a woman, or a poor person may well be an important part of that individual's lived context, but is not identical to the individual.

Under certain conditions, the act of taking the perspective of the other can come about quite "naturally" (that is, without effort). For example, well-written fiction often transports the reader into the context of the fictional characters and gives the reader their perspective on their world. In like manner, the viewer of a good film frequently identifies wholeheartedly with the screen characters and enters into their perspective unimpeded. But often it requires concentrated care and imagination to take an unaccustomed role or perhaps even a repugnant one. The totally foreign and unfamiliar perspective is not easily assumed.

One way of taking on such an unfamiliar perspective would be to utilize what Kenneth Burke has called "perspective by incongruity."[16] Burke uses the term to refer to the use of language in a certain way, such that the given order of weightedness in language is transcended so that ideas that have conventionally been considered incongruent or even mutually exclusive can be merged. As an example of this perspective by incongruity, he refers to Spengler's morphology of history by which Spengler takes a word that is usually applied in one historical setting and transfers it to another, thus violating the previous linkages and establishing new ones. This method, also used by philosophers such as Nietzsche and Bergson, invokes constructing mixed and incongruous images as a way of providing new insights into old material. Applied to the act of taking the role of the other, seeking perspective by incongruity would involve imagining oneself within radically different life experiences and apprehending them from the perspective of participant rather than observer. It would require immersing oneself within the context of the other in order to apprehend it. For example, a man trying to understand the limitations that female socialization imposes upon women might try a variety of methods to gain a perspective that is incongruous to his own experience. He might immerse himself in some particularly telling fictional account; he might try to acquire information from the literature in social psychology on sex role socialization; he might establish sympathetic communication with a woman who is willing to share her experiences with him. (The same kind of process would apply, of course, were the example reversed.) Taking perspective by incongruity would mean merging experiences, attitudes, and roles that have previously been in opposition.

The tensions inherent in self-other relations persistently reemerge and intrude into the quest for liberation. They affect one's ability to take the perspective of the other; the dialectic of self-other interaction is such that the self is at the same time both close to and far away from the experience of the other. In one sense, I know the experience of the other more immediately than I know my own because I must reflect upon my own experience in order to know it, while the experience of the other is available to me in what Alfred Schutz calls the "vivid present."[17] Mead points out that the "I/me" relation is such that the expressive action of the "I" is apprehended by the self only in retrospect, upon reflection. My own present action becomes an object of consciousness for me only in reflection because while I am expressing myself through language and gesture I am focused upon the response of the other rather than my own expression. Because I live in my own "vivid present," the immediacy of my own speaking and acting is not accessible to me as an object. Most people have had the experience of being surprised when another person points out a particular characteristic of their speech or gestures; they themselves have never noticed this characteristic because they have never viewed themselves in the immediate act of speaking. The experience of seeing oneself on camera is an interesting one precisely because it affords the individual this possibility of apprehending himself as an object in the immediacy of his expression. In this sense, I know the experience of the other more vividly than I know my own since I am present to his vivid present.

This proximity of the other is only one moment of the dialectic. The self is at the same time at a distance from the other because the consciousness of one individual is never fully accessible to another, even in the most intimate relationship. I can never totally experience the richness and and particularity of the other's consciousness because the other's emergent self, located in a particular biographical context, is a unique perspective on the world that cannot be duplicated.[18] The "here and now" of the individual, his particular self in the process of emergence at any point in time, is not something that can be captured and apprehended fully by another. The world of one intentional self is never fully accessible to the world of another. The most that can be expected is that, through the utilization of common cultural understandings, open interpersonal communications, and the reciprocity of perspectives that can emerge from imaginative efforts to take the role of the other, the self can approximate the perspective of the other. The dialectic of distance and proximity in self-other relations makes taking the role of the other more than a simple act of "putting yourself in his place." It involves a complex process of expression, imagination, reflection, and appreciation.

The two conditions for liberation are also related dialectically. In defining one's own situation and taking the perspective of the other, freedom and compassion are two moments of the same tenuously unified process. To assert one's own definition of the situation, one must first have attained a certain level of selfhood that can only come as a result of taking the perspective of others onto oneself. Similarly, to take the perspective of the other is to relate the role of the other to the roles that have already been defined as one's own. I can affirm and apprehend the other only through asserting my freedom, as my freedom is defined through my sociality. The dialectic between process and sociality is also the dialectic between freedom and compassion. [19]

As two different moments in dialectical relation to each other, the two conditions of liberation are both unified and separated. They are unified in the sense that the social act is unified. As Bergson points out, our conceptions of reality divide it into parts, in order to "fix" upon different moments of it, while that reality itself is a continuous changing process, a duration. The unification of freedom and compassion is the capacity to define one's own situation and simultaneously to apprehend the perspective of the other.

Behind this moment of unification, however, is still the tension between the two conditions in which the potential tragedy inherent in the quest for liberation lies. To seize the power to define one's own situation, under conditions in which others are attempting to impose their own definitions, might well entail ignoring their perspectives in order to assert one's own. For an oppressed individual or group to assert its freedom against its oppressors would undoubtedly be a disruptive, perhaps even a violent, act. For the workers to assert their freedom by seizing control of the means of production and redefining the work situation along different lines would require them to violate the perspective of the capitalists. For a women to assert her independence and selfhood against a domineering husband would undoubtedly require that she reject the perspective of her husband by refusing to act any longer within the situation as he defined it. For the self to assert its freedom against the tyranny of another would require that the self ignore, violate, or even obliterate the perspective of the other.

To take the role of the other, when that other is the oppressor, might entail the denial of freedom. For the slave to take the perspective of the master, and to apprehend and appreciate the master as a particular individual with a unique durational being, would be for the slave to risk forfeiting his freedom, for part of the master's perspective is that the slave should remain a slave. This particular imbalance of the dialectic of liberation is especially relevant with respect to women because the brunt of female socialization is directed toward encouraging compassion for others and minimizing self-assertion.

Another way to conceptualize this tension between the two conditions for liberation is to view it as the tension between treating the other as subject and as object. To treat the other as a subject is to enter into a personal relationship with him, to apprehend him as an intentional, acting individual, as a personality. This is the manner in which one interacts with another when one is taking the other's perspective. To treat the other as an object, however, is to view him in an impersonalized way, as an object on the horizon of one's own world. When an individual is confronting his oppressors, they necessarily appear as objects to be dealt with rather than as persons to be appreciated. This tension between freedom and compassion divides us between our need to assert our freedom against the opposition of the other and our compassion for the other as a person.

It is here that the ontological dualism between being and becoming reemerges to thwart the move toward unification. Since we depend on the other as the very source of our self-identity, when the relation with the other is also the source of our domination then we are put in an intolerable bind. From the perspective of the slave, to reject the master is to reject the very source of one's self-definition; and to accept the master is to accept the continuation of slavery. The requirements of freedom and compassion may clash, leaving us torn and uncertain. To pursue freedom, then, is to opt for temporality and shift the emphasis of the interaction to "becoming," to thrust oneself forward into the future regardless of the costs for the other. To pursue compassion, on the other hand, would be to embrace the present spatiality of social relations, the "being" that exists with others, and to sacrifice the pursuit of one's own autonomous definition of the situation. Regardless of our best intentions concerning the unification of these two conditions, they may split apart and confront us with a desperate "either/or" situation. The dialectic of being and becoming cannot be magically erased from our experience, nor can we overcome it simply by conceptual means. Ontology sets the boundary conditions for politics, and those who choose to ignore the dilemmas that result are simply not aware of the complexities of experience. At best, their recommendations for liberation will be oversimplified; at worst, they will be so one-dimensional so as to be destructive. Multidimensional persons can never be liberated by one-dimensional politics. The dialectic of freedom and compassion must be seen in all its complexity, as reflecting the dilemma of persons who are simultaneously spatial and temporal beings, both tied to what they are and able to imagine what they could be.

The search for liberation entails the search for the unity of freedom with compassion, but, in different contexts, one moment would necessarily be emphasized over the other to meet the needs of the particular situation. When the threat to freedom is most immediate, the assertion of autonomy may take precedence. In such a case, one might be most concerned with asserting and defending one's own definition of the situation. Conversely, when one's freedom is not endangered, the moment of compassion might be dominant, and the individual would be most concerned with apprehending and understanding the perspective of the other. Part of the process of seeking liberation entails making choices about whether to treat the other as subject or as object, and this decision hinges upon whether one is concerned most with asserting one's own perspective or apprehending the perspective of another.

Because of its complexity, the quest for this kind of liberation can often go awry. The results of an unsuccessful attempt to merge the two conditions might well be alienation, acquiescence, or apathy, or perhaps a lapsing back into either tyranny or subservience. It is also possible to direct the process described here in other directions and according to other motivations. One might take the perspective of the other in order to dominate and manipulate him more effectively, or one might assert one's own definition of the situation in order to widen and deepen one's power over others. The process of liberation outlined here entails a choice to embrace freedom and compassion, and the will to pursue them as intrinsic values. For those who have made such a commitment, the search, always, is for the elusive unity of the two, in which one is able to affirm oneself and the other simultaneously, to work out an authentic self-identity in the context of one's social relations. We ultimately seek the process through which being and becoming might dialectically coincide—when that which we are, in our relations with others, supports and affirms us in our attempts to move toward that which we wish to become. It is in the moments of unity between freedom and compassion that the dialectic of liberation is fulfilled.

Notes

1. George Herbert Mead, *Mind, Self and Society* (Chicago: University of Chicago Press, 1934), pp. 147-49.

2. David L. Miller, *George Herbert Mead: Self, Language and the World* (Austin, Tex. : University of Texas Press, 1973), p. 10.

3. Frantz Fanon, *The Wretched of the Earth* (New York: Grove Press, 1963), pp. 249-310.

4. Max Stirner, *The Ego and Its Own* (London: Trinity Press, 1971), p. 66.

5. I would like to thank Dr. Mulford Sibley for pointing out to me the importance of this qualification in considering the distribution of power between oppressor and oppressed.

6. For a brief but excellent discussion of the master/slave dialectic, see David Rasmussen, "Between Autonomy and Sociality," *Cultural Hermeneutics* 1 (Spring 1973): 3-45.

7. My thanks to Dr. Michael Weinstein for the clarification that his insights have lent to this discussion of the tensions within the liberation dialectic.

8. Fanon, *The Wretched of the Earth*, pp. 249-310.

9. John Steinbeck, *The Grapes of Wrath* (New York: Bantam Books, 1970), p. 40.

10. Mills describes the relation in this way:

Troubles occur within the character of the individual and within the range of his immediate relations with others; they have to do with his self and with those limited areas of social life of which he is directly and personally aware. Accordingly, the statement and the resolution of troubles properly lie within the individual as a biographical entity and within the scope of his immediate milieu—the social setting that is directly open to his personal experience and to some extent his willful activity. A trouble is a private matter: values cherished by an individual are felt to be threatened.

Issues have to do with matters that transcend these local environments of the individual and the range of his inner life. They have to do with the organization of many such milieux into the institutions of an historical society as a whole; with the ways in which various milieux overlap and interpenetrate to form the larger structure of social and historical life. An issue is a public matter; some value cherished by publics is felt to be threatened (C. Wright Mills, *The Sociological Imagination* [New York: Oxford University Press, 1959], p. 8).

11. Ibid., p. 211.

12. Betty Friedan, *The Feminine Mystique* (Middlesex, England: Penguin Books, 1963), p. 283.

13. This assumes, of course, that the perspectives and values of the worker are qualitatively different from those of the capitalist. It seems today that many, if not most, of the workers are primarily interested in pursuing their immediate interests within bourgeois society for better wages and benefits. In this they are aided by the major trade unions, most of which are thoroughly bourgeois in their goals. Those among the workers who have aspirations for their labor and their lives that go beyond the bourgeois issues involved in wage negotiations usually find themselves without any organizational base and are easily ignored or suppressed. The tendency for workers in bourgeois society to adopt bourgeois values is a familiar one to leftists, and has alternately been labeled as false consciousness or as revisionist wisdom. The accuracy of either of these labels depends upon the level of awareness on the part of the workers and the degree to which their perspectives are arrived at autonomously.

14. I am grateful to Dr. Larry Plumb and Dr. Edwin Fogelman for the fruitful discussions in which the importance of choice in relating axiology to ontology was clarified.

15. For an interesting discussion of the interplay between temporality and role-taking, see Mary Katherine Tillman, "Temporality and Role-Taking in G. H. Mead," *Social Research* 37 (Winter 1970): 533-46. She states the relation as follows:

By participating in the social process through role-playing (now understood as temporally structured), the human individual passes from system to system, even though these intersecting systems may negate one another. Through the mechanism of communication, these varied and perhaps even mutually exclusive systems of society provide a context in which the individual can project the direction of his own unique self-program (p. 544).

16. Kenneth Burke, *Permanence and Change* (Los Altos, Calif.: Hermes Publications, 1954), p. 90.

17. Schutz is much like Mead is this respect. With regard to our moment of closeness to the other, he states that "whereas I can observe my own lived experiences only after they are over and done with, I can observe yours as they actually take place" (Alfred Schutz, *The Phenomenology of the Social World* [Evanston, Ill.: Northwestern University Press, 1967], p. 102). This is particularly true when one is in close face-to-face relations with another person, in which

I literally see my partner in front of me. As I watch his face and his gestures and listen to the tone of his voice, I become aware of much more than what he is deliberately trying to communicate to me. My observations keep pace with each moment of his stream of consciousness as it transpires. The result is that I am incomparably better attuned to him than I am to myself (p. 169).

For a further discussion of Schutz's concept of closeness and its relation to the Meadian view of the self, see Gibson Winter, *Elements for a Social Ethic* (New York: Macmillan and Co., 1966). Also see David Rasmussen, "Between Autonomy and Sociality," for a brief discussion of Schutz's phenomenological account of the we-relation which makes clear his affinity with Mead's analysis.

18. Schutz also recognizes this moment of the dialectic within the we-relation. The experience of the other is available to me "in discontinuous segments, never in its fullness" (Alfred Schutz, *The Phenomenology of the Social World*, p. 107). My experience of you, in other words, is not the same as your own experience of yourself: "My lived experience of you, as well as the environment I ascribe to you, bears the mark of my own subjective Here and Now and not the mark of yours" (p. 105).

19. Ibid., p. 2.

Liberation and Womankind 5

If the dialectic of liberation proposed here is relevant to the concrete requirements of women's liberation, then it must be capable of generating an analysis that compares favorably with the major competing strands of feminist theory. As noted in Chapter 1, liberalism and Marxism, the two major paradigms of liberation in feminist theory, offer important insights into certain aspects of the nature of women's domination and the requirements for women's liberation, but neither by itself provides an adequate base for feminist theory. The only other philosophical perspective to have generated a feminist analysis of major proportion, existentialism, is highly suggestive but ultimately unsatisfactory as a philosphical base for feminism. In order to provide a context for evaluating the Meadian perspective on sexual oppression and sexual liberation, I will briefly reconsider these three competing analyses, demonstrating the advantages and disadvantages of each. I will also analyze the self-formation processes that women generally experience from a Meadian perspective and apply the view of domination and liberation developed herein to a consideration of women's liberation.

Liberal Feminism

Nearly all feminists agree that women have historically been denied the opportunity to construct their own separate identity, their own sense of selfhood and purpose apart from the definitions imposed on them by men. Where feminists differ, and radically so, is over the causes of this denial and the ways in which it can and should be changed. Liberal feminism finds its most articulate expression in Betty Friedan's analysis of the malaise of the American middle-class housewife, *The Feminine Mystique*. As noted in Chapter 1, her work fits squarely into the tradition of liberal political philosophy and reformist political tactics. She is interested in bringing women into the mainstream of American life, and to do so she doggedly tracks down the barriers to this full participation. Her analysis is not to be underrated. Friedan looks closely and carefully at the effects on women of educational policies, women's magazines' editorial lines, advertising, housework, and, most centrally, the crisis of personal identity that she labels the "problem that has no name." She exposes with skill and insight the emptiness that characterizes the lives of many middle-class women who have no sense of themselves as individuals. Her book has caused a virtual explosion of consciousness-raising among women precisely because she reveals the day-to-day consequences of sexism, of what it means to be treated as, and finally to come to regard oneself as, less than fully human. True to the liberal tradition, however, Friedan focuses on the internal dynamic of this problem of self-identity and fails to locate it in its overall institutional context. She recognizes the colossal magnitude of the identity crisis that besets women assigned the role of spectator rather than participant, but she does not place this crisis within the institutional structures that perpetuate it and that stand as barriers to liberation. As a result, her analysis is innocent to the point of naiveté concerning the workings of the dominant institutions in patriarchal capitalist societies. For example, she recognizes the workings of the "sexual sell," by which women are manipulated into conspicuous consumption throught sexually directed advertising, but she does not draw the necessary systemic conclusions about the workings of corporate capitalism. Her book includes an account of a very revealing interview with an advertising executive who earned over one million dollars a year for "manipulating the emotions of American women to serve the needs of business." From her interview with this particular hidden persuader, she concludes that the most basic function of the American housewife is to "*buy more things for the house.''* [1] This helpful gentleman quite readily explained that the vacuum created within women who live empty, purposeless lives can be manipulated into profits at the "point of purchase." Friedan concludes, quite rightly, that women are the victims of massive manipulation directed toward developing "needs" for new products that are nonessential, frivolous, inefficient, expensive, and even dangerous: "Like a primitive culture which sacrificed little girls to its tribal gods, we sacrifice our girls to the feminine mystique, grooming them ever more efficiently through the sexual sell to become consumers of the things to whose profitable sale our nation is dedicated." [2]

So far, so good. But Friedan does not follow this trail far enough. She does not see that the reasons for this kind of crass manipulation are not incidental, but reflect the logical consequences of patriarchal capitalism. Its ideology, bourgeois liberalism, is a total world view; its ethic is to consume, discard, expand; it views relationships as contracts, people as objects, needs as sources of profit. [3] *Of course*, women are degraded and manipulated by such a system— *everyone is.* Friedan avoids this conclusion by maintaining that the "sexual sell" is a malfunction of corporate capitalism, not the logical consequences of the system itself. It is "just something that happened to women when the business of producing and selling and investing in business for profit—which is merely the way our economy is organized to serve man's needs efficiently—began to be confused with the purpose of our nation, the end of life itself." [4] She thus avoids confronting the institutional context of women's oppression and concentrates instead on the requirements of an internal liberation, the realization of an autonomous self-identity. But no oppressed group, including women, can forge its own identity solely by an internal quest because its oppression is defined and maintained by the elaborate network of institutional linkages that exist outside the individual and have a facticity that cannot be denied.

Friedan's view of liberation focuses on the achievement of a true self-realizing identity as an active human being but in so doing she obscures the institutional context of this search for a self-identity. She urges women to "grow up and live their own lives," and argues that women must "exercise their human freedom, and recapture

their sense of self. They must refuse to be nameless, depersonal-
ized, manipulated, and live their own lives again according to a
self-chosen purpose. They must begin to grow."[5] Of course; who
could quarrel with this plea for women to seize their own autonomous existence? But Friedan implies that this pursuit of autonomy
is an individual process, that it involves the development of one's
internal capabilities. However, just as the self can emerge and exist
only in its relations to others, liberation must also come within the
context of our relations with others, a social context. This requires
an attack on the institutional structures that inhibit liberation and
the construction of a context that allows it. One cannot become
liberated from the pervasive mystique that Friedan describes simply by deciding to be so, although that is certainly an important
aspect of the process. As long as the existing network of institutions
perpetuates the domination of the white male elite, this pursuit of
internal autonomy will be elusive and partial. Like our very selves,
our pursuit of liberation is a social process, requiring the construction of a context within which it is possible to pursue it.

Friedan's concrete recommendations for "a new life plan for
women" are also squarely within the confines of the liberal tradition. She urges women (1) to view housework as a necessary task
to be accomplished as quickly and efficiently as possible rather than
as a career; (2) to refrain from overglorifying marriage; and (3) to
pursue and apply an education. She considers this last recom-
mendation the most important because educational credentials are
crucial to entering the world of employment. She has faith that
liberation will be achieved by opening the man's world to women:
"Now that education, freedom, the right to work on the great
human frontiers—all the roads by which men have realized themselves—are open to women, only the shadow of the past enshrined
in the mystique of feminine fulfillment keeps women from finding
their road."[6] However, if it is precisely these dominant institutions
—corporate and government bureaucracies; legal, medical, and
educational systems; marriage and the family; and the church—
which incorporate and perpetuate the subjection of women, then
integrating women into them will not bring about their reconstruction. Laws that guarantee property rights and credit to married
women do little to change the overall structure of marriage as a

commodity relationship; equal access to education does not by itself alter the socialization of students into traditional sex roles; allowing women into the managerial ranks does little to alter the structures of bureaucratic subordination; incorporating women into the ranks of military and industrial hierarchies does not prohibit the military-industrial complex from undermining or eliminating socialist experiments in Third World nations. If it is the existing institutions that must be reconstructed, then incorporating women into those institutions will not effect such a reconstruction. The liberal perspective on liberation, while insightful in many ways, does not stand as an adequate theoretical base for a theory of feminism.

Marxist Feminism

Unlike Friedan's work, which is representative of liberal feminism, there is no single analysis that stands out as representative of the Marxist feminist perspective. The best of the Marxist feminists have applied the original Marxist scheme to an analysis of the various institutional contexts that dominate women's lives, particularly marriage and the family. The worst of them have imposed rigid ideological categories and strident rhetoric onto the complexity of women's experience in an attempt to explain female oppression within a preexisting theoretical context. The limitations of the Marxist world view as a sole basis for a theory of liberation, especially one of feminist liberation, are discussed at some length in Chapters 1 and 3. Here I will simply indicate what the best of the Marxist feminists have contributed to our understanding of women's role in society and will briefly recapitulate the nature of their inadequacies.

The Marxist perspective provides a thorough critique of liberalism's anti-institutional bias by pointing out the importance of the institutional networks within which we live in defining our concepts of ourselves and others. Self-knowledge is not gained simply through an internal search, for each self is situated within a complex set of interrelationships and structures that define us in ways we cannot avoid. The Marxist feminists provide a necessary corrective to the liberal emphasis on internal liberation by showing that liberation is a social process, one that involves a radical restructuring of our relations with others in both institutional and personal contexts.

Since the institutions of marriage and the family have been a major factor in defining the role of women, it is to these that the Marxist feminists turn. They are correct in pointing out the pernicious effect that centuries of economic dependence have had on women. To be dependent on another for one's livelihood, and virtually denied any means of altering that dependency through custom, law, and violence, is to always live on the fringes of the world, unable to assert oneself directly for fear of losing that economic lifeline. This means that traditionally marriage has been a commodity relationship in the fullest sense of the term. The woman exchanges her domestic labor and sexual performance for some measure of economic security for herself and her children. The very fact that bourgeois marriage is defined as a "contract" indicates that the terms of exchange are dominant, not the quality of the relationship. The elaborate mythology of romantic love cannot hide the fact that marriage is a commodity exchange. Specific individuals may then attempt to redefine their relations to their spouses in a more humane and egalitarian manner, but the meaning of the institution in culture remains intact.

The private domestic labor that a woman exchanges in the marriage contract supports the dominant institutions of capitalism in several important ways. Given the requirements that most human beings have for survival, the tasks that traditionally are allotted to women constitute "socially necessary labor." Feeding, clothing, sheltering, and nurturing others are all important contributions to the survival of the human community. In the capitalist framework, however, these functions are downgraded because they are unpaid and thus confer no status on those who perform them. Women's position within capitalism is a "worst of both worlds" situation: women continue to perform the traditional home-related tasks that are assigned to them in many (though not all) societies but the financial and status rewards within capitalism are conferred through a system of public wages in which they do not participate. This basic inequality cannot be adequately redressed within a capitalistic system, notwithstanding conservative economist Milton Friedman who has suggested that husbands and

wives could contract with other husbands and wives for the performance of household tasks.[7] All domestic labor would then be
brought into the market, and commodity relations would be introduced into the most intimate parts of our daily lives. This may be an
ideal solution from the capitalistic point of view, but it is a human-
ist's nightmare. The last bit of spontaneity and affection is wrung
from our lives, and we find ourselves encased completely within the
impersonality of the contract.

In addition to the contribution of unpaid labor, Marxists also
point out that maintenance of the home is a necessary function for
the continuance of capitalism because it allows the male workers a
place of retreat and simultaneously encourages them to be docile in
the work place so as not to risk the safety and security of their
families.[8] In addition, the competition within the public realm between working men and working women is a classic "divide and
conquer" strategy that pits male and female workers against one
another and leaves the overall power structure intact.

The socialization of children is still another function performed
by women within the patriarchal family structure that serves well
the needs of the economic system. Traditionally, mothers hold
primary responsibility for this task, and they are expected to train
their children in the values and behavior patterns that the system
finds useful in its recruits: acceptance of hierarchical social relations, respect for private property, respect for authority, and will-
ingness to "follow the rules." It is not coincidental that childhood
socialization enforces these very values. They reflect the requirements of maintaining a certain kind of political/economic system
and demonstrate the reality of interlocking institutional networks
and reciprocal power relations. We are indebted to the Marxist
feminists for making clear the role that the institutions of marriage
and the family play within the capitalist system, and for analyzing
the constraints that these structures impose on the men and women
who participate in them. No amount of internal autonomy or
"growing up" can abolish the facticity of these institutional settings
or do away with the domination they impose.

Given the multiple insights the Marxist feminists have provided,
they must be incorporated into a broader understanding of the
dynamic of dominance and subordination. Ultimately, even the

most generous interpretation of Marx must conclude that the basic *Weltanschauung* of human beings is labor. The Marxist conceptualizes human beings as *producing* agents, not as experiencing actors, and this image will not suffice as a basis for liberation theory because of its partial nature. As is argued in Chapters 1 and 3, domination cannot be reduced to exploitation—there are sources of oppression that are not economic. In addition, the multiple possibilities for experience cannot be reduced to the options surrounding the ability to work. The insights of the Marxist feminists, while significant, are incomplete.

Recently, some socialist feminists have attempted to broaden their analysis while remaining within an overall Marxist perspective. Zillah Eisenstein argues in *Capitalist Patriachy and the Case for Socialist Feminism* that "Marxist analysis provides the tools for understanding all power relations."[9] She goes on to note that the domination of women by men and of nonwhites by whites are forms of oppression that cannot be traced solely to economic exploitation. Eisenstein clearly sees the limits of traditional Marxist analysis and rejects its one-dimensionality in favor of a more complex analysis of power relations. She also argues persuasively that much of the emphasis in radical feminist analysis on the biological base of sexism is inadequate because biology does not stand alone; it must be interpreted within a social framework. One cannot argue from nature to culture. Rather, the dynamics of culture must be used to explain the ways natural distinctions have been interpreted and applied.[10] She argues that: "patriarchy precedes capitalism through the existence of the sexual ordering of society which derives from ideological and political interpretations of biological differences. In other words, men have chosen to interpret and politically use the fact that women are the reproducers of humanity." She concludes that "the destruction of capitalism and capitalist exploitation by itself does not ensure species existence, i.e., creative work, social community, and critical consciousness for women."[11]

Certainly, this is not standard Marxist fare. Eisenstein goes far beyond most Marxist feminism in her analysis of power relations, and consequently she avoids many of the problems discussed above. However, her desire both to embrace Marxism and to modify it produces a fundamental ambiguity in her argument. She is correct that "there is nothing about the dialectical and historical analysis that limits it to understanding class relations," but then it is unclear how the analysis is a Marxist one. The dialectic of Marx is specifically materialist in direction; that is an important factor distinguishing Marx from Hegel and from the anarchists. To relieve the historical, dialectical analysis of its materialist base is to move substantially away from the Marxian method. Eisenstein wants to use Marx's method to go beyond Marx, but it is precisely the materialist commitment within his method that leads him to his conclusions. His exclusive focus on the economic base of power relations is central to his method of analysis, and is not simply incidental. Ultimately, Eisenstein cannot have it both ways. She must either abandon the Marxist label and the materialist assumptions that accompany it, or she must accept the Marxist framework and the one-dimensional analysis of power that it implies. The Marxist perspective on power, even when modified, cannot by itself provide an adequate basis for a theory of liberation.

The Existential Perspective

While it may not be the case that, as Alfred North Whitehead remarked, all philosophy is a footnote to Plato, it could well be said that all of feminist philosophy is a footnote to Simone de Beauvoir. In *The Second Sex*, Beauvoir presents a philosophical, political, and sociological analysis of women's role in society that still stands as the "master theory" of feminism. Her treatment of the role of women in society is grounded in a complex philosophical system, based on a thorough treatment of the nature of the self and of self-other relations. Her analysis is exceptional in this regard. Because it is a substantial philosophical as well as an ideological statement, it has had tremendous influence on subsequent writings in the feminist movement. While Beauvoir's analysis of male and female roles in terms of the existential categories of transcendence and immanence is ultimately incomplete, it is nonetheless highly suggestive. A critical survey of her argument can clarify both its contributions and its limitations.

The task which Beauvoir sets for herself is to inquire into the nature of woman, the causes and consequences of her development, the way she is perceived by man and the way in which she perceives herself. Grounding her analysis in an existential world view, she defines woman as "a human being in quest of values in a world of values," an autonomous moral agent with the ability to choose her destiny. "Our task is to discover how the nature of woman has been affected throughout the course of history; we are concerned to find out what humanity has made of the human female." [12]

In accordance with the perspective of Beauvoir's existentialist ethics, the individual, in order to fulfill his or her existence as an autonomous and free being, must be able to transcend the immediate situation through the enactment of chosen projects. That is, one must have the means to renew oneself by involvement in creative actions directed toward the future, which manifest one's existence in an ever-broadening scope. The history of the development of the human species is the story of this ever-continuing task—man has always been an inventor, a hunter, a conqueror, a builder. He, along with woman, played his part in the procreative process but in addition to maintaining life, he went beyond it. He has tried to mold the world and to shape it according to the values he creates, the reasons for being which he maintains. Beauvoir holds that it was the lot of woman in primitive societies to be limited to the repetition of life. Childbearing and childraising, and the accompanying domestic tasks, involve woman in no essential project of her own creative will; on the contrary, they confine her to repetitious tasks involving no lofty goals. According to Beauvoir, man has created humanity's values through action; woman, in merely reproducing life, has given it no meaning. Within the early agricultural communities, woman enjoyed a period of relatively high status because her reproductive powers were a mystery similar to the mystery of the fertile earth upon which human beings depended for food. Woman was valued as the unknown, the spirit of nature, the bringer of life. As man learned to master nature, to use it for his own purposes and to control its forces through his own activities, he transcended his fear of female fertility. In mastering the forces of nature, he mastered woman also; she was no longer a mystery because her fertility was understood, and her power was annulled. "The devaluation of woman represents a necessary stage in the history of humanity, for it is not upon her positive value but upon man's weakness that her prestige is founded."[13] When man learned to fashion tools from bronze, to tame the earth, he came to scorn woman who still was involved in immanence and in repeating life. Her incapacity for excessive physical labor, as well as her bondage to the process of life, made her appear as the other to him.

Woman's situation throughout history has been closely related to the concept of private property. The importance of private ownership is seen when one analyzes the relationship of the individual to that which he owns. Through his property, the owner projects his own existence into the material sphere. By establishing ownership he establishes his own worth. He also immortalizes himself by maintaining a part of himself which will continue to exist after his own death. This "earthly and material incorporation of the immortal soul"[14] can only take place, however, if the owner can pass the property on to individuals who belong to him and also are a projection of himself. It is to a large degree to insure the legitimacy of his heirs that man has imposed such strict rules of sexual conduct on woman. Fear that a man's wife would deceive him and present him a son who was not his own has been a large motivating factor behind the bondage of woman. Historically, the institution of private property and inheritance made marital infidelity by the wife a major offense. In addition, during many periods of history women were not allowed to own property and thereby were denied the dignity and independence that come with ownership. Often they themselves formed a part of the patrimony of a man, either father, brother, or husband.

The Industrial Revolution set the stage for the potential liberation of women. According to Beauvoir, the possibility of economic independence, together with the increasing use of *coitus interruptus* to prevent conception, began to free women from the tyranny of uncontrolled reproduction and to bring about the transformation of their role. It became possible for her to transcend the immediacy of her domestic life, to initiate projects of her own accord, and to fulfill them through her own means. But for the most part woman remained in a condition of oppression because she did not know how to take advantage of her situation. Most women have never felt solidarity with others of their sex because they have always felt they belonged to the class of their husbands and families. That is why they were so slow to organize and to demand civil rights as a group. Most upper-class and bourgeois women did not desire independence because their lives were relatively comfortable; they paid for their submission with idleness and boredom. Working-class women, on the other hand, were always on a more equal footing with their men because their labor was economically necessary to sustain the family.

Beauvoir sees the advent of factory production, and the possibilities of economic independence that the increasing employment opportunities held, as an important step toward freeing women from their subordination. However, she emphasizes that this independence was incomplete, and that the traditional role of wife and mother still was seen as the ultimately desirable goal for women. The more fully a woman embraced her traditional role, the less access she had to the avenues of creativity and transcendence. In Beauvoir's words:

The great man springs from the masses and he is propelled onward by circumstances; the masses of women are on the margin of history, and the circumstances are an obstacle for each individual, not a springboard. In order to change the face of the world, it is first necessary to be firmly anchored in it; but the women who are firmly rooted in society are those who are in subjection to it; unless designated for action by divine authority —and then they have shown themselves to be as capable as men—the ambitious woman and the heroine are strange monsters. It is only since women have begun to feel at home on the earth that we have seen a Rosa Luxemburg, a Mme. Curie appear. They brilliantly demonstrate that it is not the inferiority of woman that has caused their historical insignificance; it is rather their historical insignificance that has doomed them to inferiority.[15]

Central to Beauvoir's thesis concerning woman is the notion of the duality between self and other as a fundamental human category. Each individual defines himself by reference to other people who are different from himself, i.e., they are *other*. We view the world, as Beauvoir says, "under the sign of duality, which is not in the first place sexual in nature."[16] In this basic human relation, each participant views himself as primary, as the essential pole of the relation. Correspondingly, each views the other as secondary, as the inessential. Since all individuals approach others with this assumption of priority, their claims can be said to be "reciprocal"; that is, the inessential for another is the essential for oneself.

The category of the other is specifically appropriate to an analysis of the duality between the sexes, Beauvoir argues, because here the reciprocity between self and other has not been recognized. Man has set himself up as the sole essential, the one who is opposed to the pure other, woman. Woman has been seen by man as the mirror and audience to his acts, and not as an actor in her own right. She has been confined to the position of spectator on the world, when her existence as a human being demands that she be a free participating agent. "Now, what peculiarly signalizes the situation of woman is that she—a free and autonomous being like all human creatures—nevertheless finds herself in a world where men compel her to assume the status of the Other."[17]

Paralleling Sartre, Beauvoir argues that human consciousness includes within it "the original category of the Other and the original aspiration to dominate the Other," and that the motive underlying this urge to domination is "the imperialism of the human consciousness." It is basic to the human mind, she maintains, to attempt to project oneself outward, to proclaim one's individuality and autonomy by outwardly declaring one's existence through projection onto the world. The individual can project himself either onto an object, as in the ownership of property, or onto another human consciousness which reflects his image back to himself and which he defines as other than himself. This projection of self onto another need not always result in subjugation and oppression. If both parties resist the attempts of the other to dominate, then a state of equilibrium will be reached, albeit also a state of tension. If one of the parties is privileged in some way—as man has been over woman because of woman's lesser physical strength and her more immediate connection to the reproductive cycle—then the stronger, dominant party will be able to subject the other to its rule. Because of her ties to the species, woman has been limited to the functions of reproducing life, while man has been able to escape this mere repetition and to involve himself with other projects. "It is because humanity calls itself in question in the matter of living—that is, values the reasons for living above mere life—that confronting woman, man assumes mastery."[18]

While the subject attempts to assert his mastery over the other, he also needs the other in order to realize himself. He can only find himself through the reality of that which he is not, which limits and denies him. In Beauvoir's terms, human life is a constant struggle to lift oneself out of immanence, to transcend one's own immediacy, to cease mere being in the process of becoming something else. The category of transcendence refers to the realm of human activity and assertion, of acting in the world. Through transendence one engages in invention, projection, and creation, and attains the freedom to participate in projects of ever-widening scope. Conversely, immanence is the realm of confinement and repetition, where one is restricted to uncreative tasks and is bound to the past. Transendence is the self in action; immanence is the self at rest. In Beauvoir's view, transcendence is the more fully human category because one fulfills oneself by becoming what one is not; immanence is something to be escaped through the initiation of some objective. The existence of an other is necessary to this endeavor because the subject must define himself in terms of an alternative existence, one that is both separate from and identical to his own.

It is a heavy burden on the human consciousness that this struggle between self and other is an unending one, one in which the category of the other is filled with ambivalence. For the freedom of the other challenges, at the same time as it affirms, that of the individual who wishes to be subject. This leads to a situation of conflict, in which the consciousness of the subject attempts to affirm itself by enslaving others, making them inessential. This conflict can be alleviated if each party resists the attempt of the other to dominate him and if each party recognizes the other as a free moral agent. But Beauvoir emphasizes the difficulty of attaining this equilibrium:

It is possible to rise above this conflict if each individual freely recognizes the other, each regarding himself and the other simultaneously as object and as subject in a reciprocal manner. But friendship and generosity, which alone permit in actuality this recognition of free beings, are not facile virtues; they are assuredly man's highest achievement, and through that achievement he is to be found in his true nature. [19]

It is the burden of this constant struggle that man tries to avoid by denying it and by escaping into inauthenticity. He searches for an other that will confirm him but not oppose him, let him rest at ease and still fulfill himself. He wishes for an escape from the dialectic of reciprocity which exists in relationships of free beings, and yet he wishes to be free himself. The solution is to set up as the other a being who is endowed with consciousness and yet is not free. This fellow being, who is close enough to his own consciousness to merit his attention, and yet sufficiently different so as to enable him to exercise his power and his contempt, to indulge his fantasies—this creature is woman. Man has defined her as the other for himself so that he can fulfill himself by possessing and dominating her, and at the same time confirm his freedom through her existence as a free person. By defining woman negatively, instead of positively as she defines herself, man defines not what she is but what she appears to him to be. "Representation of the world, like the world itself, is the work of men; they describe it from their own point of view, which they confuse with absolute truth." Woman appears to man in ambiguity, for he sees and needs to see in her all that he is not. This explains the multiple images of woman that are presented in the various cultural myths that Beauvoir examines. As other, she is evil, but being necessary to him, she is also good; she both leads him to fulfillment and denies it to him. Depending upon his view of his own existence, on whether he rejoices in his carnality and life or rejects in horror his inescapable mortality, he will embrace woman in myths, dreams, and literature as the mother-earth-goddess or reject her as womb-prison-decay. It is because she is all these things, all on the plane of the inessential, that she appears so ambiguous to man. In contemporary terms, man defines woman as the ideal companion, for she confirms man's freedom without challenging it. She provides grounds for his own transcendence, his own self-definition, without threatening that process by asserting any claims of her own. "Thus the ideal of the average Western man is a woman who freely accepts his domination, who does not accept his ideas without discussion, but who yields to his arguments, who resists intelligently and ends by being convinced."[20]

In demanding that she be the other, man wishes to see woman as content with this designation. He wishes her to be the other not only for him, but for herself as well, i.e., an absolute other. In the relations between the sexes, men refuse to recognize the reciprocity of the self-other dialectic. They see women as permanent objects, permanent inessentials, irrevocably tied to immanence. This contrasts with women's own definition of themselves since people initially always posit their own subjectivity as primary. Woman's existence as a free subject is thwarted because, although she affirms it to herself, she lacks the means of proclaiming it to the world and asserting it through projects. Thus, her affirmation is lost to all except herself. Like other marginal groups (such as blacks, Indians, and Jews), her long-term subordination sometimes causes her to lose her own sense of primacy and to abandon her claims for transcendence. The dialectic of domination is complete when the suppressed acquiesce in their subordination.

Beauvoir was one of the first philosophers to point out that woman as an oppressed group have a great deal in common with other oppressed groups, particularly in the rationalizations used to justify their oppression. Philosophers, legislators, and other representatives of the dominant class have drawn on myth, tradition, biology, religion, psychology, and economic necessity to justify the subjugation of women as they have that of blacks, Jews, and other oppressed minorities. The stereotype of the "Eternal Feminine," the "Black soul," and the "Jewish character" are all different facets of the same process—the attempt by the ruling class to define those whom they have subjected so as to make them conveniently suited for their oppression. The dominant class uses the characteristics of the conditions which it itself created in order to justify the conditions. The vicious circle is completed when the group that is defined as inferior and is relegated to the position of inferior in fact becomes inferior because the opportunities open to them are so limited.

These common characteristics notwithstanding, the situation of women contains a fundamental difference. The other oppressed groups, notably the blacks, Indians, and Jews, have been oppressed through an historical *event* which resulted in the subjection of the weaker and the victory of the stronger: the transporting of blacks to America for slavery, the victories of imperialism in colonizing the "natives," and the scattering of the Jews. In contrast, women have been subjugated through an historical *development*. Hence, their condition is more like that of the proletariat than of ethnic groups, for this development explains both the situation of the class and the membership of individuals within it. Like the proletariat, woman's subjugation is a condition that developed, as a result of which her situation is seemingly the more determined. Beauvoir, however, rejects such a conclusion: "In truth, however, the nature of things is no more immutably given, once and for all, than is historical reality. If woman seems to be the inessential which never becomes the essential, it is because she herself fails to bring about this change."[21] Women's subordination is not a part of the nature of things; women need not allow themselves to be defined as the permanent other.

Woman's situation differs even from that of the proletariat, however, in that the bond that unites her to her oppressor is mutually inescapable. Both men and women are necessary components of the human community; both are needed for its continuation. Largely because of this inescapable bond, women have no solidarity as a group. The bonds that unite women go virtually unrecognized because they have much greater loyalty toward the class to which they belong by association with a male. The proletarians dream of bringing about the disappearance of the ruling class; blacks can opt for a separate society that completely frees them from association with whites; but, Beauvoir argues, woman cannot take recourse in this direction for she would be no freer apart from her oppressor than in subjugation to him.

This shared need between man and woman, if mutually recognized, could conceivably bring about a situation of equality. As is true of the master-slave relationship, however, mutual dependence does not bring about liberation. Transcendence, the ability to engage in projects of ever-expanding dimensions and thus to define oneself through one's own actions, is a continuous process that is fraught with tension. Transcendence requires the other in order to provide a social context for action; our freedom must be challenged in order to be confirmed. Thus, the other both confirms and threatens one's freedom. Without the other, there would be no context for transcendence, no grounds for self-definition; yet, the presence of the other is a threat because the other's projects threaten one's own primacy. The oppressor has at hand the power necessary to fulfill his need; his need necessitates no conscious obligation to the oppressed except to maintain his existence. The master can define the slave as absolute other and refuse to recognize that, from the slave's perspective, the master himself is the other. Thus, the mutuality of need works to the advantage of the oppressor and the disadvantage of the oppressed. If both parties recognize the reality of the other's claims on the world, reciprocity could be achieved. Reciprocity characterizes relations between equals, each of whom has recognized the subjectivity of the other, but it is based on a more fundamental conflict that has been temporarily put aside.

Thus it is that, although men and women are in a relationship of mutual need, women have never had equality with men. Woman has not established her separate identity partially because of her economic dependence and partially because of the other handicaps men have forced upon her: legal inequality, the force of custom and taboo, the strength of traditional male prestige. Within this situation, to refuse to be defined as the other would mean to give up the advantage of alliance with the upper caste. For woman to proclaim her free existence as subject in and for herself would entail a difficult, uncertain future for her. Again paralleling Sartre, Beauvoir posits a temptation toward inauthenticity in both men and women. The same inclination that leads men to establish woman as an inauthentic other tempts women to accept this designation. Immanence and passivity are frustrating conditions of life, but for some people they are more easily borne than the burden of freedom. "Thus, woman may fail to lay claim to the status of subject because she lacks definite resources, because she feels the necessary bond that ties her to man regardless of reciprocity, and because she is often very well pleased with her role as the *Other*."[22]

Beauvoir examines in some detail the "Eternal Feminine," the body of social myth that has historically been used to justify and perpetuate the oppression of women. This myth posits that certain characteristics, such as passivity, docility, and irrationality, portray the essence of woman. Those who are biologically female, but who do not fit into this category, are said to be unfeminine. The real explanation—that the category of femininity is artificial—is never offered as the explanation. The category of the Eternal Feminine designates a very specific and limited role that is proper and "natural" for woman, and it operates to confine her within a very narrow sphere of activity. By confining her to immanence, it thwarts the very real and human potential within her to escape these bonds.

As Beauvoir is quick to point out, the myth of Eternal Feminine is a very convenient one for the ruling class. By attributing woman's situation to natural, unchallengeable causes, it creates the rationalization, and even the demand, for the subjection of women and the accompanying superior position of men. Included within this concept is the notion of the mystery of woman, a notion that is also a convenient one in that it precludes the need for any kind of authentic relationship with her or any attempt to understand her. What man ignores here is, again, the reciprocity of the condition; man, as he is other to woman (albeit unrecognized by him), so is he also a mystery, an unknowable, to her. Again man perceives his own point of view as absolute truth: since woman is a mystery to him, she must also be a mystery to herself, an absolute mystery.

In their use of the basic categories of self and other, and their reliance on such concepts as immanence, transcendence, and emergence, both Beauvoir and Mead owe an immense debt to Hegel and the Hegelian tradition. However, the existentialist treatment of self-other relations diverges sharply from the Meadian view, and this divergence results in somewhat different views of the possibilities for liberation. Beauvoir assumes that the self can be completely differentiated from other selves, that it is a separate entity. Self and other are two self-contained categories set in opposition to each other: "The category of the Other is as primordial as consciousness itself. In the most primitive societies, in the most ancient mythologies, one finds the expression of a duality—that of the Self and the Other."[23] Beauvoir assumes that these two categories are mutually exclusive, that if something is self, it cannot be other also. This assertion of the total separation of selves is contrary to Mead's notion of the basic sociality of selves. Beauvoir maintains that self and other meet only in opposition, while Mead, through an analysis of anthropological data as well as of the process of childhood socialization, demonstrates that this is not initially the case. Because of the nature of the social process through which the selves arise, part of each self lies in its relationship to others. Thus, the line between selves is often hazy for they necessarily intertwine.

Because Beauvoir fails to recognize the basic interdependence of selves, she can conceive of their relation only in terms of opposition and hostility. She maintains that "the existence of the Other is a threat, a danger." The self, in her view, not only wishes to be the one, the essential, but also the *only* one, the *only* essential. Opposition takes on the meaning of conflict rather than simply of difference. When a person sets himself up as the sole essential, he precipitates conflict with other selves who desire to do the same thing, and in this conflict each self pursues that which will most benefit him. Beauvoir uses this basic hostility of self to other to account for the oppression of women. Women's inferior strength, together with her ties to reproduction, limited her ability to engage in projects of transcendence, and so the original division of labor between the sexes occurred. This division resulted in oppression and domination rather than friendly association because of "the imperialism of the human consciousness, seeking always to exercise its sovereignty in objective fashion."[24] Because, she holds, man is a being who defines himself through projection of self onto things, and exercises his individuality through domination of others, woman's condition has been one of oppression.

Beauvoir conceives of the self as an "empty ego," a blank slate without content. Thus, the self is always engaged in a quest for meaning outside itself. This quest for meaning becomes a quest for power, for the subject can only define himself as the essential one by enslaving others to himself as a testimony to his subjectivity. For Beauvoir the ego is a vacuum, and must continuously seek to fill itself through outward expansion. This does not allow for any authentic existence of the self as a whole, but only for an ego searching for power over others, so that it can claim that its projects are fulfilled and be in a position to enforce this claim. Because the self is this emptiness, it defines itself by establishing identifications outside itself. Since it has no meaning without these identifications, they become more important than the life process itself, and each subject becomes engaged in the struggle to establish his own identifications and projections as superior and to annihilate or take over those of others.

While Mead fails to consider the role of conflict in self-other relations, Beauvoir elevates the role of conflict to dogma by positing it as the only condition for self-other interaction. Her view of the self as an empty ego takes no account of the aspect of the self that Mead calls the "me." In the "I/me" relation #2, the "me" is defined as the "summed-up self"—the memories of past actions, experiences, and events that make up the personal history of each individual. It is the content of the "me" that gives a more or less stable definition of self to each individual, enabling one to identify experiences as one's own and to distinguish these experiences from the experiences of other selves. As soon as the infant emerges from the womb, it is the recipient of and participant in activities and experiences that give content and meaning to its consciousness. The individual does not exist in a vacuum, but rather in a processual relation to other selves, and the memory of these relations are retained within the "me" and fill it with meaning and content.

Because of her assumption that the desire to dominate is an original tendency in mankind, Beauvoir assumes that every person always values his own self more than the self of another. Accordingly, love and cooperation must always be secondary emotions, engendered when the original conflict is stalemated. If neither party can dominate the other effectively, then an equilibrium of sorts is reached. Beauvoir makes no allowance for an individual who might value another as much as, or even more than, he values himself. In her view, generosity, compassion, altruism, or sacrifice are not possible as primary phenomena. Rather, they rest on the basis of an underlying urge to dominate. While Mead has been taken to task in the present work for not recognizing the possibility of conflict in self-other relations, Beauvoir goes to the opposite extreme and sees only conflict. However, whereas Mead's theory can be expanded to include a consideration of power, based on his view of the social, processual self, Beauvoir's conceptualization of the self as empty and isolated irretrievably confines human beings within a ceaseless quest for power.

Beauvoir's view of the requirements for liberation rests upon her categories of immanence and transcendence, which are ethical as well as ontological categories. Women are at heart transcendent beings as much as men are, but they have been locked into immanence by their enslavement to the species:

On the biological level a species is maintained only by creating itself anew; but this creation results only in repeating the same Life in more individuals. But man assures the repetition of life while transcending Life through Existence; by this transcendence he creates values that deprive pure repetition of all value. . . .In setting himself up as a sovereign, he is supported by the complicity of woman herself. For she, too, is an existent, she feels the urge to surpass, and her project is not mere repetition, but transcendence toward a different future. . . .Her misfortune is to have been biologically destined for the repetition of Life, when even in her own view Life does not carry within itself its reason for being, reasons that are more important than life itself.[25]

Transcendence, then, is equated with the male and his role in society, while immanence is the lot of the female. Relations between transcendent beings are filled with conflict and struggle because the liberty of the other transcendent being, while it insures my own, also conflicts with it: "There is the tragedy of the unfortunate human consciousness; each separate conscious being aspires to set himself up alone as sovereign subject. Each tries to fulfill himself by reducing the Other to slavery." The desire to escape this struggle with other transcendent beings leads man to seek a being that will confirm his liberty without challenging it. This being, according to Beauvoir, is woman. By all accounts she ought to be a free being like himself, yet her situation confines her to immanence. The broad spectrum of human activity is thus parceled out according to sex, with the biggest share going to men. Beauvoir maintains that

man today represents the positive and the neutral—that is to say, the male and the human being—whereas woman is only the negative, the female. Whenever she behaves as a human being, she is declared to be identifying herself with the male. . . .Woman feels inferior because, in fact, the requirements of femininity *do* belittle her. She spontaneously chooses to be a complete person, a subject and a free being with the world and the future open before her; if this choice has a virile cast, it is so to the extent that femininity today means mutilation.[26]

Women are enticed to accept their lot by the lure of immanence; female socialization is geared toward engendering an acceptance of passivity in the young girl. Boys, on the other hand, are pushed into situations and roles that demand they exercise their freedom through activity. Since transcendence is the fully human calling, the consequences of women's confinement are devastating:

The young man's journey into existence is made relatively easy by the fact that there is no contradiction between his vocation as human being and as male; and this advantage is indicated even in childhood. Through self-assertion in independence and liberty, he acquires his social value and concurrently his prestige as male. . . .But for the young woman, on the contrary, there is a contradiction between her status as a real human being and her vocation as a female . . .a conflict breaks out between her original claim to be subject, active, free, and, on the other hand, her erotic urges and the social pressure to accept herself as passive object.[27]

Beauvoir's analysis corresponds partially to the view of liberation presented in Chapter 4. Males in contemporary society are more able to enact their own definition of the situation than are females, partially because of the dynamics of childhood socialization. Boys are taught to explore their freedom and to define their own situation, while girls are taught to be more passive and to accept the definition of the situation imposed by others. In Beauvoir's words:

The [male] constantly questions the world; he can, at any moment, rise up against whatever he is; and he therefore feels that when he accepts it, he actively ratifies it. . . .The [female] simply submits; the world is defined without reference to her, and its aspect is immutable as far as she is concerned.[28]

Girls, on the other hand, are taught to be more sensitive to other people and to take the role of the other in order to relate to others and make their way in the world. Thus, the two conditions of

liberation correspond partially to Beauvoir's categories of immanence and transcendence.

There is a danger in too closely equating transcendence and
immanence with male and female. While Beauvoir is careful to
demolish the myth of the Eternal Feminine, she is in danger of
establishing a corresponding myth of the Eternal Masculine that
also poses a barrier to liberation. She is too quick to equate human-
ness with maleness, not realizing that there is a parallel set of
restrictions imposed on the male role that make it a poor model for
the liberated human being. For example, she says that "The advantage man enjoys, which makes itself felt from his childhood, is
that his vocation as a human being in no way runs counter to his
destiny as a male. . . .It is in man and not in woman that it has
hitherto been possible for man to be incarnated."[29] The equation
of transcendence with men and immanence with women, while it
contains a partial truth, is both inaccurate historically and conceptually overstated.[30] The creation of values and the molding of
thoughts and actions are not processes that can be unreservedly
attributed to the entire male half of the population and denied to
the female half. Beauvoir is guilty both of overstating the importance
of male contributions to social development and of underesti-
mating the importance of women's role. The evidence of anthropology increasingly points to many major accomplishments on the
part of women, in spite of, or perhaps because of, their involvement
with domestic matters and reproduction. Women probably invented agriculture, weaving, pottery-making, were the first to
domesticate animals, and perhaps even invented language as an
aid in their communal work.[31] Women, although they have often
been confined to dull and repetitive tasks, are not always trapped
within them. Nor do they have a monopoly on repetitious and
boring labor. Most jobs performed primarily by men in this society
would merit a similar description. In castigating femininity and
praising in its stead "masculine values," Beauvoir overlooks those
values that also have been historically associated with male activities—ruthless competition, aggression, violence, and conquest—
and that would not by themselves be conducive to liberation.

Beauvoir locates the hope for women's liberation in the category
of transcendence because liberation requires self-confidence, self-

assertion, and spirit to regard the universe as one's own and to assume an independent relationship with the world. She states that the first step in this attainment of transcendent existence is for women to acquire economic independence. By working in the world and providing for her own support, woman takes a major step toward defining her own situation and resisting the definitions imposed by others. However, Beauvoir recognizes that economic independence by itself does not constitute liberation because it involves joining a work force that is oppressed. Especially if women employed outside the home are not relieved of at least part of their domestic tasks, their problems will not be alleviated substantially. Economic independence must be accompanied by the males' recognition of the reciprocity of the self-other dialectic. Women are not the absolute other because they are subjects for themselves. Liberation requires that men recognize women as transcendent beings, as free subjects. According to Beauvoir, a liberated society would be one in which "women raised and trained exactly like men were to work under the same conditions and for the same wages."[32] Again, liberation is equated with transcendence and transcendence with maleness.

The vision of liberation that Beauvoir offers has both similarities and differences to that which I have proposed in Chapter 4. Her category of transcendence generally corresponds to the condition of freedom. Transcendence, as self-projection into the world, requires that one be able to define one's own situation and resist attempts by others to impose their own definitions of the situation. That is, it consists of independence and the ability to resist domination. Whereas transcendence can be equated with freedom, immanence, in contrast, is not the equivalent of compassion. Beauvoir sees immanence in a very negative light, equating it solely with passivity and confinement: for her it is a barrier to liberation. I have suggested that compassion, the taking of the perspective of the other, is equally a condition for liberation. Both freedom and compassion are necessary in order to go beyond the opposition of master and slave. I have also recognized that there is a tension between the two and that according to circumstances, it is sometimes necessary to emphasize one at the expense of the other. For an oppressed individual or group to assert its own definition of the situation would probably require that it violate the perspective of the dominant party because it is from the oppressor's perspective that the oppression occurs. Similarly, for an oppressed individual or group to take the perspective of the dominant group would endanger this assertion of freedom. Thus, it is understandable that Beauvoir would emphasize transcendence over immanence and that women would choose freedom over compassion. The situation of women is such that to obtain freedom it would be necessary to violate the perspective of the males who wish to keep them subservient. This does not mean that the dialectical relation between freedom and compassion is broken, but only that the two are different moments in the process of liberation and that under certain circumstances it is necessary to pursue one at the expense of the other.

The Meadian Perspective

A theory of feminism, as a theory of liberation, should be able to address two complementary aspects of women's situation in contemporary society. It should be able both to account for women's oppression and to indicate ways it might be overcome. It has already been shown that, in *The Second Sex*, Simone de Beauvoir deals with both aspects of women's situation with remarkable thoroughness, even though her analysis is marred by the difficulties engendered by her underlying conceptualization of the self. I have argued that the Meadian view of the self proposed here, in spite of its limitations, offers a sounder and more adequate conceptualization of the self and of self-other interaction than does the existential perspective. This being the case, the Meadian view, modified by a consideration of power and liberation, should offer some insight into the general issue of women's role in society. The question to be addressed in this section, then, is the following: given this view of the self, of domination, and of liberation, what light can be shed on the issues of women's oppression and women's liberation? How does the analysis of womankind generated by the Meadian perspective compare with analyses presented by other writings on women?

In replacing the concept of "human nature" with the concept of the social, processual self, Mead argues that there is no initial substantive content to the human self, no essence of human nature underlying human behavior. The self gains meaning and content through its interactions with other selves and with the composite of accepted social norms, rules, and roles that Mead calls the generalized other. Human beings are not born with any assigned behavioral or personality traits; these traits develop through the process of social interaction. Therefore, all arguments that justify and account for women's role in society by reference to their "nature," or to some set of innate character traits, can be rejected. If all meaning and structure in the world are human creations, the result of human beings placing certain evaluations, judgments, and interpretations onto material phenomena, it must be concluded that women's role has been created, not ordained. The Meadian perspective dispenses with the arguments that appeal to "women's nature," to what Beauvoir calls the Eternal Feminine, and requires that we look to our social structures and interactions to account for women's situation.

Given the popular respectability and recognition that sociological theories asserting the priority of "nurture" over "nature" have achieved in recent years, this understanding of social structure may seem like a small accomplishment. However, long-cherished myths die hard, and the ideas about woman's innate temperament—that she possesses a "mothering instinct," that she is naturally intuitive, emotive, and supportive, while man is naturally aggressive, assertive, and dominant—are among the oldest and most dearly held of myths. In her studies of social mythology, Elizabeth Janeway provides extensive documentation of the forms this myth has taken throughout the history of Western culture. Beauvoir also discusses the impact of ideas concerning the Eternal Feminine, pointing out that such myths have been invaluable in keeping women out of the public realm by defining them as unsuitable for such participation. The realm of male privilege in politics, business, education, and religion was and is justified by arguments that women's nature makes her inherently incapable for performing in such roles.[33] It is no small contribution, then, to approach a discussion of women's place in the social order by starting from a theory of the self that refutes the myth of the Eternal Feminine.

Mead's theory urges us to understand the individual by examining the social processes of which she is a part, keeping in mind that the interaction between the individual and the generalized other is a dialectical one. The self is both created socially and creates itself through the interaction of the ''I'' and the ''me'' and through the relations each self sustains with other selves and with the social process as a whole:

The behavior of the individual can be understood only in terms of the behavior of the whole social group of which he is a member, since his individual acts are involved in larger social acts which go beyond himself and which implicate the other members of that group. [34]

The very process of communication requires taking the attitude of the other because one must take the perspective of the other toward one's own gesture and respond to it as the other responds in order to know its meaning. All selves define themselves, at least initially, by reference to the standards of particular others and of the generalized other. The very act of thinking requires the generalized other because it consists of an internalized use of symbols that are socially defined.

When women undergo this process of acquiring a self-definition by interaction with the generalized other, they are defining themselves by reference to standards that brand them as inferior. This is because the generalized other is male; it is the expression of the norms and rules governing a male-dominated society. The generalized other, as discussed in Chapter 3, is both the expression and the reflection of the institutionalized distribution of power in society. This distribution of power has been and continues to be predominantly in male hands. Thus, the generalized other is defined by men, and it generally reflects male values, standards, and perceptions. This is not to say that all social rules reflect male dominance because such a reductionist view would both overlook the multiple sources of power in society and ignore those social rules that do not benefit a particular elite (for example, traffic laws). However, given this qualification, the generalized other both expresses and reflects the primarily male-controlled power structures in society.

Women, then, are created by the society within which they live. They are the outcome of a particular definition of womankind as it is contained within the generalized other. It is their relations to particular others and to the generalized other that define them and establish their proscribed place in the world:

> The self is something which has a development; it is not initially there, at birth, but arises in the process of social experience and activity, that is, develops in the given individual as a result of his relations to that process as a whole and to other individuals within that process.[35]

Men, too, of course, are defined in reference to the generalized other, but they are more likely to have participated in establishing the definitions since they are more likely than women to occupy positions of power, authority, and prestige in society. This is not to say that all men have the freedom to assert autonomous definitions of themselves. Certainly, the definitions of the proper male role and temperament can be as crippling as those applied to the female. But the distribution of power and the content of the generalized other which expresses and reflects that power are predominantly of male manufacture.

A kind of double-bind is imposed on women by virtue of their interaction with the generalized other. All individuals define themselves by taking the attitude of the generalized other toward themselves. When women do so, they are defining themselves by reference to standards that view them as inferior. This is the "Catch-22" of women's role: the process of self-development is such that, in order to define themselves, women must take the perspective of the master toward themselves. The process of self-definition requires women to adopt a perspective toward themselves that discourages further autonomous self-definition. Interaction with the norms and rules of the generalized other is necessary for self-definition, yet it also undermines it. Paradoxically, the requirement for creativity stifles creativity. The demands of the feminine role are in conflict with the requirements for active self-assertion in the world. For women, the very process by which self-identity is attained undermines that self-identity since it requires that they define themselves by reference to standards that allow no autonomous self-definition. Thus, in the words of one feminist, "if they are normal women, they are abnormal people; while if they are normal people, with ordinary technical interests and capabilities, they are abnormal women. They can't be both."[36]

The influence of the male-defined generalized other on women is the source of the arguments within the women's liberation movement for a new self-image for women. In Beauvoir's terms, the generalized other is the perspective of the male subject as he views woman as the other. The generalized other reflects the established male view of what women are and of what they should be. In her study of the historical development of social myths, Janeway also concludes that woman's situation had always been male-defined, so that a history of women's activities consists for the most part of a history of what women have been thought to be and allowed to do by men:

What is special is not their own plans and deeds but, rather, the roles, expectations, and interpretations that have been projected onto them. . . . It is the image of women, originating in men's eyes, that alone gives her a special group identity. Which is not to say that women don't often accept such an identity. . . .[37]

The ideas and roles contained in the generalized other are so strong that they appear immutable. The male-defined portrayal of women has attained such an aura of legitimacy that challenges against it frequently go unmet, even unheard. For women to attempt to impose their own definitions of self on the existing framework as defined by men is to risk ridicule as well as defeat. Women cannot find a definition of themselves within the generalized other that corresponds to their own experience of themselves. Rather, they find definitions of themselves originating from men's experiences of them. Women are, in the words of one feminist writer, "oppressed by an overwhelming sense of not being there."[38]

Put in terms of this analysis, women are unable to define the situation within which they must act, or at least, they cannot define it as extensively and effectively as men can. Because women lack the necessary control over the relevant social objects, including the norms and rules of the generalized other that govern the conduct of the sexes, they are not in a position to define their own situation, and so they are forced to accept the definition of it that is imposed by men. Within most relationships involving the exercise of power, women are the subordinates of men: daughters to fathers, wives to husbands, female employees to male employers, and so forth.

Women do have some options before them—like the slave, they may undermine or sabotage their masters, or rebel against them. But the initial distribution of power, as it is expressed and reflected in the generalized other and as it is distributed throughout the major institutions in society, is in the hands of men.

At this point it is important to recall the differences, discussed in Chapter 4, between types of master/slave relations. Not all relationships between dominant and subordinate parties are equally coercive. When the master wishes to preserve the slave, the slave's position is less tenuous than when the master wishes to obliterate him. As Benjamin Barber argues in his book *Liberating Feminism*, genocide is not the same as sexism:

Nora's plight in Ibsen's *A Doll's House* is troubling but it is not Anne Frank's plight at Buchenwald: one is harassed, the other imprisoned, one awakening to the possibilities of her potential freedom, the other deprived of her actual freedom, one at war with inner ambivalence and cultural conditioning, the other at war with external enemies and physical persecution. Neither woman is to be denied but their situations are very different. [39]

Given this crucial distinction between oppression aimed at obliterating the subordinate party and oppression aimed at subduing her, it is still appropriate, for several reasons, to invoke the master/slave dialectic in both cases. First, Barber underrates or ignores the sheer physical violence that men have always directed and continue to direct against women. A host of contemporary studies on rape and wife beating show that the number of reported instances is growing. [40] The suffering that these victims undergo is more than a mere inconvenience, and their abuse constitutes more than discrimination or deception—it is *oppressive*. Violence has been leveled at women by men in much the same way that it has been used against workers by owners and against blacks by whites. It is not the violence of the concentration camp, but it is sheer, brute violence nonetheless.

Second, Barber's analysis underplays the cultural basis of femininity and the extent to which the feminine role is the creation of a male-dominated society. He argues that masters literally invent slaves, in order that they themselves might exist as masters, while "it can hardly be said that men invent women, and no amount of

controversy about cultural conditioning or the manipulative stereo-
types of the male literary imagination can change this paramount
fact.''[41] Barber is correct in saying that men did not invent women
as a biological category, any more than whites invented blacks or
Nazis invented Jews or settlers invented Indians. But sex, like race,
means little outside of some cultural context that places it within
linguistic, social, and political categories. That cultural context is
and has been a male defined one; the parameters of the feminine
role have been invented by men as surely as whites invented
"niggers" and settlers invented "savages." In dreams, myths, and
language, from ancient tribal societies to the modern industrial
world, the image of woman has been shaped by the beliefs and
desires of men. Barber's analysis fails to come to terms with the
manifold evidence from sociology and anthropology which suggests that our concept of femininity is quite literally invented and
that it reflects the characteristics men have felt to be undesirable in
themselves and convenient in their subordinates.[42]

Third, there is a common dynamic in all power relations that
makes them sufficiently similar as to justify a common analysis.
Power, whatever its specific form, is the ability to define the situation within which another person acts by controlling the relevent
social objects. Freedom and compassion are the elements of the
liberation dialectic, and they involve defining one's own situation
and taking the perspective of the other. The dynamic of the relation
between oppressor and oppressed is a process of common dimensions regardless of the specific participants involved. While the
differences Barber points to are significant, and while they alter the
tensions within the liberation dialectic in crucial ways, they ought
not to blur the shared dynamic of power relations.

One important indicator of the power that male-dominated institutions exercise over women lies in the methods by which representatives of these institutions define the situation so as to obscure
the link between the private troubles of individual women and the
broader public issues these troubles reflect. The traditional nuclear
family, with the isolation it imposes on women, and the psychiatric
profession, which defines troubled women as neurotic rather than
oppressed, are particularly blatant examples of this point.[43] Husbands and psychiatrists alike are in a position to convince their
wives/patients (it is sometimes difficult to separate the two roles)

that their problems are unique and that the answers they seek are personal—in the embrace of a protective spouse or on the couch of a solicitious therapist. Thus, the representatives of these institutions teach women to look either inside themselves, or to their relations with individual men, for a resolution of their dissatisfaction, instead of translating it into public issues that require political action. Their troubles are potentially public because they are *shared*, but until that common situation is recognized there exists no ground for collective action. Power can be exercised most blatantly against those who have no defense because they have been convinced they deserve their subordination, because their problems are defined as within themselves.

This idea of the unequal distribution of power is a familiar one in the feminist literature. Again, Beauvoir was one of the first to articulate its effect on sexual politics. Utilizing the language of immanence and transcendence, she argues that, since the major portion of activity in the world is the prerogative of men, women have suffered by being confined to inactivity. They are unable to establish any definition of themselves because they are unable to *act*:

Woman is not allowed to *do* something positive in her work and in consequence win recognition as a complete person. However respected she may be, she is subordinate, secondary, parasitic. The heavy curse that weighs upon her consists in this: the very meaning of her life is not in her hands. [44]

In her book *Sexual Politics*, Kate Millett describes the many ways in which men define the situation for women and prohibit or discourage them from effecting definitions of their own. The image of women that is incorporated in the generalized other, reflecting what Millett recognizes as a patriarchal distribution of power, is of male manufacture. [45] Within the various roles that a woman commonly occupies—wife, mother, teacher, secretary, waitress, or another of the "helping professions"—she is nearly always subordinate to a man. If the particular man involved is generous enough to avoid exercising his male prestige, then she still has to contend with the forces of tradition and custom that place her within a subordinate role and attempt to keep her in it.

While women are generally unable to define their own situation, they are often forced to take the role of the other. Women are frequently credited with an intuitive ability to "tune in" to other people's desires and needs, and to hold social interactions together by "managing interpersonal relationships." This capacity to take the role of the other effectively has nothing to do with any innate social instincts, but with the requirements of women's role. The subordinate in most power relationships is well advised to develop a strong sense of interpersonal relationships, to be sensitive to the dynamic of "social atmospherics."[46] Recent studies of interpersonal behavior between the sexes have found that female participants in group interactions are generally more responsive to non-verbal cues from others than are male subjects. Men are more likely to initiate interactions and to control them once begun, and are more likely to initiate discussions of intimate topics, than are women. Yet women are expected to be more personable, to reveal more emotion and to be more self-expressive:

Women in our society are expected to reveal not only more of their bodies than men but also more of themselves. . . .Self-disclosure is a means of enhancing another's power. When one has greater access to information about another person, one has a resource the other person does not have. Thus not only does power give status, but status gives power. And those possessing neither must contribute to the power and status of others continuously.[47]

Further, the studies found that men are more likely to touch women than vice versa, and that men talk more than women, both in single sex and mixed sex groups. Women are more likely to look into men's eyes than vice versa; the authors argue that in general subordinates maintain more eye contact with those from whom they expect or require approval, and that such eye contact is a method for obtaining non-verbal cues and judging appropriate behavior. (However, women are likely to back down from eye contact once the "look" becomes a gesture of dominance. This clearly, is consistent with the interpretation of the interaction as one between superordinate and subordinate figures.)[48]

Since the situation within which they operate is of male definition, women must acquire this capacity in order to anticipate the requirements of the dominant party and to avoid negative sanctions. Furthermore, it is difficult to enact anything directly when one lives on the edge of events, playing a passive rather than an active role. It is therefore necessary to "manage emotional relationships" in order to accomplish anything. If one cannot act directly, then one must act by manipulating others. This is the truth behind the stereotype of the nagging, pushy wife, the domineering mother, and the adage that "behind every successful man stands a successful woman." If one is able to act autonomously, then such considerations are of secondary importance; but if one can act only through others, then this sensitivity to human context and interaction is essential. The definition of women's role as expressed through the generalized other impels women to take the role of the other.

An important aspect of woman's role as the manager of interpersonal relations is the expectation that she will protect and foster the growth of others at the expense of her own. This is the central component of the motherhood role, and it is so generally accepted socially that any individual who performs a tender, compassionate, or supportive act toward another is said to be "mothering" him. While the family is the center for the development and sustenance of woman's protective, nuturing role, it is also a characteristic of the dominantly female professions—nursing, secretarial work, teaching, social work, counseling, speech and physical therapy, and so on. "The compassion trap," as it has been called by one feminist writer,

incorporates the insidious notion that the needs, demands, and difficulties of other people should be woman's major, if not exclusive, concern, and that meeting these must take precedence over all other claims. Implicit in the role that derives from this conviction is the virtue of subordinating individual needs to the welfare of others and the personal value and supposed reward of deriving a vicarious satisfaction from this exercise. . . .[49]

Given this understanding of the expectation concerning women's role, it can be seen that many typically "female" professions are simply extensions of the role expectations dominant within the family. Thus, a woman may achieve some economic independence as a secretary or teacher while still being exploited psychologically by an emotional indenture that requires the same kind of sacrifice and equally prohibits autonomy.

Another characteristic that often accompanies women's ability to grasp the dynamic of emotional currents within relationships, and to be supportive of the endeavors of men, is the ability to please. Of course, pleasing others can be a valuable human trait; most people, men and women, find it desirable to please those whom they love and admire. But pleasing others as a general policy, pleasing indiscriminately as a way of making one's way in the world, is a role particularly relegated to women. It is an attitude commonly expected of those in subordinate positions, as the stereotype of the shuffling, grinning "Uncle Tom" testifies. The same trait can also be found in the image of the diffident, self-effacing "yes-man" of middle management, whose success in the marketplace depends on his ability to capitulate appropriately to his superiors. The trait is therefore not limited to women, but it is often particularly important for women to please men, both in order to placate them and so defend themselves against the exercise of power and to manipulate others into taking actions that women themselves cannot take directly:

The powerful need not please. It is subordinates who must do so—or at least it is subordinates who are blamed if they don't—and especially subordinates who live at close quarters with their superiors. . . .Socially then, the need to please marks women as subordinates, though often they are petted subordinates, for pleasing is of course a delightful gift to receive. Success at anything is enjoyable, and a woman who knows how to please others may well be pleased with herself.[50]

A policy of pleasing others indiscriminately as a way of getting along in the world has debilitating consequences for all parties involved. The secondary status that most women occupy vis-a-vis the male makes them vulnerable to his disapproval, and this vulnerability often gives rise to flattery as women try to maintain their precarious position. As Leonore Weitzman points out in her summary of the sex-role socialization literature, our culture's definition of femininity is such that a woman cannot know if she is being successfully "feminine" unless she has a reaction from another person. Femininity requires continued interaction with and feedback from others, so that the woman can "know" if she is being sufficiently nurturant, supportive, attractive, etc.[51] It is, then, not unexpected that many studies of small group interactions conclude that women in organizations and groups are most concerned with maintaining satisfying personal relations, while men are most concerned with furthering their career aspirations.[52] Given that women are more likely to be dependent on the approval of others, their concern for positive group relations appears to be a realistic response to the demands and constraints of their situation. Those who are powerless are generally more likely to seek the approval of others; those who depend upon the good will of superiors in order to maintain an otherwise precarious position are likely to be concerned about sustaining an appropriate image, presenting themselves in an approved way, etc. They need an appropriate image because it is their only defense against the more direct power of their superiors.[53]

One of the essential functions of flattery is that it assists the male in avoiding the difficult, sometimes painful, process of seeking self-knowledge by convincing him *a priori* of his worth. Since admiration from others is a pleasant gift to receive, men cling to this definition of women as flatterer, but in fact women do men no favor by performing this function. Indiscriminate admiration for the male, simply because he is male, may prop up a fragile ego, but it does little to help him understand himself. Flattery keeps both parties from confronting themselves and is thus the height of inauthentic relations. As Simone de Beauvoir notes, flattery requires the participation of both parties in pretense, since it is less effective if it lacks subtlety:

The ideal of the average Western man is a woman who freely accepts his domination, who does not accept his ideas without discussion, but who yields to his arguments, who resists intelligently and ends by being convinced.[54]

The overriding concern with image management, the ability to please others and to be acutely responsive to non-verbal instructions, to manipulate others through flattery, and so forth, are all traits that characterize the role of the subordinate. The subordinate must take the perspective of the powerful in order to anticipate commands and avoid punishments. The powerful need not do so, because they are able to enforce their definition of the situation without such tactics. Women must take the perspective of men onto themselves in order to absorb the dominant definition of the situation and respond to it. This often includes acting to please the man and thereby accomplish her aims indirectly. Most women are so well socialized since childhood in the art of pleasing others that their smile is quick, constant, and often involuntary, and they are often incapable of directly expressing anger. Women are more likely than men to smile at others, even when they are angry or frustrated.[55] Smiling as a policy is a tool by which the subordinate placates the powerful. The burden of that hated, involuntary smile is so great that one feminist has half seriously proposed a "smile boycott"[56] so that women can attempt to rid themselves of this symbol of acquiescence to their oppression.

The compassion trap has had insidious effects on women. By learning that she must subordinate her own needs to the needs of others, woman is taught to forfeit her own legitimate demand for an active, assertive life, for her own projects, for her own "place in the sun." Through the lure of the compassion trap, which at least represents a role that she can count on and in which she will be recognized as doing well, women are often trapped into defining themselves as inessential and as secondary to others, usually to a man. To please others, she is often required to make such sacrifices, and she then awaits the recognition and approval of the man for her sacrifice. The wife who puts her husband through college, the mother who sacrifices her career for her children, the daughter who cares for her aging parents while her brothers go out into the world—these are all examples of common feminine roles in which woman's position as nurturer and supporter relegates her to the level of the inessential. Small wonder that wives leave their husbands, that mothers nag their children and make their lives miserable, that daughters resent their parents. This is the price that both men and women pay for holding women in immanence and denying them transcendence.

The compassion trap also prohibits many women from expressing anger over their subordination. While this limitation characterizes all people who have internalized the requirements of the subordinate role, it is particularly true of women because from childhood they are taught that such expressions are "unladylike" and inappropriate. Generally, anger is more likely to be expressed toward subordinates than toward superiors; "anger runs in channels of least resistance."[57] Those who are perpetually dependent are likely to suppress their anger, often turning it inward on themselves. This inhibition also affects woman's political role. More than one Marxist has lamented the difficulty of organizing women for political action. This difficulty is at least partially attributable to the reluctance most women feel about expressing their resentment toward others. Many women are so well schooled in taking the role of the other that they find it impossible to violate the perspective of the other, to go against the other's views. This is a case where taking the perspective of the other stands in the way of autonomy.

The institutionalized dependence on others that characterizes the feminine role even affects the manner in which women use language. Women are often credited with possessing more tact and diplomacy than men, and with an ability to smooth hurt feelings and maneuver others through skillful politeness. This trait reflects the need of the subordinate to employ verbal finesse in place of direct action. Women learn to get what they want through the clever verbal manipulation of men. The very words we use, and the way we use them, reflect the power relations around us. In a fascinating case study of language use in a Spanish village, anthropologist Susan Harding has discovered that women, unlike men, tend to talk around issues, circling the main point in a discussion and focusing on detail, while they maneuver the other in the direction they wish to go. To make a demand directly, when one is powerless, is to risk refusal. Thus, women "fragment their demands into tiny pieces" and employ a socially learned verbal subterfuge in place of a direct command over resources.[58] For the powerful, this indirect and vague approach to communication is unneccessary and often annoying. For the powerless, it is a thoroughly rational response to the constraints of subordination.

Harding has also studied the status of the information networks of men and women, and her conclusions further substantiate the political implications of linguistic differences. She has found that both sexes view the exchange of information, observations, and opinions among men as harmless and appropriate behavior, while the same activity among women is universally condemned as malicious and wicked gossip. As an explanation for this distinction, Harding argues that such an exchange constitutes a political action in which statements about others are made publicly. Since political action is not seen as appropriate for women, such exchanges are condemned. She argues that

in gossiping, women are behaving politically because they are tampering with power. Their words are the stuff that reputations are made of, and in small communities reputations are powerful because they, in part, determine one's relations and behavior. But power is not the cultural prerogative of women; it is men's. Gossip is potentially a challenge to the male hierarchy, a challenge to men's control of the hierarchy. It is the politics of the officially powerless, and thus is imbued with the connotation of malice, wickedness, sin and pollution. [59]

The dialectic of liberation is the dialectic between the two moments of freedom and compassion, of defining one's own situation and taking the perspective of the other. This interaction, it will be remembered, calls for a synthesis of the roles of master and slave since it is the master who defines the situation within which the two act, while it is the slave who takes the perspective of the other. Liberation requires that both the master and the slave be abolished as roles and that they be replaced with the perspective of one who is neither master nor slave, who neither dominates others nor is dominated by them, who is both autonomous and sympathetic. Liberation, then, would require abolishing the roles of both masculine and feminine and replacing them with the fully human—that is, with a role definition that includes both possibilities, and does not define them or allocate them according to sex.

The distribution of characteristics of temperament, role, and status according to the categories of masculine and feminine imposes oppressive limitations on both men and women because defining the human in terms of polarities eliminates certain possibilities for both. Such exclusive gender categories require the suppression of similarities between people of different sexes and the exaggeration of differences. As one anthropologist notes, it imposes the "repression in men of whatever is the local version of 'feminine' traits; in women, of the local definition of 'masculine' traits." [60] In our culture, a man who attempts to be tender, considerate of others, or nurturant is condemned as effeminate, while a women who is assertive and uncompromising is said to be imitating the male. Thus, the full realm of human possibility is so divided that both roles are limiting of individual creativity, expression, and choice.

This description of masculine and feminine is a description of *roles*, rather than of each specific individual within those roles. Of course, not every man and woman fits neatly into these categories, nor do these distinctions refer to any "essence" of men and women. They are descriptions of the accepted, culturally specific boundaries of traditional sex roles, of the limitations that are conventionally applied and that plague individuals of both sexes. Similarly, one individual does not usually totally define the situation for both, while the other is totally subordinate. The party that is dominant defines the situation more often and more effectively than the other. The imbalance of power may not be total, but it clearly is unequal.

Given these qualifications, there is a great deal of evidence in the literature of sex role socialization supporting this split between masculine and feminine.[61] For example, in his book *The Duality of Existence: Isolation and Communion in Western Man*, David Bakan describes the basic duality of morality and behavior in Western culture and the distinction between the socially defined notions of appropriate male and female behavior. The terms Bakan uses for these distinctions are "agency" and "communion." By agency he means the same kind of activities and attitudes that characterize the defining of one's own situation—independence, self-assertion, and autonomy. Communion corresponds to the behavioral manifestations of taking the perspective of others—cooperation, nurturance, and union. Bakan describes the costs that are incurred when one role is separated from the other. Agency without communion results in the repression of emotion, while communion without agency leads to dependence:

Agency manifests itself in self-protection, self-assertion, and self-expansion; communion manifests itself in the sense of being at one with other organisms. Agency manifests itself in the formation of separation; communion in the lack of separations. Agency manifests itself in isolation, alienation and aloneness; communion in contact, openness and union. Agency manifests itself in the urge to master; communion in non-contractual cooperation. Agency manifests itself in the repression of thought, feeling and impulse; communion in the lack and removal of repression.[62]

There has been much speculation about the original causes of the division of temperament, role, and status into gender categories. Granted that the distinctions are accurate and their behavioral manifestations clear, what accounts for the origins of such distinctions? Some anthropologists view the patriarchal family as the primordial form of human social organization, and they assert that it is the original and "natural" form of human association. By this argument, the physical strength of the male, the requirements of a hunting culture, and the effects of pregnancy, childbearing, and lactation on the female led to this original division of labor and culture. Since these distinctions are rooted in biology, they are assumed to be natural and therefore not open to change. Some feminists, anxious to counter the argument of the inevitability of patriarchy, posit an original matriarchal culture, a prepatriarchal form ruled by Mother-right.[63]

Both of these arguments present many problems. First, there is no reason to assume that there is any *one* cause for the distinctions of masculine and feminine, or any *one* particular original situation to explain. Second, such arguments ignore the difficulty of arguing from nature to culture. As Beauvoir, Eisenstein, and others point out, the material existence of certain biological distinctions does not by itself demonstrate anything about human association, for such distinctions must be interpreted, evaluated, and acted upon before they acquire such significance. For example, if pregnancy and childbirth are held in high esteem, and child-care responsibilities are assumed collectively, then female biological functions pose no particular limitations. Similarly, if male strength and capacity for aggression are devalued and scorned within a particular social setting, then male physiology grants no status.

Third, the anthropological evidence is by no means conclusive and has been interpreted in many different ways. Data drawn from primate behavior show that gender role differences are varied among nonhuman primates, and they do not indicate any fixed biological base for particular role distinctions.[64] At any rate, it is generally recognized that such data can give only tentative insights into human behavior precisely because they are not drawn from human subjects. Theories drawing on early human societies for evidence provide a wide spectrum of explanations. Some anthropologists see the mothering function at the base of gender role differences; others attribute the differences to the exchange of women by men for the purpose of creating social bonds; still others attribute them to differential geographic mobility or to levels of participation in social production and food provision, or to the development of private property, or to the emergence of the state.[65] Furthermore, feminist anthropologists argue that much of the data and theory in their field is permeated by sexist assumptions regarding women's role, and that Western male anthropologists bring a cultural bias to their work that substantially undermines its validity.[66] The search for original conditions, then, is an inconclusive one, and, while it may be interesting for other reasons, it is not relevant to the analysis at hand because the questions being asked here are not "Why did it happen?" or "When did it happen?," but "How does it happen now?," "How is it perpetuated?," and "How might it be changed?"

Whatever the origin of the distinction between sexual roles, the costs of such distinctions in human terms are readily apparent. From the woman's perspective, to be caught in a position within which one is prohibited from defining one's own situation is to be denied transcendence and to be limited to immanence. It is to be a spectator rather than an actor in the world. In *The Feminine Mystique*, Betty Friedan cogently describes the sense of futility and uselessness, and the lack of personal identity, that accompany the imposition of the restrictive feminine role. Friedan calls it the "problem that has no name" because it is a malaise that supersedes more conventional political and social categories. The women Friedan studied were not economically oppressed or disenfranchised, nor did they lack legal "rights" or material "things." They often had too many "things." But they were plagued by a sense of emptiness, futility, and meaninglessness in their everyday lives. Their own descriptions of their conditions are revealing: "I feel empty somehow . . .incomplete," "I feel as if I don't exist," "I just don't feel alive," "Who Am I?" "Very little of what I've done has been really necessary or important."[67] This alienation is shared by men to some extent, since in bourgeois society both men and women suffer from a lack of control over their lives. But men in our culture, regardless of their occupational and class standing, are still the beneficiaries of male privilege; they have "manhood" in their favor. The "problem that has no name" is fundamentally the crippling loss of human potential that accompanies the female role. As with the slave, taking the role of the other without being able to define one's own situation leads to sacrifice and loss of self.

This malaise within the feminine role is bound to have pernicious effects on women's relationships with men. In his book *The Un-committed*, Kenneth Keniston argues that the tendency of some mothers to displace their own frustrated desires for achievement onto their sons is a logical extension of the limitations of women's role.[68] Similarly, the obsession that many middle-class women have with endless shopping and with decorating and redecorating their homes can be explained by the fact that these women are bogged down in immanence. They *do* nothing, so they seek refuge in what they *have*.

The division of human capacities into sexual categories is no less devastating for men. The role of the master, while it does not have the same limitations as the role of the slave, has limitations nonetheless. In order to oppress women, men must act as oppressors. To do so is to engage in certain kinds of behavior and to forego others, which requires suppressing or destroying impulses that would lead to unacceptable behavior. It also leads to a denial of those possibilities associated with taking the role of the other. This is not to say that the effects of oppression are the same for master and slave. If one is examining the situation from the perspective of the oppressed, it is the imbalance of power that is the most important, and in this regard men clearly come out on top. But male socialization incurs heavy costs on many men. The compulsion to dominate, the need to assert oneself over others and to achieve and succeed at any cost, and the fear of failure or defeat are also stifling of human possibility. In a recent book directed toward the liberation of men from their traditional roles, Warren Farrell documents these costs and traces them to an insensitivity to others and inability to take the role of the other.[69] The act of taking the perspective of the other requires only a little imagination, some generosity, and the recognition of the reality of other people's needs, but it is blocked by the urge toward domination and success that characterizes the male role.

Given the Meadian perspective on the nature of self-other interaction, on domination, and on liberation, any attempt to alter women's situation in society must take into account the particular nature of the dialectic between defining one's own situation and taking the perspective of the other. While the connection between them is an intimate one, in that liberation requires both, there is also the tension between them that continually resurfaces in concrete interactions. In situations within which women's lives are defined and dominated by men, the immediate task at hand is for women to demand and attain the ability to define their own situation and to enforce their definition against attempts to undermine it. While in the final analysis the ability to take the role of the other is equally a condition for liberation, it is not women's immediate concern because it is a capacity that is more readily available to her. Thus, it is understandable that most recommendations for women's liberation emphasize the freedom component of liberation, for it is the aspect which is most frequently and consistently denied to women.

How, then, might women be enabled and encouraged to define their own situation? After they attain legal equality (a task not yet accomplished), women should next concentrate on achieving economic independence through total and equal integration into the economy. Laws interfering with each individual woman's control over her own reproductive processes are blatant obstacles to women's autonomy and freedom, and they must also be erased. These paths of reform are well-trodden, and the arguments in their favor are familiar. While they are indispensable, it must be recognized that they are not by themselves sufficient to ensure liberation. Encouraging women to economic and legal independence, while it is a necessary and laudable step, is not the same as enabling them to reject the psychological burden of the male-defined view of themselves and to assert an autonomous self-definition.

In order to understand how a new self-definition for women might come about, it is necessary to go back to the Meadian perspective on the self. The dialectical relationship between the "I," the creative capacities of the self, and the "me," the established content of the "summed-up self," is such that the self is created both through the active assertion of the "I" and the internalization of social definitions of self through the "me." Liberation, then, must involve both the assertion of the "I" in taking different perspectives on the self and the response to the social situation within which those other selves are located. Sociality, the capacity for emergence, is the ability to exist in more than one perspective at a time. Through expression one projects one's own experience into the world; through reflection one incorporates the experiences of others into one's own. Everyone takes different perspectives on themselves at some time in order to interact socially since that is how we initially gain our sense of self. For example, a young man sees himself as someone's son by taking the perspective of his parents, as a student by taking the perspective of his teacher, as a minor by taking the perspective of the law, as a boy by taking the perspective of a girl, and so forth. But women who are trapped within their traditional role have access only to a limited number and scope of perspectives on themselves: to her husband, a woman is a wife; to her children, she is a mother; to the media, she is a consumer; to her boss (if she is employed outside the home), she is a subordinate. All of these perspectives channel her in essentially the same direction, reinforcing each other in defining woman according to conventional standards. None of them provides any different options for self-definition.

Accordingly, in order for women to be able to define their own situation, a diverse number of roles must be available to them. They must be made more aware of the alternatives to their traditional roles in order to be able to project themselves outside of these roles. To some extent, contemporary American society already fulfills this requirement since it is a heterogeneous social setting. Instead of a single unified generalized other, there are multiple generalized others, multiple reference groups for any given individual. Unless a person has led an extraordinarily sheltered life, he is likely to have a certain assortment of roles and models available. Even very young children are usually aware that, in addition to mothers and fathers, there are also teachers, doctors, nurses, lawyers, firemen, and policemen in the world (or, from a different class perspective, junkies, numbers-runners, gang leaders, and prostitutes). The problem is that, even in this wider variety of roles and models, the segregation by sex is readily apparent. In addition, if those adults who are closest to children during their primary socialization years do not encourage them to internalize and act upon a variety of self-definitions, such alternatives will in all likelihood go unnoticed.

One implication of this argument is that alternatives to the conventional nuclear family are desirable as a way of broadening the pattern of self-definition that children receive. The wider the number and variety of adults that are available to provide the child with concrete alternatives for self-definition, the more likely that child is to break out of traditional roles and visualize alternatives for herself. This is the principle behind the recent move within the "counterculture" toward extended families and communal living arrangements, as parents realize the multiple advantages that such a situation provides to both their children and themselves. Many people have also advocated changes within the nuclear family itself. Much thought has been given to the possibilities of egalitarian marriages that could provide humane and supportive living contexts for both adults and children. All of these experiments are to be applauded as part of a necessary search for expanded possibilities in family arrangements.

This proposal for a new self-image for women is not new. The most vocal spokespersons for the women's liberation movement have been arguing for years that women must achieve for themselves a self-image that is of their own design. The ubiquitous language of consciousness-raising becomes more concrete when viewed from the perspective of the need to define one's own situation by first defining oneself. Indeed, the women's liberation movement itself has been instrumental in providing, or at least demanding, alternative role models by which women might define themselves. This analysis provides an overall view of the self, domination, and liberation that can integrate the standing feminist demands into a more complete concept of human liberation.

There are, of course, multiple obstacles to women's attempts to assert their own definitions of their situation. Women who attempt to break out of their traditional role are a threat both to the women who have internalized it and to the men who benefit by it. Feminists are likely to be threatened with the fate of losing their "femininity," of ceasing to attract men. More fundamentally, women who challenge the imbalance of power in male-female relations are also challenging the general distribution of power throughout society, for the subordination of female to male parallels the subordination of the weak to the strong in any social situation. Women's demands for equality threaten the superiority of male status per se, the prestige that many men claim because they have their sex in their favor. Finally, there is an element of truth in Beauvoir's assertion that there are temptations to be found in the position of immanence. After all, there are certain rewards to be reaped from pleasing others, from providing nurturance and support to others. For those who lack self-confidence, as many women do, vicarious achievement is better than no achievement at all.

In addition, the institution of the nuclear family provides its own obstacles to women's liberation by isolating women. Women spend much of their time alone with their children, as a result of which both lack any other adult perspective on their situation. Such women do not have the sense of commonality, of shared situation, that work in the public sphere offers. Marx's insight that the oppressed must share a common experience of their oppression in order to rebel against it is relevant here. Nothing is as debilitating to women as the feeling that they are alone, and as Friedan discovered, nothing is so revealing to them as the knowledge that their desperation is shared.

It is difficult to reckon the costs that are incurred when women challenge the conventional definition of themselves and attempt to forge their own. At the very least, they are likely to be ridiculed. They also jeopardize their chances for achieving the marginal reward that their traditional role offers; they are likely to feel internal conflict and a sense of personal crisis; and in some cases they run the risk of being declared insane.[70] The costs of demanding autonomy are not slight; neither, as I have argued, are the costs of forfeiting it.

The dialectical balance between the two conditions for liberation is fraught with tension because as human beings we lead a fractured existence. Self confronts other, woman confronts man, "I" confronts "me." To develop a liberation consciousness is to become aware of the ambiguous ethical situations confronting those who wish that both themselves and others be free. The potential tragedy of liberation lies in the deceptiveness of our perceptions of social reality; all is not always as it appears to be; ambiguity is endemic. To claim the right to define one's own situation may violate the perspective of the other, perhaps a beloved other; to forfeit the right is to turn compassion into martyrdom. No theory of liberation can abolish these tensions because they exist in the very structure of experience. They are, ultimately, the tensions between being and becoming, between necessity and possibility, between what we are and what we could be. The perniciousness of contemporary sex role definitions is that they attempt to externalize this dualism of being and becoming into female and male rather than seeing it as endemic to each individual self. To reunite these two poles of the dialectic into a precarious balance within each individual, to make freedom and compassion simultaneous possibilities for both women and men—this is the elusive and necessary goal of a truly *human* liberation.

Notes

1. Betty Friedan, *The Feminine Mystique* (Middlesex, England: Penguin Books, 1963), pp. 182, 181.
2. Ibid., p. 203.
3. The perspective on liberalism presented here and in Chapter 1 draws primarily upon the Anglo-American tradition of liberal theory as represented by Locke, Mill, Madison, Jefferson, and others. There are, of course, exceptions to these generalizations. As the ideas of T. H. Green, L. T. Hobhouse, and the later J. S. Mill indicate, the liberal tradition is a varied one, and not all of its members are equally guilty of the bourgeois vices.
4. Friedan, *The Feminine Mystique*, p. 181.
5. Ibid., pp. 264, 267-68.
6. Ibid., p. 283.
7. I have been informed by a colleague that Professor Friedman made this suggestion during an interview on "Meet the Press" in 1978.
8. In this connection, Erving Goffman notes that psychological bondage to conventional ideas of masculinity and femininity may be even more restrictive than the spiritual domination of religious authority. He argues that "Gender, not religion, is the opiate of the masses" (Erving Goffman,

"The Arrangement Between the Sexes," *Theory and Society* 4 [Fall 1977]: 315).

9. Zillah Eisenstein, "Developing a Theory of Capitalist Patriarchy and Socialist Feminism," in Zillah Eisenstein, ed., *Capitalist Patriarchy and the Case for Socialist Feminism* (New York: Monthly Review Press, 1979), p. 6.

10. Eisenstein refers explicitly here to Shulamith Firestone's *The Dialectic of Sex* (New York: Bantam Books, 1970), a relatively early radical feminist analysis in which biological differences are held to be innately oppressive and are seen as the cause of women's subordination.

The problem of arguing from nature to culture is discussed further below with regard to anthropological analyses of women's position in society.

11. Eisenstein, "Developing a Theory of Capitalist Patriarchy and Socialist Feminism," pp. 25, 11.

12. Simone de Beauvoir, *The Second Sex* (New York: Alfred A. Knopf, 1952), p. 47.

13. Ibid., p. 69.

14. Ibid., p. 75.

15. Ibid., p. 122.

16. Ibid., p. 63.

17. Ibid., p. xxviii.

18. Ibid., pp. 52, 60.

19. Ibid., p. 130.

20. Ibid., pp. 133, 172.

21. Ibid., p. xviii.

22. Ibid., p. xxi. (Italics Beauvoir's.)

23. Ibid., p. xvi.

24. Ibid., pp. 73, 52.

25. Ibid., pp. 58-59.

26. Ibid., pp. 71, 383-84. (Italics Beauvoir's.)

27. Ibid., p. 314.

28. Ibid., p. 310.

29. Ibid., pp. 641, 671.

30. Other commentators on Beauvoir's feminism have noted this imbalance. In her insightful analysis of Beauvoir's treatment of women in both fictional and nonfictional form, Jean Leighton observes that the fully human complexity of some of Beauvoir's female protagonists—for example, Anne in *The Mandarins* and Françoise in *L'Invitée*—is seemingly lost in the oversimplifications of *The Second Sex*:

> *The Second Sex* staunchly insists that transcendence, action, creativity and power are the masculine virtues par excellence, and these are

what determine human value. Being, passivity and immanence are feminine prerogatives and they diminish the human value of those trapped in this mode of existence. Action and transcendence are male and good; being and immanence are feminine and bad (Jean Leighton, *Simone de Beauvoir on Women* [Cranbury, N. J.: Fairleigh Dickinson University Press, 1975], p. 213).

31. Robin Morgan, ed., *Sisterhood Is Powerful* (New York: Random House, 1970), p. xxxii.

32. Beauvoir, *The Second Sex*, p. 683.

33. The discipline of psychology has contributed much to the maintenance of these myths through the writings of such eminent figures as Bruno Bettelheim, Joseph Rheingold, Eric Erikson, and, of course, Freud. As one feminist notes, these men "have set about describing the true nature of women with a certainty and a sense of their own infallibility rarely found in the secular world" (Naomi Weisstein, "Psychology Constructs the Human Female," in Vivian Gornick and Barbara K. Moran, eds., *Woman in Sexist Society* [New York: New American Library, 1971], p. 207).

34. George Herbert Mead, *Mind, Self and Society* (Chicago: University of Chicago Press, 1934), p. 7.

35. Ibid., p. 9.

36. Elizabeth Janeway, *Man's World, Woman's Place* (New York: Delta Books, 1971), p. 104.

37. Elizabeth Janeway, *Between Myth and Morning: Women Awakening* (New York: William Morrow and Co., 1975), p. 18.

38. Sheila Rowbotham, *Woman's Consciousness, Man's World* (Baltimore: Penguin Books, 1973), p. 35.

39. Benjamin Barber, *Liberating Feminism* (New York: Seabury Press, 1975), p. 30.

40. See, for example, Susan Brownmiller, *Against Our Will: Men, Women and Rape* (New York: Bantam Books, 1975); Nancy Gager and Cathleen Schurr, *Sexual Assault: Confronting Rape in America* (New York: Grosset and Dunlap, 1976); Department of Health, Education and Welfare, *Victims of Rape* (Washington, D.C.: U.S. Government Printing Office, 1976); Roger Langley and Richard C. Levy, *Wife Beating: The Silent Crisis* (New York: E. P. Dutton, 1977); Suzanne Steinmetz and Murray A. Strauss, eds., *Violence in the Family* (New York: Dodd, Mead and Co., 1974).

41. Barber, *Liberating Feminism*, p. 33.

42. Simone de Beauvoir, *The Second Sex*, and Elizabeth Janeway, *Man's World, Woman's Place*, both provide a thorough and fascinating account of this historical process. It is documented anthropologically in

Rayna R. Reiter, ed., *Toward an Anthropology of Women* (New York: Monthly Review Press, 1975).

43. A recent resolution of the Women's Caucus of the Radical Caucus of the American Psychiatric Association recognized this power. It states that

> research and therapy should at this time in history view women's mental health problems as arising from: (1) the unequal power relationship between men and women, in which women are at the bottom, and (2) the women's position as legal domestic in the home or as exploited public workers. . . .

It "urged psychiatrists to stop rationalizing the situation of women by labeling its victims as neurotic rather than oppressed" (Jessie Bernard, "The Paradox of the Happy Marriage," in Gornick and Moran, eds., *Woman in Sexist Society,* p. 158).

44. Beauvoir, *The Second Sex*, p. 430.

45. Kate Millett, *Sexual Politics* (New York: Avon Books, 1971).

46. Janeway, *Man's World, Woman's Place*, p. 112.

47. Nancy Henley and Jo Freeman, "The Sexual Politics of Interpersonal Behavior," in Jo Freeman, ed., *Women; A Feminist Perspective* (Palo Alto, Calif.: Mayfield Publishing Co., 1975), pp. 394-95.

48. Ibid., passim.

49. Margaret Adams, "The Compassion Trap," in Gornick and Moran, eds., *Woman in Sexist Society*, p. 559.

50. Janeway, *Man's World, Woman's Place*, p. 114.

51. Leonore J. Weitzman, "Sex-Role Socialization," in Freeman, ed., *Women: A Feminist Perspective*, p. 118.

52. Rosabeth Moss Kanter, "Women and the Structure of Organizations: Explorations in Theory and Behavior," in Marcia Millman and Rosabeth Moss Kanter, eds., *Another Voice* (New York: Doubleday and Co., 1975), p. 54.

53. The ability to please others is probably related to class as well as sex. Research by Flora suggests that working class women are less likely to be skilled at manipulating symbols and presenting appropriate images. (Cornelia Butler Flora, "Working Class Women's Political Participation: Its Potential in Developed Countries," in Marianne Githens and Jewel L. Prestage, eds., *A Portrait of Marginality* [New York: David McKay, Co., 1977], p. 79.)

54. Beauvoir, *The Second Sex*, p. 172.

55. D. Bugental, L. Love, and R. Gianetto, "Perfidious Feminine Faces," *Journal of Personality and Social Psychology* 17 (1971): 314-18. Cited in Arlie Russell Hochschild, "The Sociology of Feeling and

Emotion: Selected Possibilities," in Millman and Kanter, eds., *Another Voice*, p. 294. For an insightful discussion of the relation of flattery to dominance, see Abigail L. Rosenthal, "Feminism Without Contradictions," *The Monist* 57 (January 1973): 42.

56. Firestone, *The Dialectic of Sex*, p. 90.

57. Hochschild, "The Sociology of Feeling and Emotion: Selected Possibilities," in Millman and Kanter, eds., *Another Voice*, p. 295.

58. Susan Harding, "Women and Words in a Spanish Village," in Eisenstein, ed., *Capitalist Patriarchy and the Case for Socialist Feminism*, p. 292.

59. Ibid., pp. 302-3.

60. Gayle Rubin, "The Traffic in Women: Notes on the Political Economy of Sex," in Eisenstein, ed., *Captalist Patriarchy and the Case for Socialist Feminism*, p. 180.

61. Mead clearly recognized the importance of childhood socialization as a way of acquiring a self-perception, although he did not apply his insight to the distinctions discussed here. Through participation in various social acts, the child incorporates and internalizes a view of himself that is presented by those others who engage in the social acts also. Thus, the little girl takes the attitude toward herself which she finds others taking toward her, and this is most frequently an attitude that includes these definite ideas about appropriate male and female behavior. Similar analyses in the field of child psychology are so numerous as to be inexhaustible. They include Nancy Chodorow, "Family Structure and Feminine Personality," in Michele Z. Rosaldo and Louise Lamphere, eds., *Woman, Culture and Society* (Stanford, Calif.: Stanford University Press, 1974)—Chodorow analyzes the differences in response that parents make toward little girls and little boys, and shows its connection to the expectations for manhood and womanhood; David Gutmann, "Women and the Concept of Ego-Strength," *Merrill-Palmer Quarterly of Behavior and Development* 2 (1965): 229-40—Gutmann suggests that female socialization leads women to have "more flexible ego boundaries," and less stringent self-other distinctions, so that women more easily take the role of the other; Rae Carlson, "Sex Differences in Ego Functioning: Exploratory Studies of Agency and Communions," *Journal of Consulting and Clinical Psychology* 37 (1971): 267-77—Carlson finds confirmation of Bakan and Gutmann in empirical tests; Rosalie A. Cohen, "Conceptual Styles, Culture Conflict, and Nonverbal Tests of Intelligence," *American Anthropologist* 71 (1969): 828-56—Cohen, focusing on different "cognitive styles," finds that women are more embedded in social relationships and have closer interactional patterns with others than do men.

62. David Bakan, *The Duality of Existence: Isolation and Communion in Western Man*, quoted in Nancy Chodorow, "Family Structure and Feminine Personality," in Rosaldo and Lamphere, eds., *Woman, Culture and Society*, pp. 55-56.

63. See Millett, *Sexual Politics*, pp. 108-10, for a brief discussion of the sources of these two views.

64. Lila Leibowitz, "Perspectives on the Evolution of Sex Differences," in Reiter, ed., *Toward an Anthropology of Women*, pp. 20-35.

65 These various interpretations are proposed and defended by anthropologists of differing opinions in Reiter, ed., *Toward an Anthropology of Women*, and in Rosaldo and Lamphere, eds., *Woman, Culture and Society*. They are also summarized by Heidi Hartmann, "Capitalism, Patriarchy and Job Segregation by Sex," in Eisenstein, ed., *Capitalist Patriarchy and the Case for Socialist Feminism*, pp. 206-47.

66. Rayna R. Reiter, "Introduction," in Reiter, ed., *Toward an Anthropology of Women*, p. 12.

67. Friedan, *The Feminine Mystique*, pp. 18-25.

68. See Janeway, *Man's World, Woman's Place*, pp. 147-62, for a summary of Keniston's argument.

69. See Warren Farrell, *The Liberated Man* (New York: Bantam Books, 1974).

70. In her study of women in asylums, Phyllis Chesler concludes that much of what is conventionally called madness in women is "an expression of female powerlessness and an unsuccessful attempt to reject and overcome this state" (*Women and Madness* [New York: Avon Books, 1972], p. 15). Similarly, sociologists Walter Gove and Jeannette Tudor conclude from their study of mental illness in modern industrial nations that women's role is more limiting and frustrating for them than is the male counterpart and that women are more likely to be discontented with it. Women who object to or cannot deal with the limitations of their role are then treated by the mental health establishment as individual dysfunctionals (Gove and Tudor, "Adult Sex Roles and Mental Illness," *American Journal of Sociology* 72 [January 1973]: 812-35).

Bibliography

Abel, Reuben. "Pragmatism and the Outlook of Modern Science," *Philosophy and Phenomenological Research* 27 (September 1966): 45-54.

Altbach, Edith Hoshino, ed. *From Feminism to Liberation*. Cambridge, Mass.: Schenkman Publishing Co., 1971.

Ames, Van Meter. "Buber and Mead," *Antioch Review* 27 (1967): 181-91.

———. "Mead and Husserl on the Self," *Philosophy and Phenomenological Research* 15 (March 1955): 320-31.

———. "Mead and Sartre on Man," *Journal of Philosophy* 53 (March 15, 1956): 205-19.

Annas, Julia. "Mill and the Subjection of Women," *Philosophy* 52 (April 1977): 179-94.

Barber, Benjamin. *Liberating Feminism*. New York: Seabury Press, 1975.

Bartky, Sandra Lee. "Toward a Phenomenology of Feminist Consciousness," *Social Theory and Practice* 3 (Fall 1975): 425-39.

Baumann, Bedrich. "Parallels Between the Theoretical and Artistic Presentation of the Social Role Concept," *Social Research* 34 (Autumn 1967): 563-607.

Beauvoir, Simone de. *The Second Sex*. New York: Alfred A. Knopf, 1952.

Behnke, Elizabeth A. "Space-Time Concepts as World Dimensions," *Main Currents* 31 (September-October 1974): 13-17.

Bell, Caroline Shaw. "Economics, Sex and Gender," *Social Science Quarterly* 55 (December 1974): 615-31.

Bell, Roderick; Edwards, David V.; and Wagner, R. Harrison. *Political Power*. New York: The Free Press, 1969.

Berger, Peter L., and Luckmann, Thomas. *The Social Construction of Reality*. New York: Doubleday and Co., 1966.

Bergson, Henri. *Time and Free Will*. London: George Allen and Unwin, 1910.

Betz, Joseph. "George Herbert Mead on Human Rights," *Transactions of the Charles Peirce Society* 4 (Fall 1974): 199-223.

Bittner, C. J. "George Herbert Mead's Social Concept of the Self," *Sociology and Social Research* 16 (September-October 1931): 6-22.

Blackstone, William T. "Freedom and Women," *Ethics* 85 (April 1975): 243-48.

Blumer, Herbert. "Sociological Implications of the Thought of George Herbert Mead," *American Journal of Sociology* 71 (March 1966): 535-45.

———. *Symbolic Interactionism*. Englewood Cliffs, N. J.: Prentice Hall, 1969.

Bolton, Charles D. "Behavior, Experience and Relationships: A Symbolic Interactionist Point of View," *American Journal of Sociology* 64 (July 1958): 45-58.

Bookchin, Murray. *Post-Scarcity Anarchism*. San Francisco: Ramparts Press, 1971.

Brewester, John M. "A Behavioristic Account of the Logical Function of Universals," *Journal of Philosophy* 33 (September 10, 1936): 505-14.

Brotherston, B. W. "Genius of Pragmatic Empiricism," *Journal of Philosophy* 40 (January 21, 1943): 29-39.

Brown, Bruce. *Marx, Freud, and the Critique of Everyday Life*. New York: Monthly Review Press, 1973.

Brownmiller, Susan. *Against Our Will: Men, Women and Rape*. New York: Bantam Books, 1975.

Buchler, Justus. *Toward a General Theory of Human Judgment*. New York: Columbia University Press, 1951.

Burke, Kenneth. *Permanence and Change*. Los Altos, Calif.: Hermes Publications, 1954.

Carden, Maren Lockwood. *The New Feminist Movement*. New York: Russell Sage Foundation, 1974.

Carlson, Rae. "Sex Differences in Ego Functioning: Exploratory Studies of Agency and Communion," *Journal of Consulting and Clinical Psychology* 37 (1971): 267-77.

Chafe, William H. "Feminism in the 1970's," *Dissent* 21 (Fall 1974): 508-17.

Chafetz, Janet Saltzman. *Masculine, Feminine or Human?* Itasca, Ill.: F. E. Peacock Publishers, 1974.

Chesler, Phyllis. *Women and Madness*. New York: Avon Books, 1972.

Clayton, Alfred S. *Emergent Mind and Education.* New York: Bureau of Publications, Columbia University, Teachers College, 1943.

Clements, Barbara Evan. "Emancipation Through Communism: The Ideology of A. M. Kollontai," *Slavic Review* 32 (June 1973): 323-38.

Cohen, Rosalie A. "Conceptual Styles, Culture Conflict, and Nonverbal Tests of Intelligence," *American Anthropologist* 71 (1969): 828-56.

Cole, G. D. H. *The Meaning of Marxism.* Ann Arbor, Mich.: University of Michigan Press, 1966.

Cook, Gary A. "The Development of George Herbert Mead's Social Psychology," *Transactions of the Charles Peirce Society* 4 (Summer 1972): 167-86.

Cottrell, Robert D. *Simone de Beauvoir.* New York: Frederick Ungar Publishing Co., 1975.

Cronk, George F. "Symbolic Interactionism: A 'Left-Median' Perspective," *Social Theory and Practice* 2 (Spring 1973): 313-33.

De Laguna, Grace A. "Communication, the Act and the Object with Reference to Mead," *Journal of Philosophy* 43 (April 25, 1946): 225-38.

Doan, Frank M. "Notations of George Herbert Mead's Principle of Sociality with Special Reference to Transformations," *Journal of Philosophy* 53 (September 27, 1956): 607-15.

————. "Remarks on George Herbert Mead's Conception of Simultaneity," *Journal of Philosophy* 55 (February 27, 1958): 203-9.

Duncan, Hugh Dalziel. *Symbols and Social Theory.* New York: Oxford University Press, 1969.

Effrat, Andrew, ed. *Perspectives in Political Sociology.* New York: Bobbs-Merrill Co., 1974.

Eisenstein, Zillah R., ed. *Capitalist Patriarchy and the Case for Socialist Feminism.* New York: Monthly Review Press, 1979.

Epstein, Cynthia Fuchs, and Goode, William J. *The Other Half: Roads to Women's Equality.* Englewood Cliffs, N. J.: Prentice Hall, 1971.

Fanon, Frantz. *The Wretched of the Earth.* New York: Grove Press, 1963.

Faris, Ellsworth. "The Social Psychology of George Herbert Mead," *American Journal of Sociology* 43 (November 1937): 391-401.

Farrell, Warren. *The Liberated Man.* New York: Bantam Books, 1974.

Findlay, J. N. "Husserl's Analysis of the Inner Time-Consciousness," *The Monist* 59 (January 1975): 3-20.

Firestone, Shulamith. *The Dialectic of Sex.* New York: Bantam Books, 1970.

Fleck, Leonard. "G. H. Mead on Knowledge and Action," *Proceedings of the American Catholic Philosophical Association* 47 (1973): 76-86.

Freeman, Jo. "The Origins of the Women's Liberation Movement," *American Journal of Sociology* 78 (January 1973): 792-811.

———. *The Politics of Women's Liberation*. New York: David McKay Co., 1975.

———, ed. *Women: A Feminist Perspective*. Palo Alto, Calif.: Mayfield Publishing Co., 1975.

Friedan, Betty. *The Feminine Mystique*. Middlesex, England: Penguin Books, 1963.

Gerth, Hans, and Mills, C. Wright. *Character and Social Structure*. London: Routledge and Kegan Paul, 1954.

Gillin, Charles T. "Freedom and the Limits of Social Behaviorism: A Comparison of Selected Themes from the Work of G. H. Mead and Martin Buber," *Sociology* 9 (January 1975): 29-47.

Gintis, Herb. "Activism and the Counterculture: The Dialectics of Consciousness in the Corporate State," *Telos* (Summer 1972): 42-62.

Githens, Marianne, and Prestage, Jewel L., eds. *A Portrait of Marginality*. New York: David McKay Co., 1977.

Goffman, Erving. "The Arrangement between the Sexes," *Theory and Society* 4 (Fall 1977): 301-33.

———. *Asylums*. New York: Anchor Books, 1961.

Gornick, Vivian, and Moran, Barbara K., eds. *Woman in Sexist Society*. New York: New American Library, 1971.

Gouldner, Alvin. *The Coming Crisis in Western Sociology*. New York: Basic Books, 1970.

Gove, Walter R., and Tudor, Jeannette F. "Adult Sex Roles and Mental Illness," *American Journal of Sociology* 78 (January 1973): 812-35.

Hacker, Andrew. "Cutting Classes," *New York Review of Books* 23 (March 4, 1976): 15-18.

Hegel, G. W. F. *The Phenomenology of Mind*. New York: Harper and Row, 1967.

———. *The Philosophy of Right*. London: Oxford University Press, 1967.

Hobbes, Thomas. *Leviathan*. Middlesex, England: Penguin Books, 1968.

Hobhouse, L. T. *Liberalism*. London: Oxford University Press, 1964.

Hole, Judith, and Levine, Ellen. *Rebirth of Feminism*. New York: Quadrangle Books, 1971.

Holmes, Eugene Clay. *Social Philosophy and the Social Mind: A Study of the Genetic Methods of J. M. Baldwin, G. H. Mead, and J. E. Boodin*. Published by the author, Howard University, Washington D.C., 1942.

Honeycutt, Karen. "Clara Zetkin: A Socialist Approach to the Problem of Women's Liberation," *Feminist Studies* 3 (Spring/Summer 1976): 131-44.

Huber, Joan. "Symbolic Interaction as Pragmatic Perspective: The Bias of Emergent Theory," *American Sociological Review* 38 (April 1973): 274-84.

―――. "Toward a Sociotechnological Theory of the Women's Movement," *Social Problems* 23 (April 1976): 371-88.

Israel, Joachim. *Alienation: From Marx to Modern Sociology*. Boston: Allyn and Bacon, 1971.

Jagger, Alison. "On Sexual Equality," *Ethics* 84 (July 1974): 275-91.

James, William. *Essays in Radical Empiricism and a Pluralistic Universe*. New York: E. P. Dutton and Co., 1971.

Janeway, Elizabeth. *Between Myth and Morning: Women Awakening*. New York: William Morrow and Co., 1975.

―――. *Man's World, Woman's Place*. New York: Delta Books, 1971.

Jaquette, Jane, ed. *Women in Politics*. New York: John Wiley and Sons, 1974.

Kaing, Howard P. "A Non-Marxian Application of the Hegelian Master-Slave Dialectic to Some Modern Politico-Social Developments," *Idealistic Studies* 3 (September 1973): 285-302.

Kolb, William L. "A Critical Evaluation of Mead's 'I' and 'Me' Concepts," *Social Forces* 22 (March 1944): 291-96.

Kuhn, Thomas. *The Structure of Scientific Revolutions*. Chicago: University of Chicago Press, 1962.

Lee, Donald S. "The Construction of Empirical Concepts," *Philosophy and Phenomenological Research* 27 (December 1966): 183-98.

Lee, Harold N. "Mead's Doctrine of the Past," *Philosophy and Phenomenological Research* 27 (December 1966): 52-75.

―――. "Time and Continuity," *Southern Journal of Philosophy* 10 (Fall 1972): 295-99.

Leighton, Jean. *Simone de Beauvoir on Women*. Cranbury, N. J.: Fairleigh Dickinson University Press, 1975.

Lew, Raymond. "Hegel and Consciousness." Unpublished paper, Department of Political Science, University of Minnesota (September 1973).

Lichtman, Richard. "Symbolic Interaction and Social Reality: Some Marxist Queries," *Berkeley Journal of Sociology* 15 (1970): 73-93.

McKinney, John C. "The Contribution of George Herbert Mead to the Sociology of Knowledge," *Social Forces* 34 (December 1955): 144-49.

―――. "George H. Mead and the Philosophy of Science," *Philosophy of Science* 22 (October 1955): 264-71.

MacMurray, John. *Persons in Relations*. London: Faber and Faber, 1961.

―――. *The Self as Agent*. London: Faber and Faber, 1956.

MacPherson, C. B. *The Political Theory of Possessive Individualism*. London: Oxford University Press, 1962.

Magas, Branka (with comments by Robin Blackburn and Lucie Rey). "Sex Politics; Class Politics," *New Left Review* 66 (March-April 1971): 69-96.

Manis, Jerome G., and Meltzer, Bernard N., eds. *Symbolic Interaction*. Boston: Allyn and Bacon, 1972.

Marx, Karl. *Capital and Other Writings*. Max Eastern, ed. New York: Modern Library, 1932.

———. *Early Writings*. T. B. Bottomore, trans. New York: McGraw-Hill Co., 1963

———. *The Grundrisse*. David McLellan, ed. New York: Harper and Row, 1971.

Marx, Karl, and Engels, Frederick. *The German Ideology*. C. J. Arthur, ed. New York: International Publishers, 1970.

———. *Marx and Engels*. Louis Feuer, ed. New York: Doubleday and Co., 1959.

Mead, George Herbert. "A Behavioristic Account of the Significant Symbol," *Journal of Philosophy* 19 (March 16, 1922): 157-63.

———. "The Definition of the Psychical," *Decennial Publications of the University of Chicago*. First series, 3: 77-112.

———. "The Genesis of the Self and Social Control," *International Journal of Ethics* 35 (April 1925): 251-77.

———. "The Mechanism of Social Consciousness," *Journal of Philosophy* (formerly *Journal of Philosophy, Psychology and Scientific Method*) 9 (July 18, 1912): 401-6.

———. *Mind, Self and Society*. Chicago: University of Chicago Press, 1934.

———. *Movements of Thought in the Nineteenth Century*. Merritt M. Moore, ed. Chicago: University of Chicago Press, 1936.

———. "National-Mindedness and International-Mindedness," *International Journal of Ethics* 39 (July 1929): 385-407.

———. "Natural Rights and the Theory of the Political Institution," *Journal of Philosophy* (formerly *Journal of Philosophy, Psychology, and Scientific Method*) 12 (March 18, 1915): 141-85.

———. "The Nature of Aesthetic Experience," *International Journal of Ethics* 36 (July 1926): 382-93.

———. "The Objective Reality of Perspectives," *Proceedings of the Sixth International Congress of Philosophy*. New York: Longmans, Green and Co., 1927.

———. "The Philosophical Basis of Ethics," *International Journal of Ethics* 8 (April 1908): 311-23.

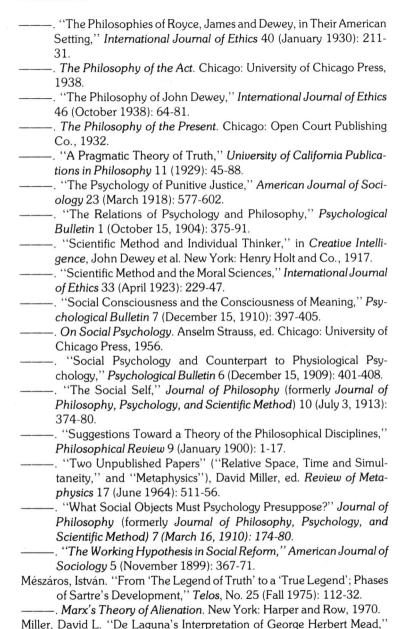

———. "The Philosophies of Royce, James and Dewey, in Their American Setting," *International Journal of Ethics* 40 (January 1930): 211-31.

———. *The Philosophy of the Act.* Chicago: University of Chicago Press, 1938.

———. "The Philosophy of John Dewey," *International Journal of Ethics* 46 (October 1938): 64-81.

———. *The Philosophy of the Present.* Chicago: Open Court Publishing Co., 1932.

———. "A Pragmatic Theory of Truth," *University of California Publications in Philosophy* 11 (1929): 45-88.

———. "The Psychology of Punitive Justice," *American Journal of Sociology* 23 (March 1918): 577-602.

———. "The Relations of Psychology and Philosophy," *Psychological Bulletin* 1 (October 15, 1904): 375-91.

———. "Scientific Method and Individual Thinker," in *Creative Intelligence*, John Dewey et al. New York: Henry Holt and Co., 1917.

———. "Scientific Method and the Moral Sciences," *International Journal of Ethics* 33 (April 1923): 229-47.

———. "Social Consciousness and the Consciousness of Meaning," *Psychological Bulletin* 7 (December 15, 1910): 397-405.

———. *On Social Psychology.* Anselm Strauss, ed. Chicago: University of Chicago Press, 1956.

———. "Social Psychology and Counterpart to Physiological Psychology," *Psychological Bulletin* 6 (December 15, 1909): 401-408.

———. "The Social Self," *Journal of Philosophy* (formerly *Journal of Philosophy, Psychology, and Scientific Method*) 10 (July 3, 1913): 374-80.

———. "Suggestions Toward a Theory of the Philosophical Disciplines," *Philosophical Review* 9 (January 1900): 1-17.

———. "Two Unpublished Papers" ("Relative Space, Time and Simultaneity," and "Metaphysics"), David Miller, ed. *Review of Metaphysics* 17 (June 1964): 511-56.

———. "What Social Objects Must Psychology Presuppose?" *Journal of Philosophy* (formerly *Journal of Philosophy, Psychology, and Scientific Method*) 7 *(March 16, 1910): 174-80.*

———. *"The Working Hypothesis in Social Reform,"* *American Journal of Sociology* 5 (November 1899): 367-71.

Mészáros, István. "From 'The Legend of Truth' to a 'True Legend'; Phases of Sartre's Development," *Telos*, No. 25 (Fall 1975): 112-32.

———. *Marx's Theory of Alienation.* New York: Harper and Row, 1970.

Miller, David L. "De Laguna's Interpretation of George Herbert Mead," *Journal of Philosophy* 44 (March 13, 1947): 158-62.

————. "George Herbert Mead's Conception of the 'Present'," *Philosophy of Science* 10 (January 1943): 40-46.

————. *George Herbert Mead: Self, Language and the World.* Austin, Tex.: University of Texas Press, 1973.

————. "Josiah Royce and George H. Mead on the Nature of the Self," *Transactions of the Charles Peirce Society* 11 (Summer 1975): 67-89.

Millett, Kate. *Sexual Politics.* New York: Avon Books, 1970.

Millman, Marcia, and Kanter, Rosabeth Moss, eds. *Another Voice.* New York: Doubleday and Co., 1975.

Mills, C. Wright. *The Power Elite.* London: Oxford University Press, 1956.

————. *Power, Politics and People.* London: Oxford University Press, 1939.

————. *The Sociological Imagination.* New York: Oxford University Press, 1959.

————. *Sociology and Pragmatism.* New York: Oxford University Press, 1969.

Mitchell, Juliet. "Marxism and Women's Liberation," *Social Praxis* 1 (1973): 23-33.

————. *Psychoanalysis and Feminism.* New York: Vintage Books, 1974.

————. *Women's Estate.* New York: Vintage Books, 1973.

Moreno, Francisco José. *Between Faith and Reason.* New York: New York University Press, 1977.

Morgan, Robin, ed. *Sisterhood Is Powerful.* New York: Random House, 1970.

Morris, Charles W. "Peirce, Mead, and Pragmatism," *The Philosophical Review* 47 (March 1938): 109-127.

————. *The Pragmatic Movement in American Philosophy.* New York: George Braziller, 1970.

————. "Pragmatism and Metaphysics," *The Philosophical Review* 43 (November 1934): 549-64.

Mothersill, Mary. "Notes on Feminism," *The Monist* 57 (January 1973): 104-14.

Murphy, Arthur E. "Concerning Mead's *Philosophy of the Act*," *Journal of Philosophy* 36 (February 16, 1939): 85-103.

Natanson, Maurice. "George Herbert Mead's Metaphysics of Time," *Journal of Philosophy* 50 (December 3, 1953): 770-82.

————. "Phenomenology and Social Role," *Journal of the British Society for Phenomenology* 3 (October 1972): 218-30.

————. *The Social Dynamics of George Herbert Mead.* Washington, D.C.: Public Affairs Press, 1956.

Ollman, Bertell. *Alienation.* London: University of Cambridge Press, 1971.

Perinbanayagam, R. S. "The Significance of Others in the Thought of Alfred Schutz, G. H. Mead, and C. H. Cooley," *Sociological Quarterly* 16 (Autumn 1975): 500-21.

Petras, John W. "George Herbert Mead's Theory of Self: A Study in the Origin and Convergence of Ideas," *Canadian Review of Anthropology and Sociology* 10 (May 1973): 148-59.

Pfeutze, Paul E. *The Social Self.* New York: Bookman Associates, 1954.

The Philosophical Forum 5 (Fall/Winter 1973-1974).

Plato. *The Republic of Plato.* Francis M. Cornford, trans. New York: Oxford University Press, 1945.

Rasmussen, David. "Between Autonomy and Sociality," *Cultural Hermeneutics* 1 (Spring 1973): 3-45.

Read, Herbert. *Anarchy and Order.* Boston: Beacon Press, 1971.

Reck, Andrew J. "The Philosophy of George Herbert Mead," *Tulane Studies in Philosophy* 12 (1963): 5-51.

Reed, Evelyn. *Problems of Women's Liberation: A Marxist Approach.* New York: Pathfinder Press, 1971.

Reiman, Jeffrey H. "Privacy, Intimacy and Personhood," *Philosophy and Public Affairs* 6 (Fall 1976): 26-44.

Reische, Diane, ed. *Women and Society.* New York: H. W. Wilson Co. 1972.

Reiter, Rayna R., ed. *Toward an Anthropology of Women.* New York: Monthly Review Press, 1975.

Reynolds, Janice M., and Reynolds, Larry T. "Interactionism, Complicity, and the Astructural Bias," *Catalyst*, No. 7 (Winter 1973): 76-85.

Rohrlich-Leavitt, Ruby, ed. *Women Cross Culturally: Change and Challenge.* The Hague: Mouton Publishers, 1975.

Ropers, Richard. "Mead, Marx, and Social Psychology," *Catalyst*, No. 7 (Winter 1973): 42-61.

Rosaldo, Michelle Zimbalist, and Lamphere, Louise, eds. *Women, Culture and Society.* Stanford, Calif.: Stanford University Press, 1974.

Rosenthal, Abigail L. "Feminism Without Contradictions," *The Monist* 57 (January 1973): 28-42.

Rosenthal, Sandra B. "Activity and the Structure of Perceptual Experience: Peirce and Mead Revisited," *Southern Journal of Philosophy* 15 (Summer 1977): 207-14.

―――. "Pragmatism, Scientific Method, and the Phenomenological Return to Lived Experience," *Philosophy and Phenomenological Research* 38 (September 1977): 56-65.

―――, and Bourgeois, Patrick L. "Mead, Merleau-Ponty, and the Lived Perceptual World," *Philosophy Today* 21 (Spring 1977): 56-61.

Rossi, Alice S., ed. *The Feminist Papers: From Adams to de Beauvoir.* New York: Columbia University Press, 1973.

————. "Women—Terms of Liberation," *Dissent* 21 (Spring 1974): 317-28.

Roszak, Betty, and Roszak, Theodore. *Masculine/Feminine.* New York: Harper Colophon Books, 1969.

Rowbotham, Sheila. *Woman's Consciousness, Man's World.* Baltimore: Penguin Books, 1973.

————. *Women, Resistance and Revolution.* New York: Vintage Books, 1974.

Rucker, Egbert Darnell. *The Chicago Pragmatists.* Minneapolis: University of Minnesota Press, 1969.

Russell, Bertrand. *The ABC of Relativity.* New York: New American Library, 1959.

Rytina, Joan Huber, and Loomis, Charles P. "Marxist Dialectic and Pragmatism: Power as Knowledge," *American Sociological Review* 35 (April 1972): 308-18.

Sanday, Peggy R. "Toward a Theory of the Status of Women," *American Anthropologist* 75 (October 1973): 1682-1700.

Sartre, Jean Paul. *No Exit and Three Other Plays.* New York: Vintage Books, 1946.

Schaff, Adam. *Marxism and the Human Individual.* New York: McGraw-Hill Co., 1970.

Schermerhorn, Richard A. *Society and Power.* New York: Random House, 1961.

Schneir, Miriam, ed. *Feminism, The Essential Historical Writings.* New York: Vintage Books, 1972.

Schutz, Alfred. *The Phenomenology of the Social World.* Evanston, Ill.: Northwestern University Press, 1967.

Scott, Hilda. *Does Socialism Liberate Women?* Boston: Beacon Press, 1974.

Shanley, Mary L., and Schuck, Victoria. "In Search of Political Women," *Social Science Quarterly* 55 (December 1974): 632-44.

Shaskolsky, Leon. "The Development of Sociological Theory in America: A Sociology of Knowledge Interpretation," in Janice M. Reynolds and Larry T. Reynolds, eds. *The Sociology of Sociology.* New York: David McKay Co., 1970.

Sibley, Mulford Q. *Political Ideas and Ideologies.* New York: Harper and Row, 1970.

Simpson, Evan. "Socialist Justice," *Ethics* 87 (October 1976): 1-17

Smith, T. V. "The Social Philosophy of George Herbert Mead," *American Journal of Sociology* 37 (November 1931): 368-85.

Stephen, Karin, *The Misuse of Mind.* London: Kegan Paul, Trench, Trubner, and Co., 1922.

Stirner, Max. *The Ego and Its Own*. London: Trinity Press, 1971.

Stone, Olive M. "The Rebirth of the Women's Movement," *Contemporary Review* 221 (August 1972): 74-81.

Szymanski, Albert. "Race, Sex and the U.S. Working Class," *Social Problems* 21 (June 1974): 706-25.

Terkel, Studs. *Working*. New York: Avon Books, 1972.

Thayer, H. S. *Meaning and Action*. New York: Bobbs-Merrill Co., 1968.

Thompson, Mary Lou, ed. *Voices of the New Feminism*. Boston: Beacon Press, 1970.

Tibbets, Paul. "Mead, Phenomenalism, and Phenomenology," *Philosophy Today* 17 (Winter 1973): 329-36.

———. "Mead's Theory of the Act and Perception: Some Empirical Confirmations," *Personalist* 55 (Spring 1974): 115-38.

———. "Mead's Theory of Reality and the Knower-Known Transaction," *Dialectica* 27 (1973): 27-41.

———. "Peirce and Mead on Perceptual Immediacy and Human Action," *Philosophy and Phenomenological Research* 36 (December 1975): 222-32.

Tillman, Mary Katherine. "Temporality and Role-Taking in Mead," *Social Research* 37 (Winter 1970): 533-46.

Tiryakian, Edward A. *Sociologism and Existentialism*. Englewood Cliffs, N. J.: Prentice Hall, 1962.

Tremmel, William C. "The Social Concepts of George Herbert Mead," *Emporia State Research Studies* 15 (June 1957): 1-36.

Troyer, William L. "Mead's Social and Functional Theory of Mind," *American Sociological Review* 11 (April 1946): 198-202.

University of Chicago Archives. George Herbert Mead File.

Ware, Cellestine. *Woman Power*. New York: Tower Publications, 1970.

White, Morton. *Social Thought in America*. New York: Viking Press, 1952.

Winter, Gibson. *Elements for a Social Ethic*. New York: MacMillan and Co., 1966.

Wood, Ellen M. *Mind and Politics*. Berkeley, Calif.: University of California Press, 1972.

Workmeister, W. H. *A History of Philosophical Ideas in America*. New York: Ronald Press Co., 1940.

Zeitlin, Irving. *Rethinking Sociology*. New York: Appleton, Century, Crofts, 1973.

Index

Agency, 168-69

Alienation, 104, 124, 170-71

American Women Suffrage Association, 19 n. 4

Anarchism, 99 n. 34, 111, 136

Anger, 165-66

Anthony, Susan B., 19 n. 4

Appreciation, 106, 108-9, 119-23

Asylums (Goffman), 73

Autonomy, 17, 106, 109, 111, 115, 124, 156, 166-67, 172, 175; in liberalism, 6-7, 130-31

Axiology, 113-14. *See also* Values

Bakan, David, *Duality of Existence*, 168

Barber, Benjamin, *Liberating Feminism*, 158-59

Beauvoir, Simone de, 18, 136-54, 157, 160, 164, 169, 175; on conflict, 148-50; on consciousness, 140-41; on the economic status of women, 138-39, 152; on emotions, 148; on the Eternal Feminine, 143, 145-46, 151, 154; on immanence/transcendence, 137-39, 141-43, 144-46, 149-53, 160, 175; on liberation, 138, 149-52; on the oppression of women, 143-44, 147; on the roles of women, 137-40, 146, 149-52; *The Second Sex,* 18, 136, 153; on self and other, 139-49

Behaviorism, 41-42, 46, 62 n.33, 96 n.5

Bentham, Jeremy, 6

Berger, Peter, *The Social Construction of Reality*, 78-83, 93-94

Bergson, Henri, 28, 44-45, 64, 120, 122

Bourgeois feminist, 19 n.4

Bureaucracy, 54, 70, 74, 90-92, 94, 111, 131-32

Burke, Kenneth, 120

Capitalism, 5-6, 8, 49, 74, 94, 112, 122, 129-30, 133-35

Capitalist Patriarchy and the Case for Socialist Feminism (Eisenstein), 99 n.34, 135

Cognitive self, 55-57, 59n.13, 66-67, 102-3
Communion, 168-69
Community, 14, 24, 46, 108
Compassion, 17, 106, 108-9, 110-11, 113-14, 122-25, 152-53, 159, 167, 176
Compassion trap, 162, 165
Conflict, 53, 89, 141, 147-49
Consciousness, 25-26, 28, 55, 65-66, 93, 140
Contract theory, 6, 14, 24, 40-41
Control, 15-16, 31-32, 56, 69-71, 73, 75, 91-93, 103, 108, 112. *See also* Power
Creativity, 15, 33, 34, 118, 156
Culture, 29, 30, 135; cultural myths, 142, 154, 157-59

Dewey, John, 16
Dialectic, 15, 23-24, 26, 29, 31, 33, 44, 65-66, 68, 81, 83, 84, 105, 107, 108, 118-19, 121, 122, 124, 125, 159, 167, 173, 175, 176
Dominance/subordinance, 12, 14, 17, 70, 73-77, 83, 91-95; in existentialism, 140, 142-44, 146-47, 153; and liberation, 103-10, 112, 114-18, 124-25, 157-58, 160-61, 163-68, 172, 175; in Marxism, 8-9, 89-90, 132-36
Duality of Existence (Bakan), 168

Economical and Philosophical Manuscripts (Marx), 87
Education, 117-18, 131-32

Eisenstein, Zillah, 169; *Capitalist Patriarchy and the Case for Socialist Feminism*, 99n.34, 135-36
Emergence, 44-46, 104-5, 119, 121, 146, 173
Emotions, 56-57, 102-3, 148
Engels, Frederich, *The Origins of the Family, Private Property, and the State*, 5, 7
"Eternal Feminine," 143, 145-46, 151, 154
Ethics, 47-52
Existentialism, 18, 128, 136-53
Expression/reflection, 35, 65-66, 68, 94, 121-22, 155-56, 173
Externalization, 81

Family, 8, 74, 132-34, 159, 162, 169, 174-75
Fanon, Frantz, *The Wretched of the Earth*, 104, 110
Farrell, Warren, 171
Feminine Mystique, The (Friedan), 5, 112, 129, 170
Femininity, 146, 149-51, 158-59, 163, 165-69, 171, 175, 176n.8
Feminism, 4-12, 18, 19n.4, 19-20n.6, 21-22n.20, 153, 169, 175; liberal, 5, 7, 129-32; Marxist, 5-6, 7-9, 132-36; radical, 5-6, 9-10, 12, 135
Firestone, Shulamith, 9, 177n.10
Freedom, 6, 10-11, 17, 31-32, 46, 50, 105-14, 122-25, 130, 142, 144-45, 152-53, 159, 167, 172, 176
Freeman, Jo, 9, 19-20n.6
Freud, Sigmund, 77-78

Friedan, Betty, 5, 112, 129-32, 170; *The Feminine Mystique*, 5, 112, 129, 170
Friendship, 72, 105, 108-9, 141

Gender. *See* Sex roles
Generalized other, 16, 26, 30-32, 38, 51, 58-59 n. 12, 66, 102, 154-56; diversity in the, 32, 59 n. 15, 37, 98 n. 31, 103, 116-17, 173-74; and the "I/me" relation, 35-36, 41, 67-68, 82, 115-16; and individual freedom, 31-32; and social control, 31, 32, 37, 55-56, 68, 71, 74-75, 82-83, 94-95, 156-58, 160
Genocide, 158
German Ideology, The (Marx), 85
Goffman, Erving, *Asylums*, 73

Habitualization, 79-82, 93
Hegel, G. W. F., 15, 23, 81, 85, 107-8, 110, 136, 146; *The Philosophy of Right*, 85
Hierarchy. *See* Bureaucracy
Hobbes, Thomas, 14
Human nature, 12-14, 65, 74-76, 84-87, 97-98 n. 25, 153-54

"I/me" relation, 15-16, 32-33, 55, 59-60 n. 16, 65-66, 115-19, 121, 148, 155; dual meaning of the, 34-37, 67-68, 82-83, 115-16; and Freudian thought, 61-62 n. 27, 77-78; and liberation, 173; and phenomenology, 60 n. 18
Immanence, 136, 141, 143, 145-46, 149-52, 160, 165, 170-71, 175
Inauthenticity, 142, 145, 164

Institutionalization, 79-83, 93-94
Institutions, 7, 52, 54, 56, 75, 80; and domination, 7, 129, 130-34, 159-60; and social acts, 68-69, 71-74, 83, 94
Internalization, 81, 103

James, William, 47, 52, 57-58 n.3, 60-61 n. 18, 62 n. 35
Janeway, Elizabeth, 154, 156

Knowledge, 17, 26, 37-39, 61 n. 25, 67, 119
Kollantai, Alexandra, 19 n. 4
Kuhn, Thomas, *The Structure of Scientific Revolutions*, 53

Labor, 7-9, 85-89, 133-35; division of, 7, 85, 147, 169
Language, 66, 121, 151, 166-67
Liberalism, 3-7, 10-11, 21-22 n.20, 128-30, 132; American tradition of, 16; in conflict with Marxism, 3-4, 6-7, 10-11, 132-33
Liberating Feminism (Barber), 158
Liberation, 3-9, 114-15, 119, 129-33, 144, 146, 150, 159, 167; conditions for, 104-7, 111-12, 122, 151-52, 172-75; liberal theory of, 3-4, 5, 6-7; Marxist theory of, 3, 5, 6, 7-10; tensions in, 10-11, 108-11, 121-25, 152-53, 175-76; theory of, 11-12, 14, 17-18, 23, 39, 47, 52, 57, 135-36
Liberation movements, 3-4
Locke, John, 6
Luckmann, Thomas, *The Social Construction of Reality*, 78-83, 93-94

Marriage, 74, 131-34, 174

Marx, Karl, 7, 77-78, 79, 81, 83-
89, 91, 107, 136, 175; *Economical and Philosophical Manuscripts*, 87; *The German Ideology*,
85; on nature, 87; on needs, 85-
86, 97-98 n.25; on society, 87,
97 n.23

Marxism, 3-11, 79, 84, 88, 111-12,
128, 132-36, 166; in conflict with
liberalism, 3-4, 6-7, 10-11; and
feminism, 5-6, 9-10; as a science,
84, 88; as a theory of liberation,
6-10

Mead, George Herbert, 15-18, 23-
57, 64-69, 71-72, 76-79, 81, 83-
84, 86-89, 91-93, 101-5, 115,
117, 119, 121, 146-48, 153-54,
172; on behaviorism, 41-42, 46;
on change, 38, 42, 52-53, 56;
and the cognitive self, 55-56,
59 n. 13, 66-67, 78, 101-4; and
communication, 15, 24, 26, 39,
41-42; on conflict, 53-54; on
consciousness, 25-26, 28, 55,
65-66; on contract theory, 40; on
creativity, 15, 32-36, 44, 47-48,
50, 65, 115; on emergence, 15,
36, 43-46, 104; on emotions, 56-
67, 102-3; on environment, 42-
43, 48, 50; on evolution, 43; on
freedom, 31-33, 46-47, 50,
59 n. 13; and Sigmund Freud, 77-
78; on the generalized other, 16,
26, 30-32, 35-38, 41, 51, 55-56,
58-59 n. 12; on history, 43; on
impulses, 49-50; and institutions,
52, 54, 68-69, 79; on knowledge, 26, 37-39, 61 n.25, 67;
and Karl Marx, 77, 79, 83-84,
86-89, 91; on meaning, 25, 43,

65, 69, 88; on mind, 40; *Mind,
Self and Society*, 36; *Movements
of Thought in the Nineteenth
Century*, 79; on perception, 42;
on perspective, 37-38, 43,
45-46; philosophical tradition of,
16; *The Philosophy of the
Present*, 36, 67, 92; and process,
15, 23, 24, 27-28, 30, 33-35, 37,
38, 39-46, 48, 50, 64-68, 88;
and psychology, 26, 41, 66; on
the role of the other, 15, 26, 32,
37, 57, 79, 93, 101-2; and
science, 38-39, 45, 50-54; on
self, 15-17, 23-28, 30-43, 45-46,
55, 64-67, 78, 87, 102, 104-5,
146-48; on social acts, 15-16,
26-31, 32, 34, 40, 42, 68-69, 93;
on social control, 15, 31-32, 56,
92, 103; on social objects, 27-29,
31, 42-43, 47, 92-93; on sociality, 24-39, 45-46, 146; and
symbolism, 24-26, 42, 155, on
thinking, 37, 55, 78, 102; on
time, 28, 34-35, 39-40, 43-45,
64; on values, 28-29, 47-52, 65

Meaning, 25, 43, 65, 69, 88, 147,
154

Mill, John Stuart, 5, 6, 176 n.3

Millett, Kate, *Sexual Politics*, 160

Mills, C. Wright, 90, 99 n.33, 111-
12, 126 n. 10

Mind, Self and Society (Mead), 36

Mitchell, Juliet, 8

Morality. *See* Ethics

*Movements of Thought in the Nine-
teenth Century* (Mead), 79

National Conference on New Politics, 9

National Organization for Women (NOW), 4, 19n.6
National Women Suffrage Association, 19n.4
New York Radical Feminists, 5
Nietzsche, Frederich W., 107, 120
Norms and rules, 27, 29, 31-37, 55-56, 67, 71, 75, 83, 93-95, 101, 103, 112-13, 155-57

Objectification, 80-81, 93
Ontology, 10-11, 113-14, 123-24, 149
Oppression, 11, 16, 18, 21-22n.20, 145, 147, 158, 171, 175. *See also* Dominance/subordinance
Origins of the Family, Private Property, and the State, The (Engels), 5

Patriarchy, 5, 7, 135, 169
Perception, 42
Perspective, 37-38, 45-46, 114, 119-25, 155-56, 164-65, 167, 171-73. *See also* Role of the other
Perspective by incongruity, 120
Philosophy of the Present, The (Mead), 36, 67, 92
Philosophy of Right, The (Hegel), 85
Plato, 2, 7, 12-14
Possessive individualism, 6-7, 130
Power, 9, 11-12, 14, 16-17, 37, 54, 56, 69-76, 80, 83, 89-94, 99-100n.30, 101, 104, 106-7, 109-10, 122, 125, 147, 159-61, 163, 167; contextual approach to, 70-71, 76; definitions of, 69-70, 74; distribution of, 9, 16-17, 56, 70-73, 83, 90-92, 94-95,

134-35, 155-56, 157-60, 175; psychological dimensions of, 104, 110; sources of, 73-76, 89-92, 94, 99n.33, 99n.34, 110n.37
Process, 15-17, 23, 24, 27-28, 30, 33-35, 36, 37, 39-46, 48, 50, 57-58n.3, 64-68, 76, 78, 84, 87-88, 95n.3, 104-6, 109, 122, 153
Proletariat, 8, 19n.4, 144
Property, 7, 9, 138

Reciprocity, 80, 82, 140, 142-43, 145-46, 152
Redstockings, 4
Reflection. *See* Expression/ reflection
Reformers, 3-4, 10-11, 19n.6
Reification, 81, 89
Rethinking Sociology (Zeitlin), 77
Revolutionaries, 4, 10-11
Role models, 103, 116-18, 173-74
Role of the other, 15, 26, 32, 37-38, 51, 57, 70, 79, 93, 98n.31, 101-2, 106, 109, 111, 113-14, 119-20, 122-23, 126-27n.15, 150, 152, 161-62, 165, 172
Ropers, Richard, 83-84, 86-89, 97n.21
Rowbotham, Sheila, 8
Rules. *See* Norms and rules

Sartre, Jean Paul, 140, 145
Schutz, Alfred, 121, 127n.17, 127n.18
Science, 45, 52-54
Second Sex, The (Beauvoir) 18, 136, 153
Self, concept of, 12-18, 24, 46, 60-61n.18, 64, 67-68, 74, 81-82, 84, 102, 108, 114, 121, 131-32,

146-48, 153-57; classical definition of, 12-14; and emotions, 56;
liberal definition of, 6-7, 24, 40;
Marxist definition of, 8, 85-87;
Meadian definition of, 15-17, 23-
28, 30-43, 45-46, 49, 55, 61-
62n.27, 64-67, 78, 87, 146-47;
modern definition of, 14
Self development, 7, 114, 119,
156, 173-74
Sex roles, 6-7, 9, 12, 17, 94, 117,
129-30, 133-34, 140-41, 150-
52, 154-76, 179n.53, 181n.70
Sexual Politics (Millett), 160
Significant symbol, 24-26, 42, 155
Social acts, 15-16, 26-31, 32, 34,
40, 42, 56, 68-69, 71-73, 91-94,
122
Social change, 52-54, 56-57
Social Construction of Reality, The
(Berger and Luckmann), 78-83
Social objects, 17, 27-30, 31, 42-
43, 47, 68-69, 73, 75, 92-93,
112-13
Sociality, 15, 17, 24-39, 45-46, 66,
78, 79, 104-5, 108-9, 114, 122,
173
Sociological imagination, 111, 112
Stanton, Elizabeth Cady, 19n.4
Stirner, Max, 107
Stone, Lucy, 19n.4
Students for a Democratic Society
(SDS), 9-10
Subordinance. *See* Dominance/
subordinance

Temporality, 34-35, 45, 62n.35,
64-65, 95n.1, 104-5, 114, 124
Time. *See* Temporality

Transcendence, 136-39, 141-47,
149-53, 160, 165, 170

Values, 28-29, 47-52, 56, 113-14,
134, 151
Violence, 9, 110, 158

Watson, John. *See* Behaviorism
Weber, Max, 90
Whitehead, Alfred North, 136
Women; anthropological studies
of, 9, 151, 166, 169-70; and
desire for approval, 163-65;
definitions of, 8-9, 137, 142-43,
155-57, 163-64; domination of,
18, 134, 142, 144; economic
position of, 8, 133, 145, 152; and
language, 9, 166; and mothering, 134, 137-38, 140-41, 154,
160, 162, 165, 169, 174-75;
oppression of, 7-9, 129-30, 139,
143-45, 147; roles of, 7-9, 114,
117, 123, 133-34, 137-38, 146,
149-51, 153-54, 156-76
Women's Equity Action League
(WEAL), 4
Women's International Terrorists
Conspiracy from Hell (WITCH),
5
Women's liberation. *See* Feminism
Women's liberation movement, 4-
5, 8, 19n.4, 19-20n.6, 157
Women's rights groups, 4-5
Woolf, Virginia, 18
Wretched of the Earth, The
(Fanon), 104-10

Zeitlin, Irving, *Rethinking Sociology*, 77-78, 83-84

About the Author

KATHY FERGUSON is assistant professor of Political Science at Siena College in Loudonville, New York. Her earlier writing has appeared in *Liberalism and the Modern Polity*, edited by Michael J. McGrath.